IMAGES
of America

MONROEVILLE

LITERARY CAPITAL OF ALABAMA

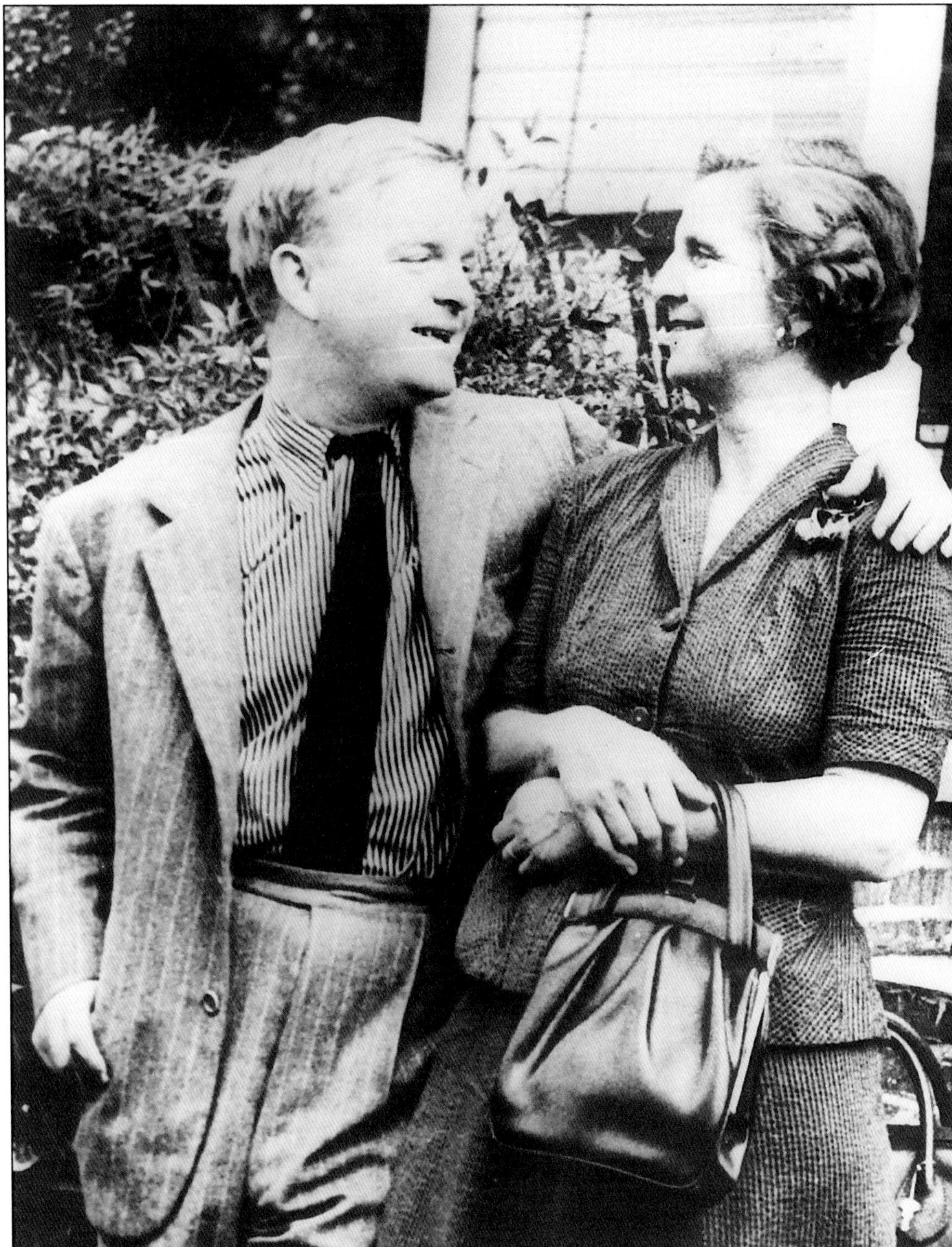

Truman Capote with his Aunt, Mary Ida Faulk Carter, in the Early 1960s at her Home outside Monroeville. The photo was taken while he was working on the book, *In Cold Blood*.

IMAGES
of America

MONROEVILLE

LITERARY CAPITAL OF ALABAMA

Kathy McCoy

ARCADIA
PUBLISHING

ISBN 978-0-7385-5437-2

Published by Arcadia Publishing
Charleston, South Carolina

Printed in the United States of America

Library of Congress Catalog Card Number: 98-87570

For all general information contact Arcadia Publishing at:
Telephone 843-853-2070
Fax 843-853-0044
E-Mail sales@arcadiapublishing.com
For customer service and orders:
Toll-Free 1-888-313-2665

Visit us on the Internet at www.arcadiapublishing.com

Contents

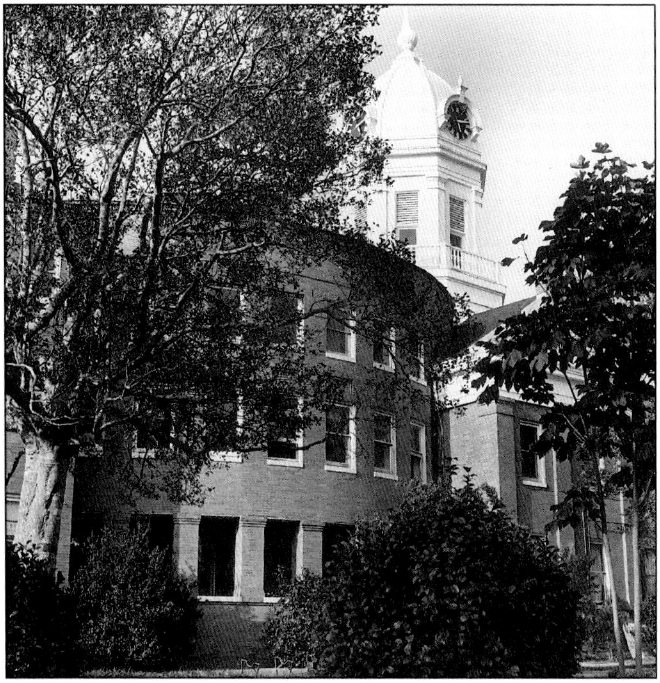

The Old Monroe County Courthouse. At least five Monroeville-based courthouses have served the people of Monroe County over the years. More than any other Southern town, Monroeville is most easily identified by mention of its domed courthouse. The first and second Monroeville courthouses burned and were replaced by what is now known as the Old Monroe County Courthouse, which was built in 1903. This second public structure, located on the downtown square next to the modern-day courthouse, served as the model for the movie setting of the trial in *To Kill A Mockingbird*.

Acknowledgments

In 1999 Monroeville will celebrate its 100th year as an incorporated city. However, Monroeville's history actually covers over 160 years, with the county seat of Monroe County being moved from Claiborne, a river town, to the interior of the county in 1832. Over these years Monroeville has seen many transformations, but has retained the character and values of a small Southern town, while other towns have become more homogeneous places. That character is shown in the faces of the many people who call Monroeville, Alabama home. It is also shown in the great literary works of Truman Capote and Nelle Harper Lee.

The author gratefully acknowledges the support of the Monroe County Heritage Museums' board and staff. Special thanks to Dawn Crook for "organizing" and Sandra Standridge, whose patience exceeds the bounds of human limitation!

I would also like to especially thank Aaron White. A preserver of historical photography, Aaron purchased the late Max McAliley Collection. McAliley photographed the people and places of Monroeville and the county from the mid-1940s until the 1980s. Aaron graciously shared with the museum many of the photos used in this book and which are now in the museum archives. He himself is a professional photographer who has photographed Monroe County's people and places for over 28 years. In 1993 Aaron's photo of the old courtroom in the courthouse was chosen for the cover of Shelby Foote's republished book *Follow Me Down*.

Finally, acknowledgments need to be made to those who have throughout the years worked so hard to preserve the heritage of Monroeville. Among these are the Monroe County Conservation Club, the present-day Old Courthouse Restoration Committee, Probate Judge Otha Lee Biggs, the Monroe County Commission, and the city and mayor of Monroeville.

INTRODUCTION

The year 1832 found Monroeville a small village with several hundred people living in the coastal plains of the piney woods. Monroeville's big sister to the west, Claiborne, was a city by the standards of the time. Claiborne boasted being the second-largest city in Alabama in the 1820s. Population estimates for Claiborne in "her golden age" (1820s–1830s) range as high as 6,000. In reality, the population possibly reached 3,000 or 4,000. Incorporated as early as 1820, Claiborne was an important river trading point. When Monroe County was created in 1815, by proclamation of Gov. Holmes of the Mississippi territory, Claiborne had been chosen the county seat. By 1832 a more central point in the county was desired for the "seat of justice," and a commissioned survey group traveled through central Monroe County to locate a spot. According to local legend (and the *Montgomery Advertiser*, April 27, 1916), the geographical center of the county was actually located northwest of present Monroeville (Limestone Swamp), but due to a "jug of rum," the county seat is at the present location.

At the present site of Monroeville was a crossroads (some have called this the Walker's Mill community), where a sociable blacksmith kept an inn for chance travelers through the area. His house and shop were located on the west side of the present square where today sits the state employment office and Skinner's Furniture (the first old jail building).

The commissioned group stopped to spend a night with the blacksmith. When he learned of their mission, he began to "lavish hospitality upon them." The next morning before their departure, the blacksmith offered the group a jug of rum. They each took a drink and lingered, chatting with him. After a third round of rum, they convened to the house, where they continued the discussion of their purpose and after finishing the entire jug of rum, the gentlemen agreed that this should be the center of Monroe County and therefore the county seat. The name of the man supposedly responsible for this feat remains unknown.

The town was named Centerville and was later changed to Monroeville after James Monroe. The United States government deeded 80 acres to Judge Henry Taylor for county purposes and appointed him as probate judge of Monroe County.

This probate judge selected the site for the first of five courthouses and had the courthouse and jail built of logs. The actual site of the first courthouse is where the parking lot between the two present courthouses is located. The jail was located where Skinner Furniture is now. The log courthouse burned in 1833. Some time after the fire, a brick kiln was built to fire handmade bricks for the new courthouse. The building date of the third courthouse is 1854, but according to local tradition, it was built by slaves. It was from this courthouse that Probate Judge T.M.

McCorvey rode to meet the Yankees on the outskirts of town in April 1865. Judge McCorvey and Mrs. Spottswood pleaded with the Yankee raiders for deliverance. The raiders' commander agreed not to harm the helpless civilians, and this first group passed through the city without doing more than looting of public buildings, while private homes were left untouched. A second wave of raiders eventually passed through. The cotton house on the north side of the square was burned, smokehouses and barns were plundered, and most of the food and livestock—including horses and mules needed for farming and transportation—were taken. Already impoverished by four years of war, citizens were left with virtually nothing after the raid.

The Monroe Journal, the county's oldest and longest-running newspaper, was founded in 1866 at Claiborne and was moved to Monroeville by 1870. Over the years it has consistently won press awards and has been listed by the *Encyclopedia of Southern Culture* as the best small weekly in the state. In its early days, the *Journal* reflected the temperament of Monroeville during the Reconstruction era. Falling just south of the Black Belt, Monroe County was not truly part of the plantation region of the state. However, prior to the war, slaves comprised about 53 percent of the county's population. Monroe ranked 12th in the state's 52 counties in the percentage of slaves to total population and 21st in the state in the number of slave-holding families, with 676. After the war, Monroeville citizens and others in the county regarded Reconstruction bitterly. This is well illustrated in early letters to the editor condemning the northern dictates to the Alabama Legislature. One anonymous writer (writing under the pen name "Tight Eye," which indicated intoxication) wrote, "Let a man hold his head up as long as he is honest, no matter how poor he is and—because a fellow whips you, it's no reason why you should be afraid of him."

The *Journal* continued its outright condemnation of Reconstruction efforts, remaining staunchly pro-white and pro-Southern. That is a stark contrast to the 1950s-era *Journal* which blasted the Ku Klux Klan and taunted the robed antagonists to direct its attacks at the *Journal* and other strong business interests rather than trying to intimidate local black citizens.

Monroeville was incorporated on April 15, 1899. Its first mayor was T.S. Wiggins, and councilmen were John DeLoach, J.F. Deer, W.S. Wiggins, Q. Salter, and J.W. Fore. These family names and many others prominent in the community prior to the turn of the century are still evident in modern-day Monroeville.

In the early part of the 20th century, Monroeville had four schools, several established churches, a bus company, an established bank, a furniture-manufacturing plant, and several businesses. It is obvious, however, that Monroeville's economic, social, and population "boom" came June 21, 1937, with the completion of the Vanity Fair silk mill. Vanity Fair Mills, now the world's leading manufacturer of women's intimate apparel, doing business internationally under the name Vanity Fair and many other labels, remains a primary employer of Monroe County.

Since Alabama River Pulp Company opened at Claiborne in 1979, the forest-products mill complex has grown and flourished into the Alabama River Companies and has brought new citizens from other states and other countries into Monroeville.

Today, Monroeville's grand old courthouse sits quietly on the square like a prime maiden aunt. Visitors from around the country and around the world simply "drop in" at the courthouse—still the centerpiece of the county—which has become something of a monument to every intangible from social justice to Southern gentility. It is a symbolic touchstone for budding writers and lovers of great literature. Each year, a play based on *To Kill A Mockingbird* is performed by a local cast, produced by the Monroe County Heritage Museums, in the famous courtroom.

Monroeville is known as the childhood home to authors Harper Lee, Truman (Persons) Capote, Mark Childress, and journalist Cynthia Tucker. Some have speculated many more unpublished authors live out their "novels" in Monroeville today.

One

Crossroads

"The streets of Monroeville were much like those red, muddy streets
described in Harper Lee's *To Kill a Mockingbird*."
—George T. Jones
Native of Monroeville and newspaper columnist

This road is not passable
Not even jackassable.
So when you travel
Take your own gravel.
—Unknown 19th-century Alabama poet

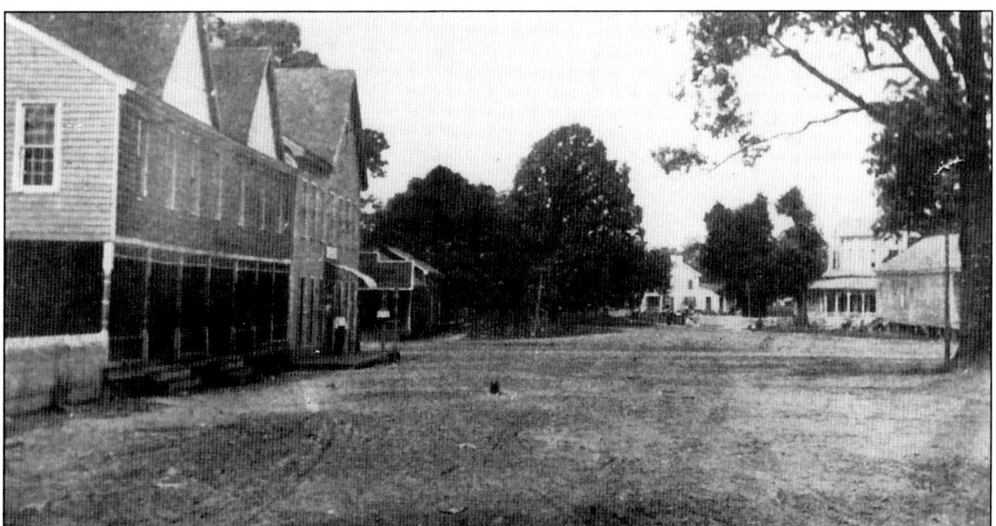

Street Scene of Monroeville Looking West off the Square.

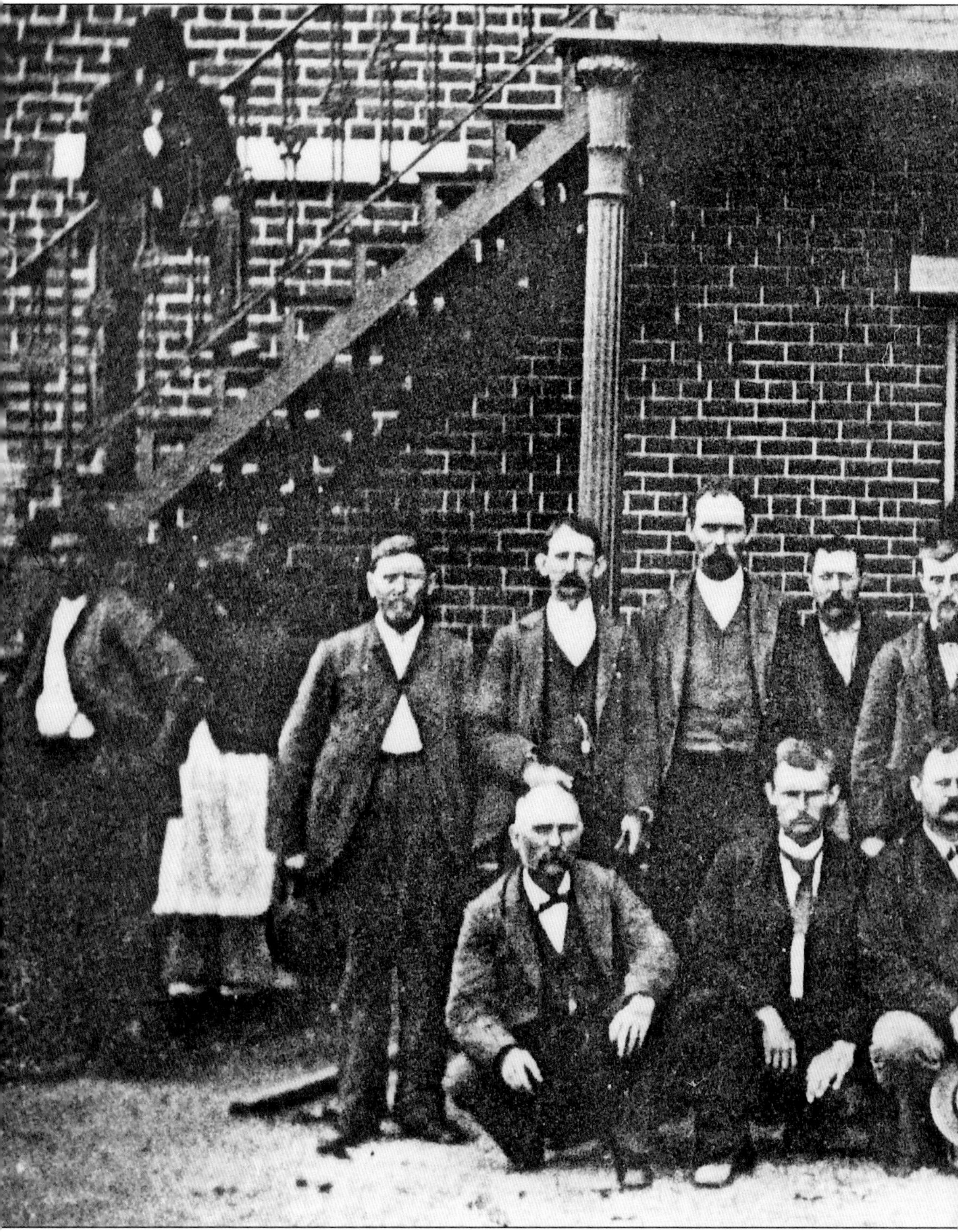

The Second Monroe County Courthouse. The courthouse was built by slaves, as legend goes, prior to the War Between the States. The bricks were handmade on the premises. In 1929, the old courthouse was burned down by an arsonist. The arsonist was reputedly the step-son of

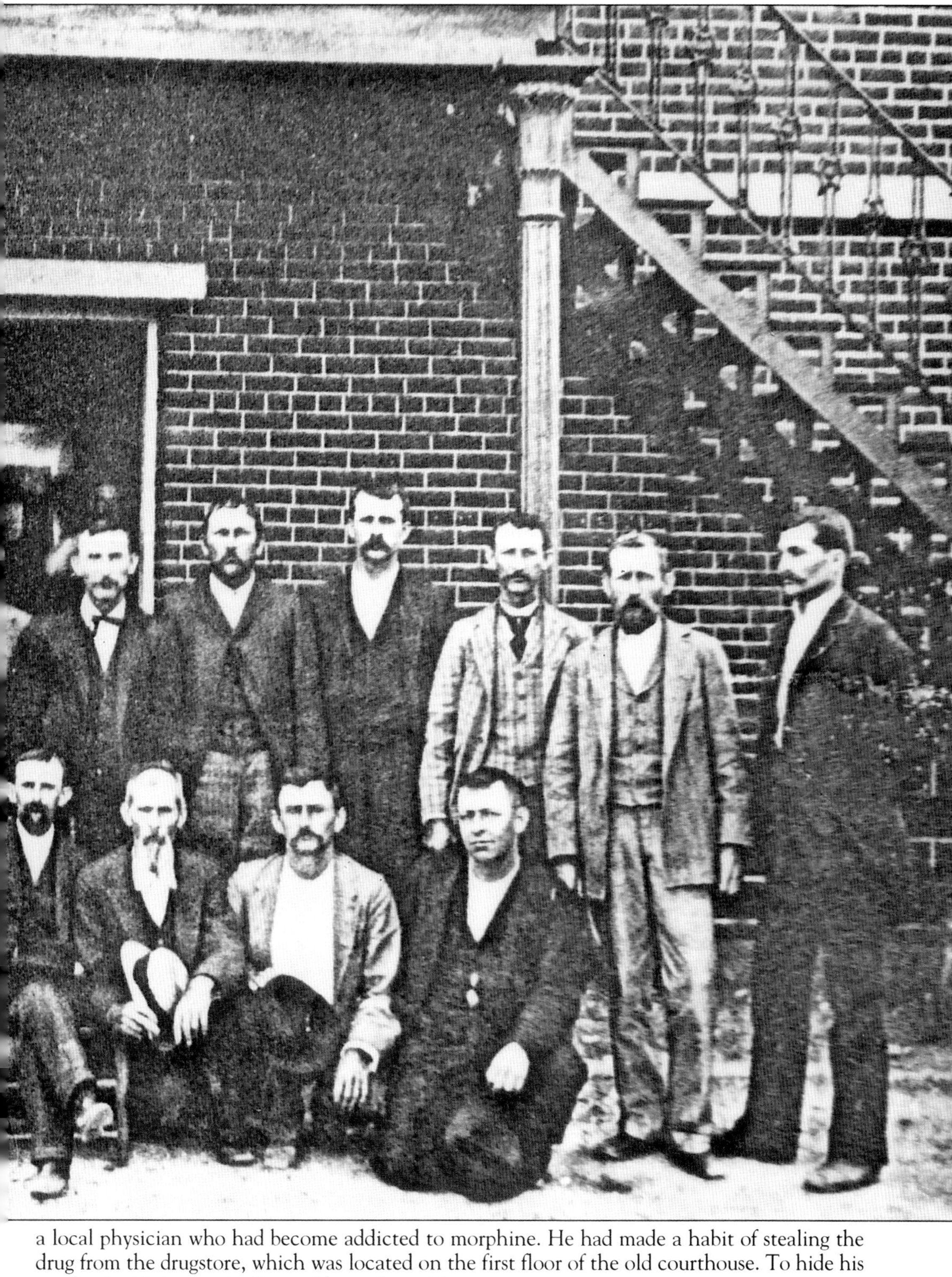

a local physician who had become addicted to morphine. He had made a habit of stealing the drug from the drugstore, which was located on the first floor of the old courthouse. To hide his act, he decided to set it afire and burn the evidence.

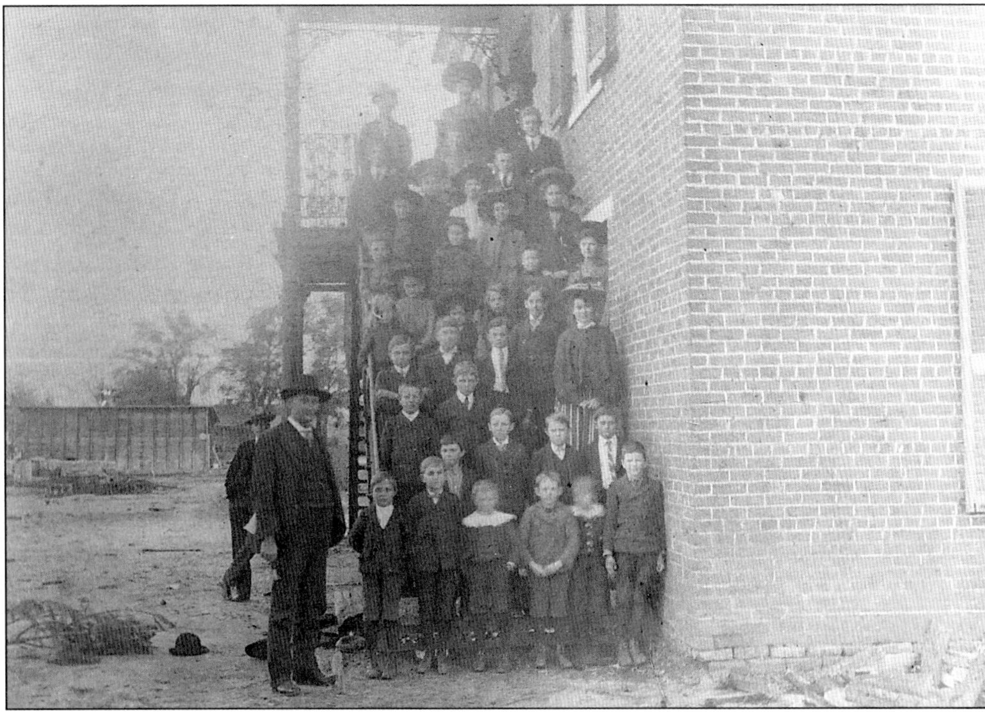

A GROUP OF BLIND SCHOOL CHILDREN AT THE OLD PRE-CIVIL WAR COURTHOUSE. The photo was taken in the early 1900s.

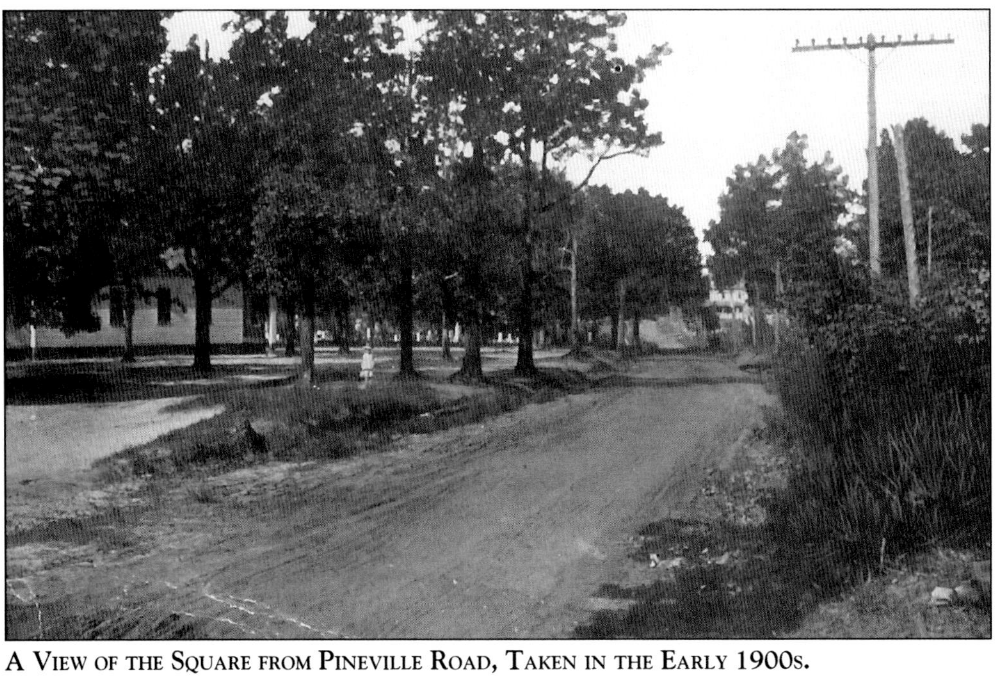

A VIEW OF THE SQUARE FROM PINEVILLE ROAD, TAKEN IN THE EARLY 1900S.

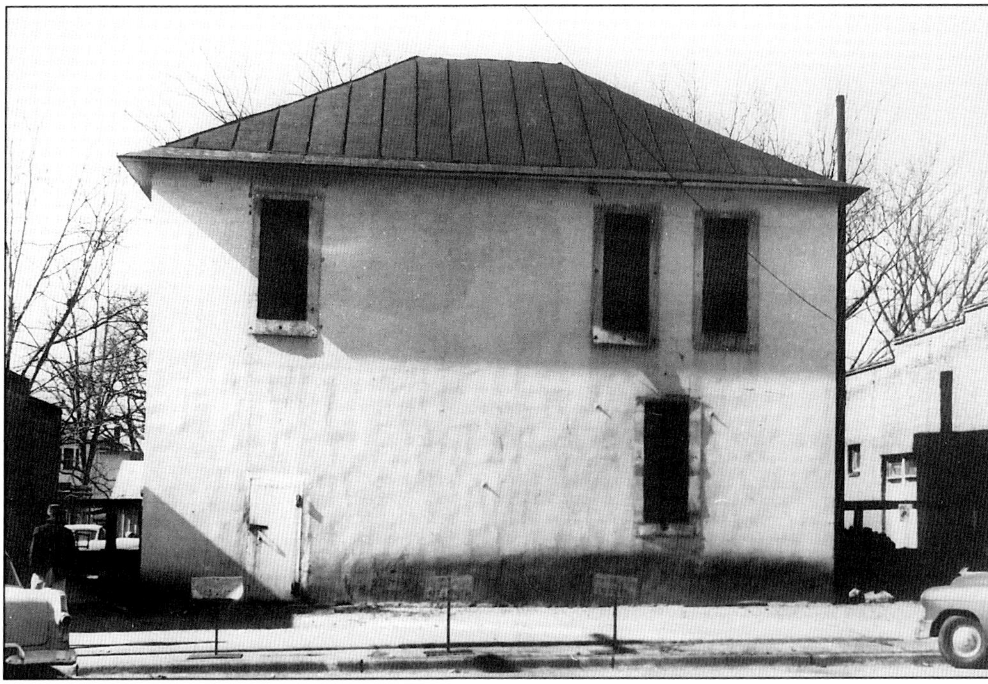

The Old Monroe County Jail. The building still stands behind the 1903 courthouse. This jail, built prior to the 1880s, was used in the 1930s and was described in the book *To Kill A Mockingbird*.

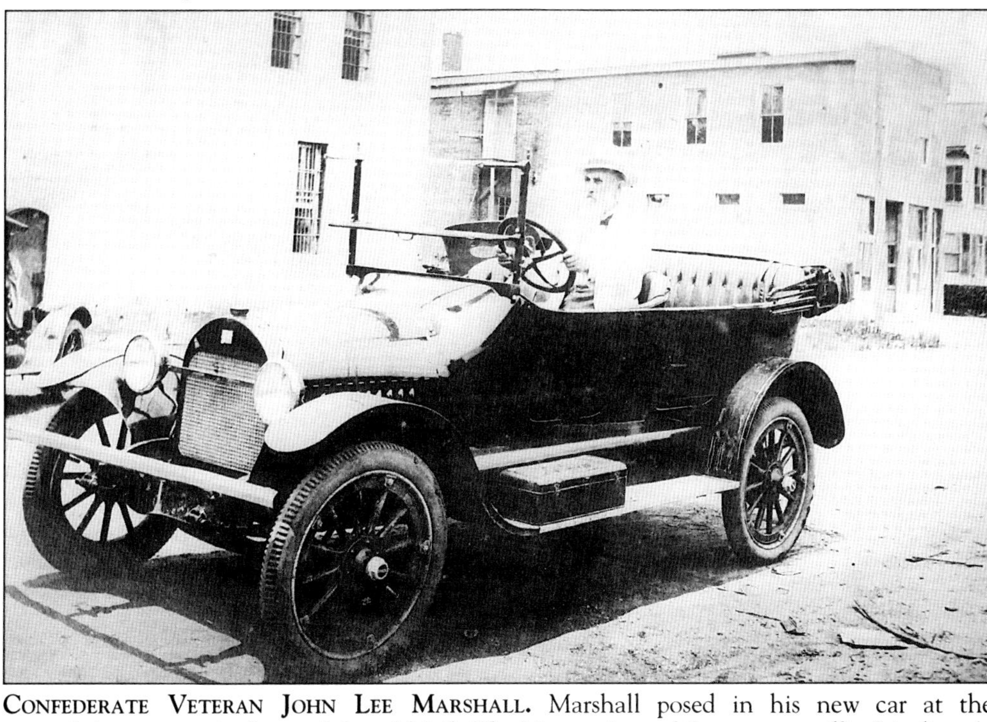

Confederate Veteran John Lee Marshall. Marshall posed in his new car at the turn of the century in front of the old jail. *The Monroe Journal* "newspaper office" is directly beside the jail.

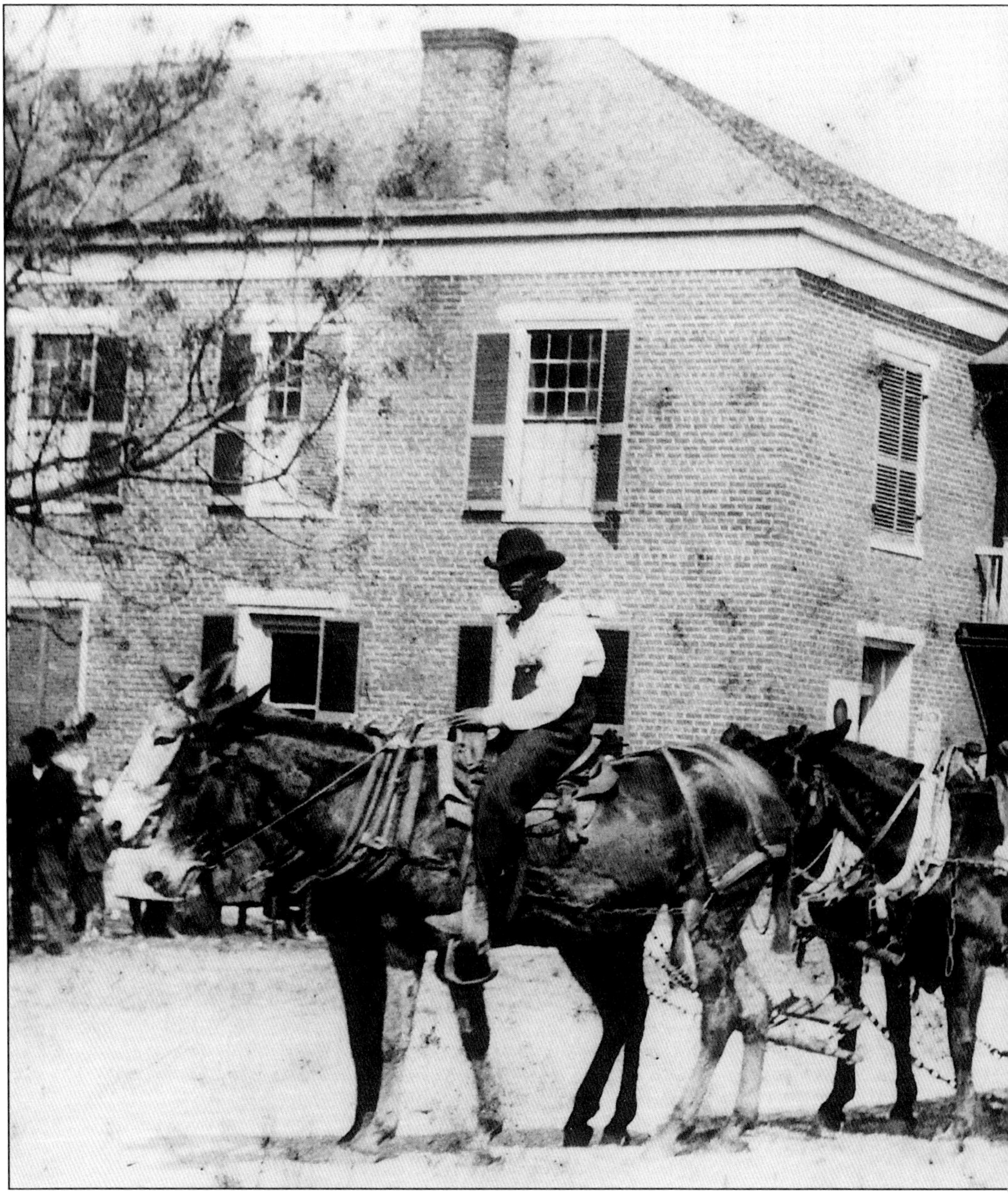

A PHOTOGRAPH TAKEN 1908 DURING A "LAND-GRABBING" EVENT IN FRONT OF THE OLD ANTEBELLUM COURTHOUSE.

In 1903, Andrew Bryan, prominent Southern municipal architect, was contracted by Probate Judge Nick Stallworth to design a new courthouse (shown on page 16). A contractor from Louisville, Kentucky, M.T. Lewman, was contracted to build the structure for $29,000. During the negotiations, one of the court officials pointed out that blueprint plans for a foundation were missing. These plans were added, along with a basement, causing the cost of the new courthouse to rise. Supplies, shipped in by rail, included manufactured heart-pine and yellow poplar windowsills and rolled tin for the second-floor ceiling. The courthouse was floored with heart pine, and all balustrades in the courtroom and stairways were pine. Stair handrails were oak.

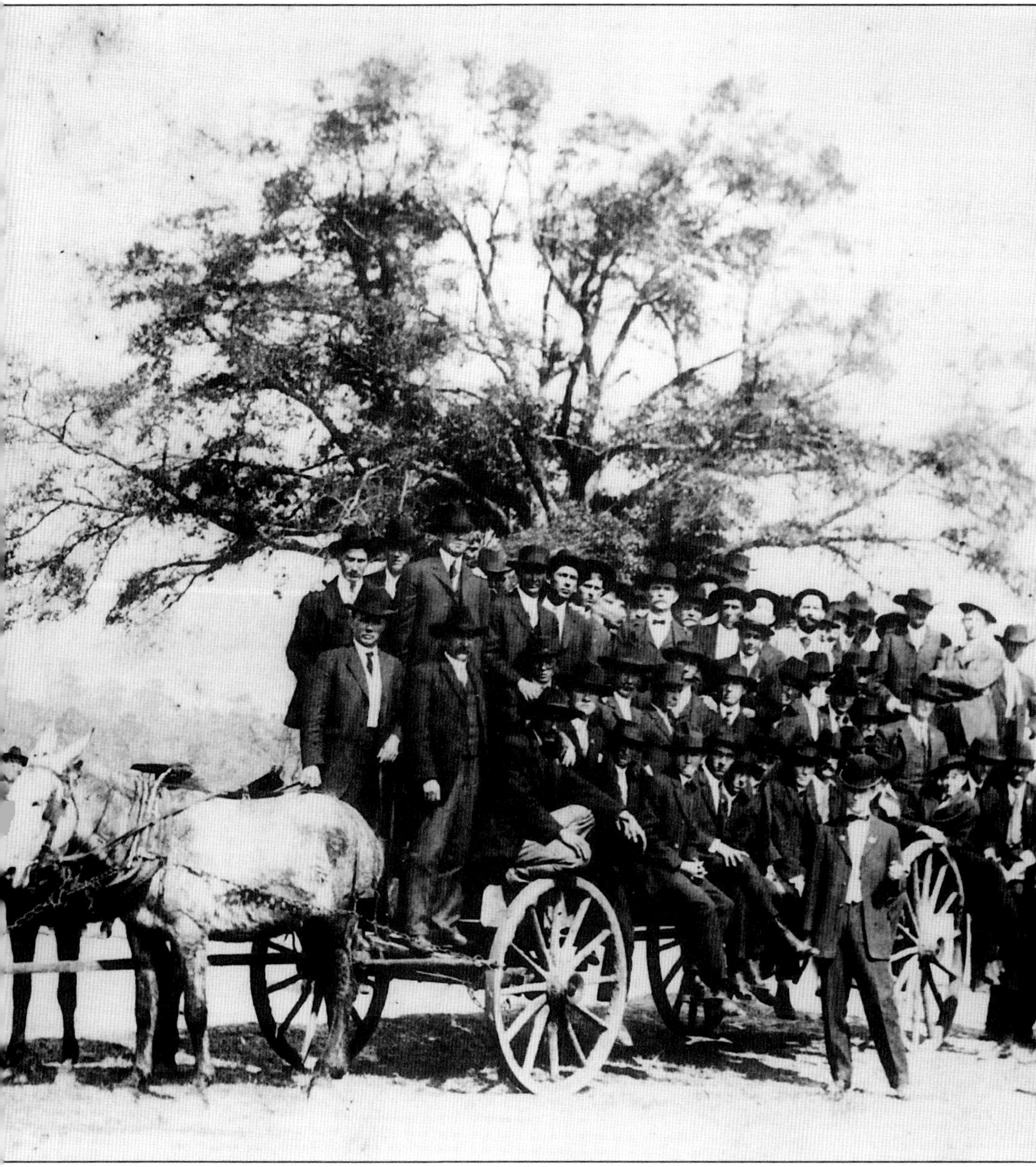

There has always been a controversy over whether the courthouse actually had doors on the bottom floor entrances. Old-timers don't remember any, but during restoration, evidence was found that doors had existed during some period. Evidence was also found that the woodwork in the courthouse had once been stained cherry. Today the courthouse boasts mahogany doors and the original woodwork, stained and painted. The courthouse also had the latest in heating: coal-burning fireplaces with metal inserts backed with fire brick. Two large, pot-bellied stoves heated the courtroom. The "dome" is of sheet metal and has been painted both silver and white at different times. The clock encased in the dome strikes on the hour and is mentioned in Truman Capote's *A Christmas Memory* as "the courthouse bell sounded so cold and clear."

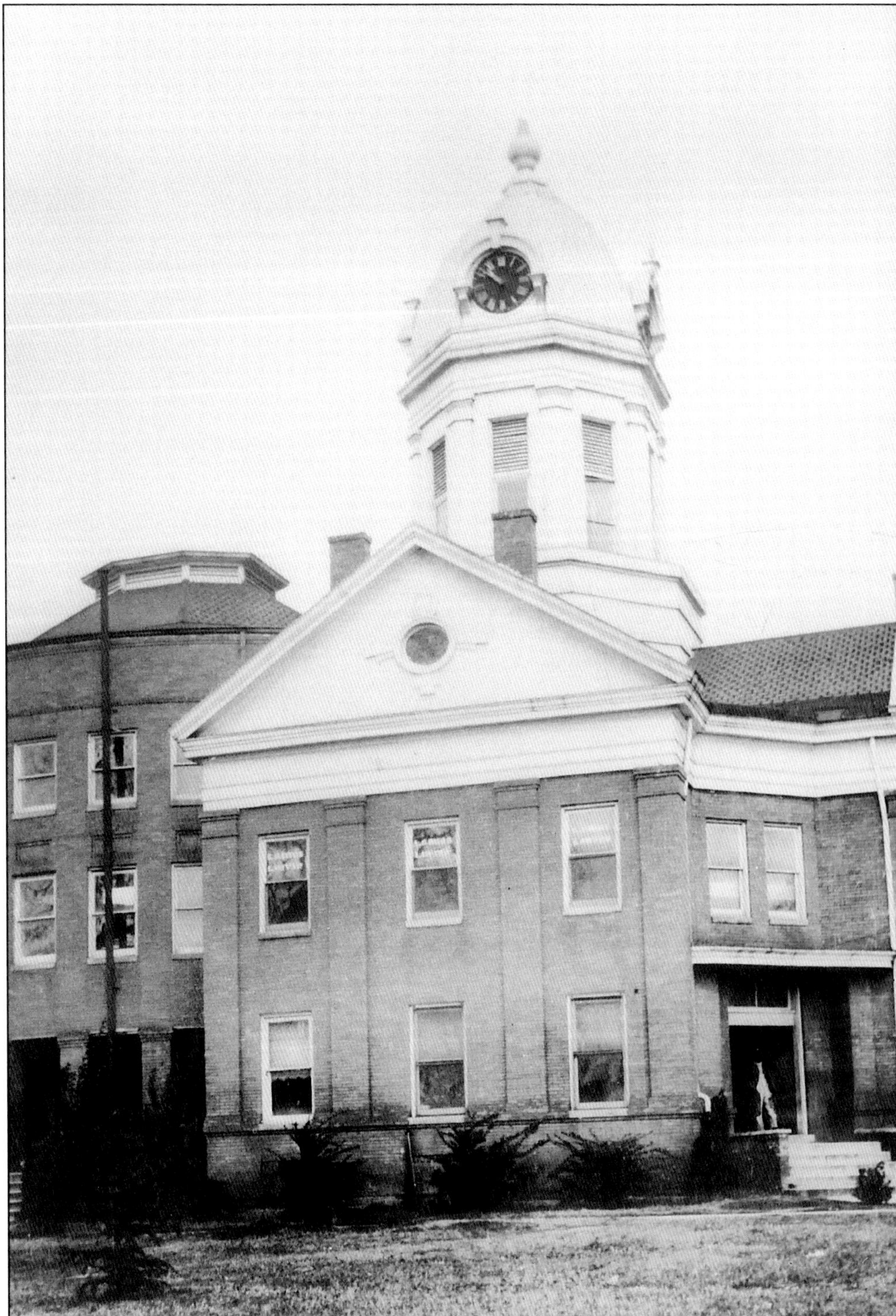

The Earliest Photo Known of the 1903 Courthouse on Monroe County Square. This courthouse is now the home of the Monroe County Heritage Museums.

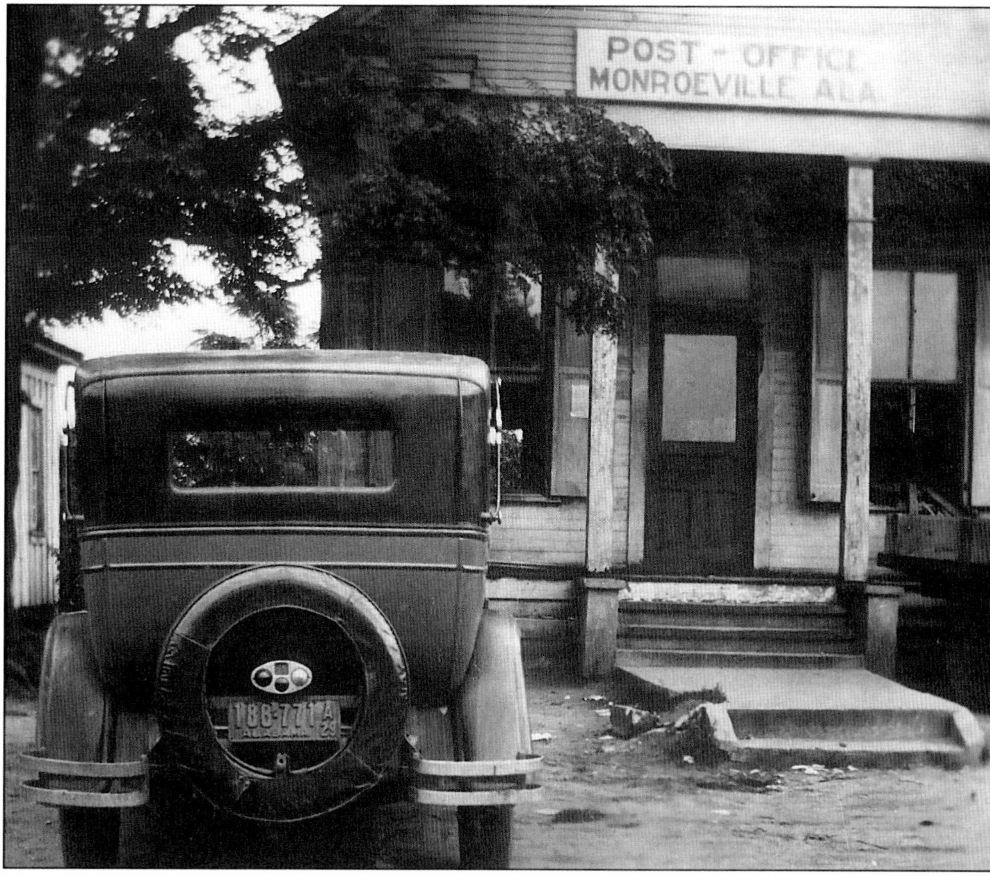

The 1926 Post Office, Located on the North Side of the Square.

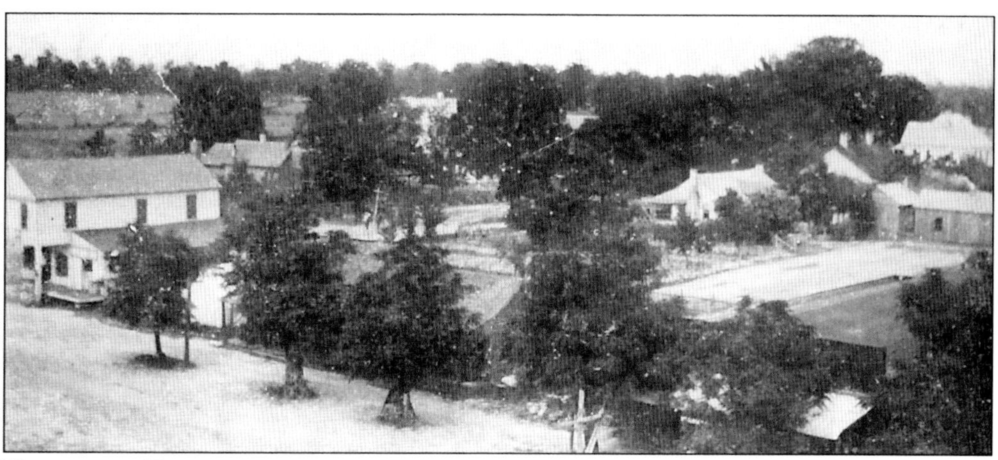

View of the Town Looking Northeast from the Courthouse Dome.

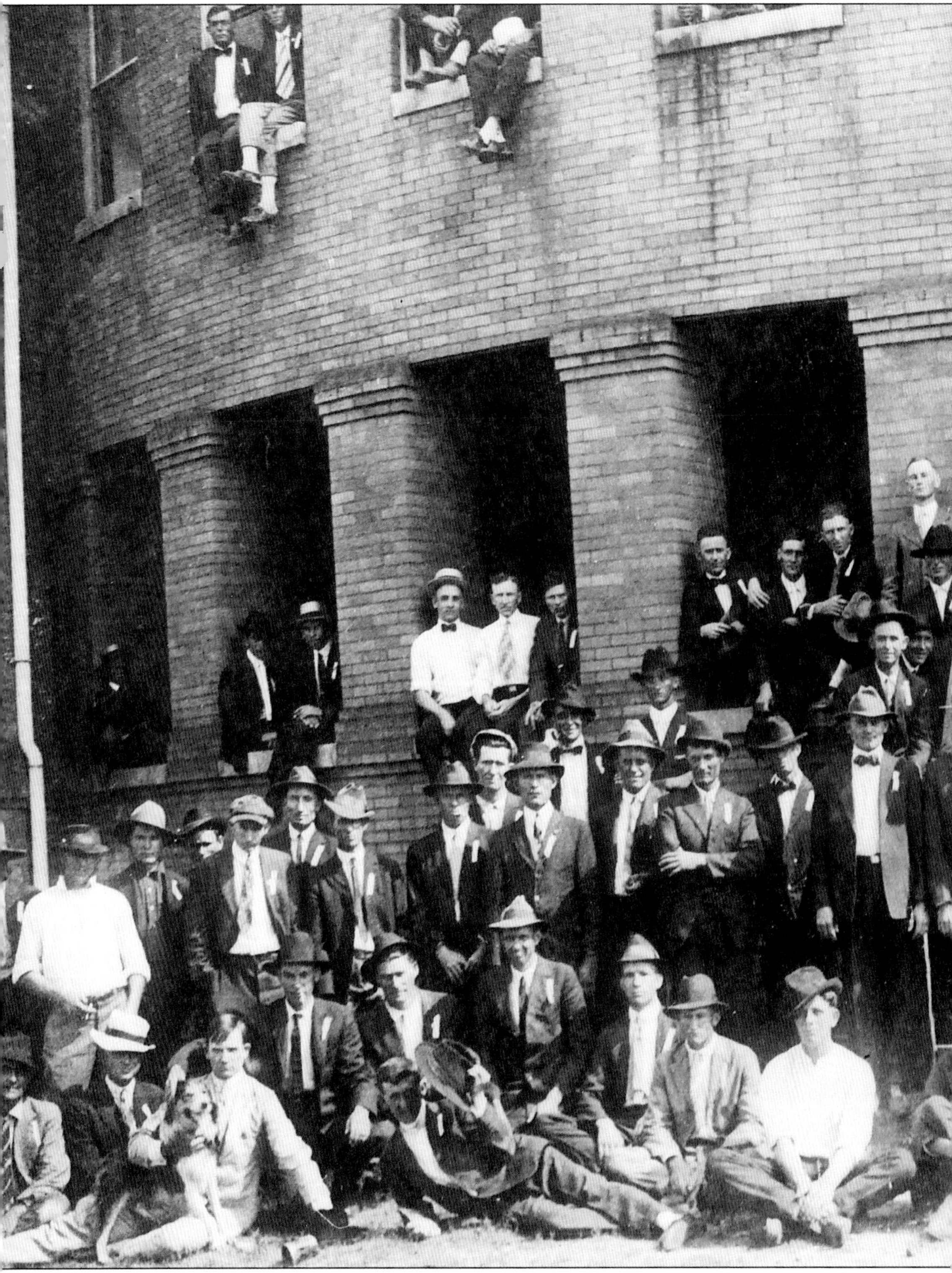

WORLD WAR I INDUCTEES FROM MONROE COUNTY ON THEIR WAY TO EVERGREEN, ALABAMA

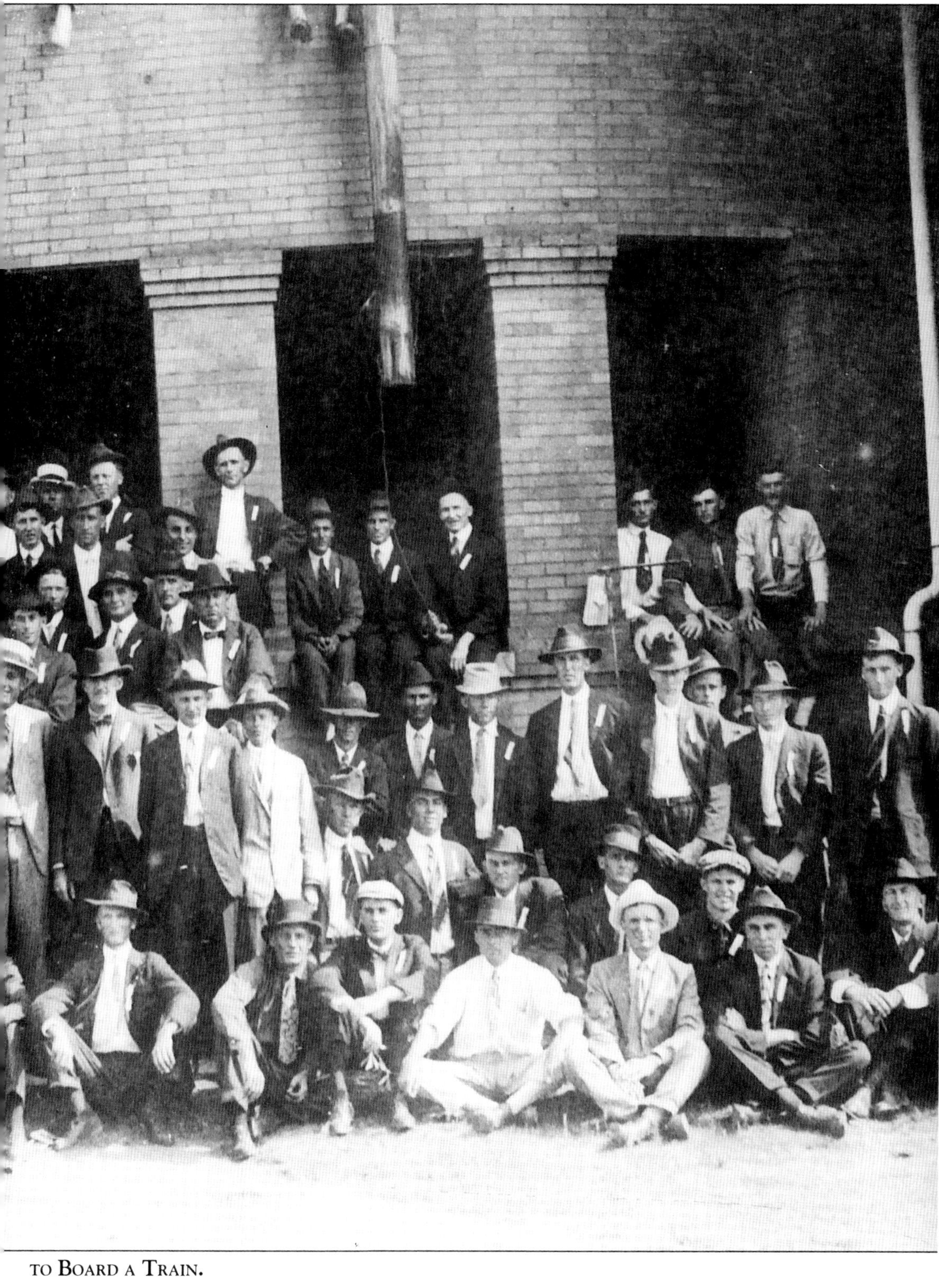

TO BOARD A TRAIN.

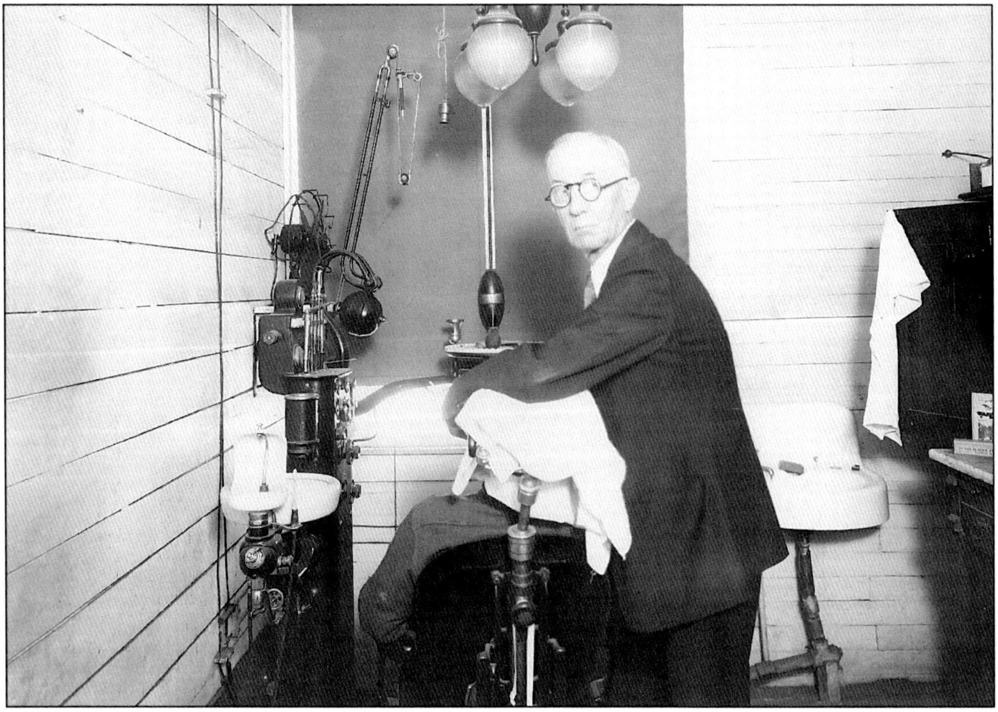

James Wallace Johnson Jr., in his Dental Office on the Square.

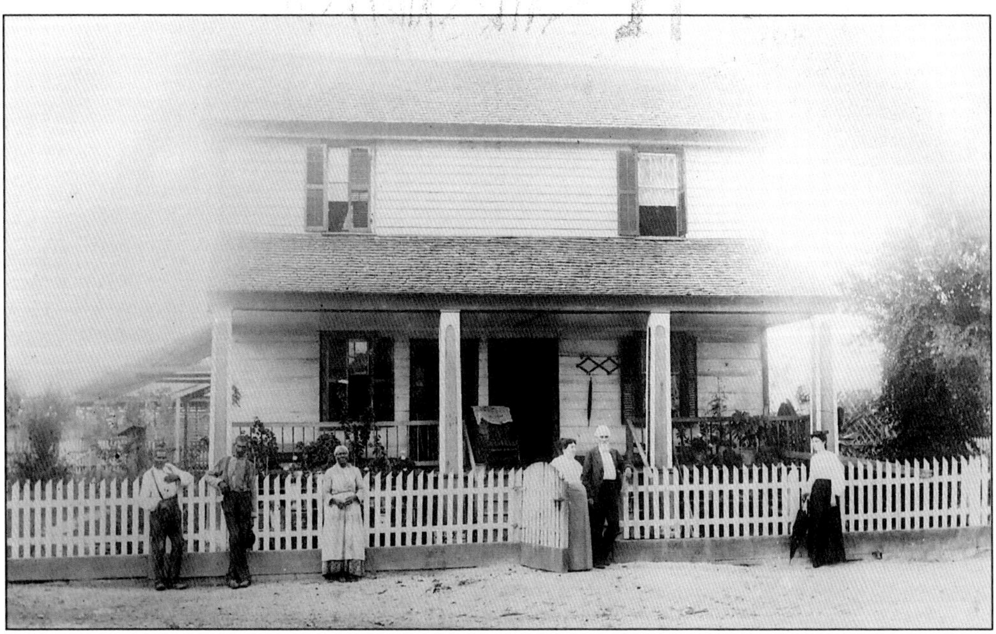

The Home of Captain William Stephen Wiggins on West Claiborne Street, Just West of Present Darby's Red & White Store. From left to right are: Asberry Wiggins, Will "Dock" Preyear, Lucy Snyder (servants), Mrs. Wiggins (Lucy "Lula" Hixon Wiggins), Captain Wiggins, and Miss Edna Newberry.

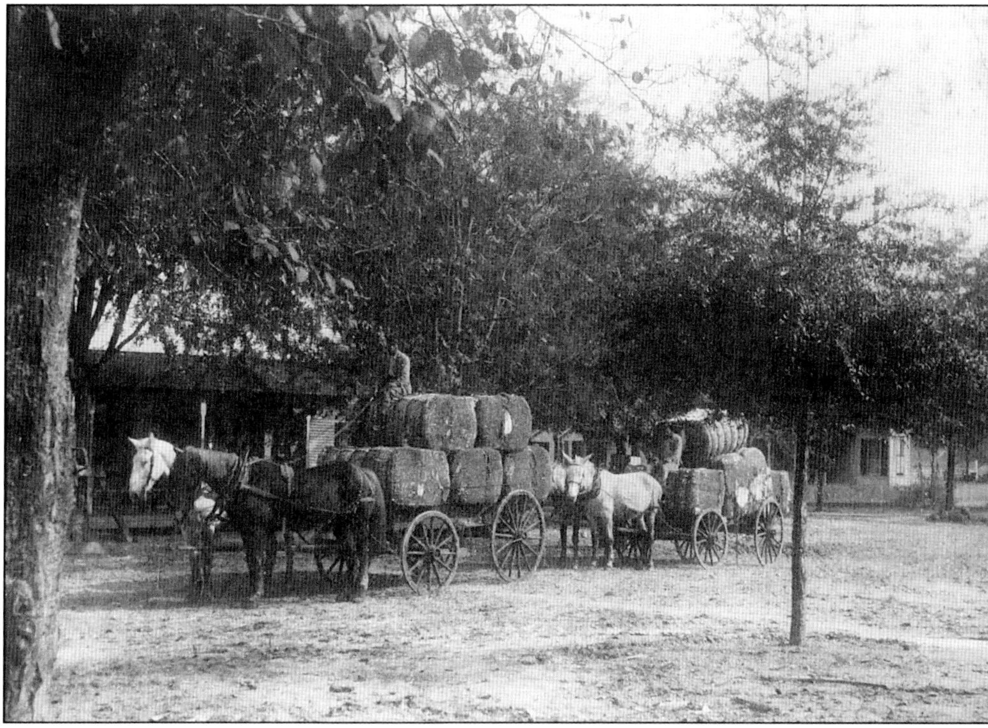

COTTON ON THE WAY TO MARKET. Cotton production began again in Monroe County following the war. Slaves became tenant farmers, and the South was taxed heavily on cotton shipped North, which continued until the 1960s.

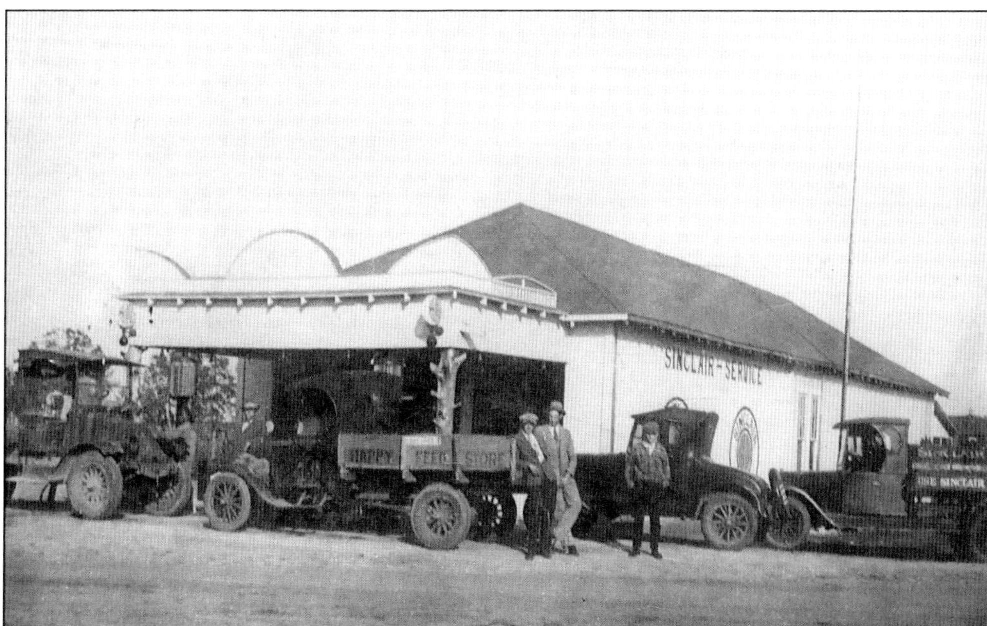

AN EARLY 1900S SINCLAIR SERVICE STATION LOCATED ON SOUTH ALABAMA AVENUE OFF THE SQUARE. Note the tree "pillars" in front.

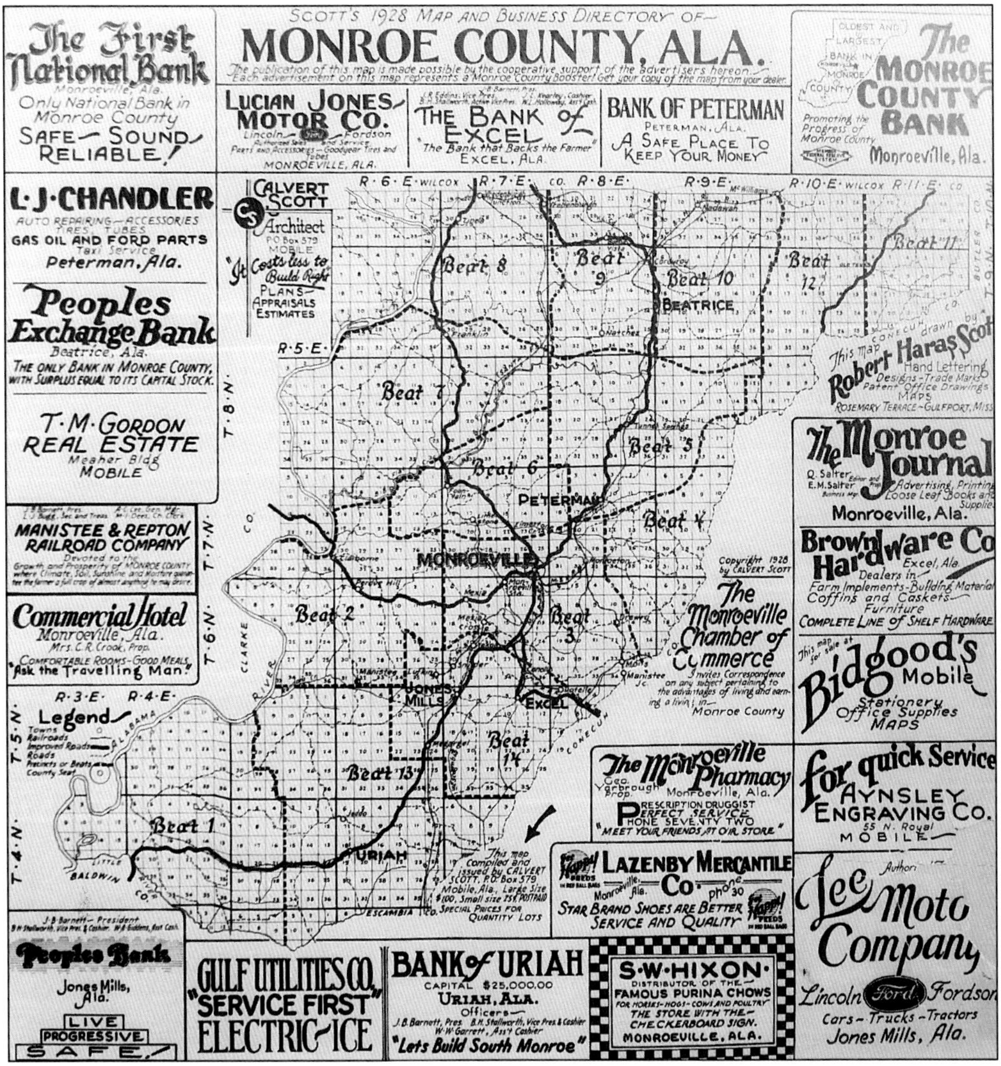

1928 Map and Business Directory. Notice the Manistee and Repton Railroad ad in which Harper Lee's father, A.C. Lee, was listed as general manager. When southerners shipped raw materials by rail to the North, the rail rates were less than when the finished products were shipped back to the South. The northerners gained on the cheap rate, leaving the southerners to pay the higher rate.

Two

PEOPLE

"Before the Civil War, the symbol of progress for towns along the Coosa-Alabama waterway was the steamboat: The more vessels serving a community, the more important that community was. After the war railroads slowly but steadily claimed the field, and the river became less important as a gauge for measuring advancing Alabama."
—Dr. Harvey H. Jackson, III from his book *Rivers of History*

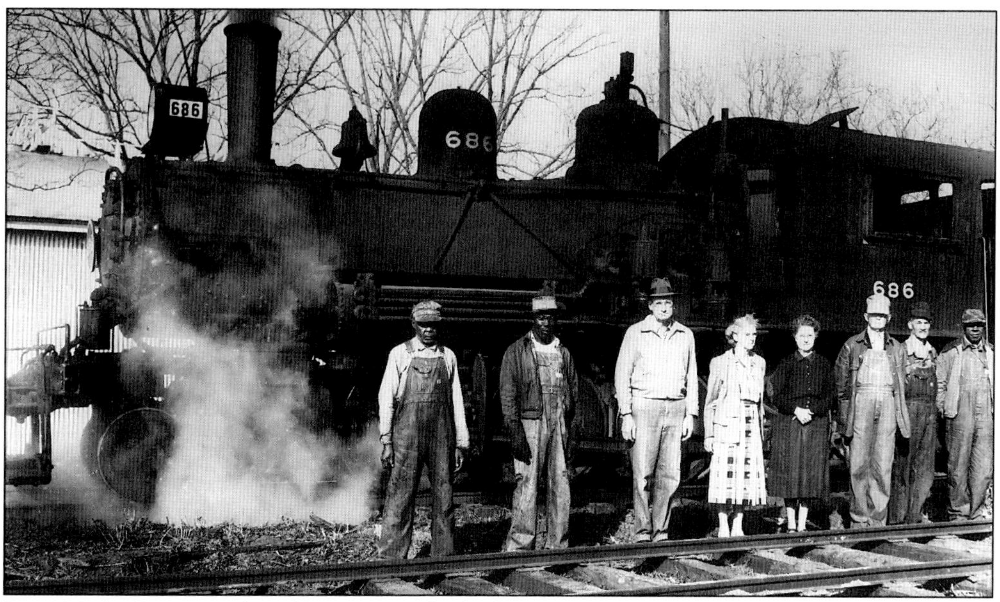

In 1900 the Bear Creek Mill Company built the Manistee & Repton Railroad to connect its big but isolated sawmill with the L&N Railroad 20 miles to the east at Manistee Junction. In 1912 the M&R Railroad was extended 5 miles to reach Monroeville in the middle of the county. A few years later, the M&R connected with the Gulf, Florida & Alabama Railway. The Manistee & Repton Railroad, although a great benefit for Monroeville, was never profitable, and eventually the original trackage was completely abandoned in favor of a new 4.5-mile connection into Monroeville from the L&N's Selma-Pensacola main line.

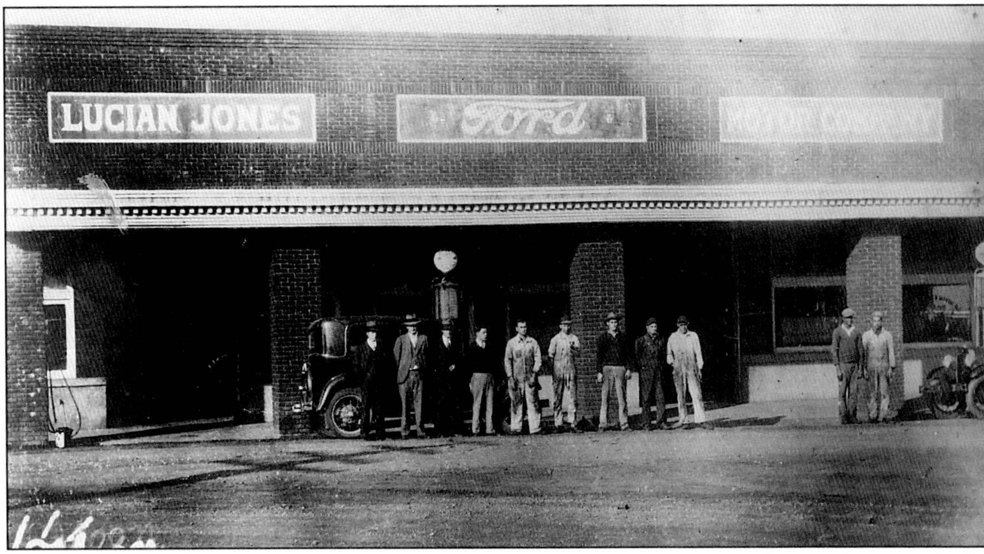

The Lucian Jones Ford Dealership in 1930 on the Square. From left to right are: Charles Cole, salesman and later mayor of Monroeville; Mr. Riley, salesman; Lucian Jones, owner; William Simmons, parts manager; Clyde Marshall, mechanic; Jessie Crutchfield, mechanic and later chief of police; Royal Skinner; unknown; unknown; Johnny Nettles; and Charlie Cheese.

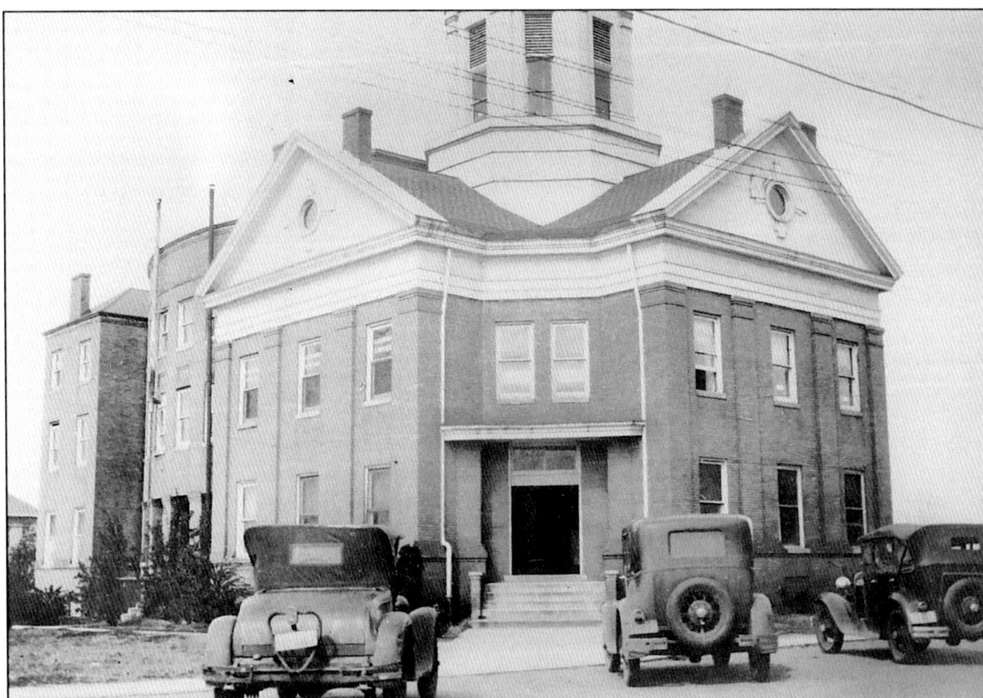

The New Courthouse. According to *The Monroe Journal* in 1904, "The new courthouse is one of the handsomest and most conveniently appointed in the state and one that would do credit to a county far exceeding Monroe in wealth and population . . . "

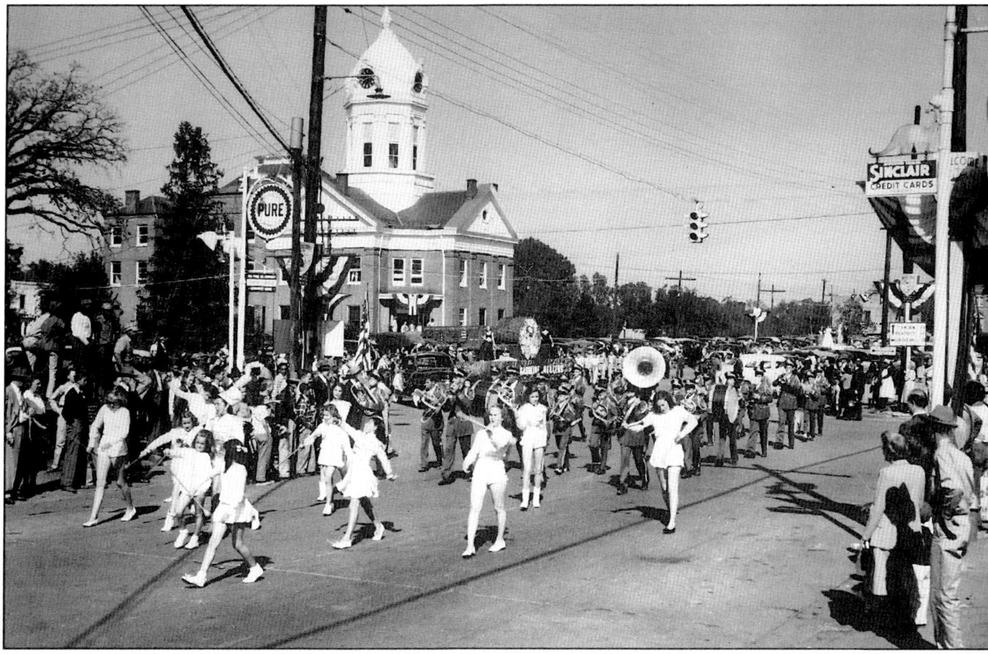

THE ANNUAL HOMECOMING PARADE IN THE EARLY 1950S. Even though the courthouse became the center of activities for the town, Nicholas Stallworth lost his bid for re-election after it was built. At that time, Monroe Countians called the old courthouse "Stallworth's folly" because of the high price of $29,000.

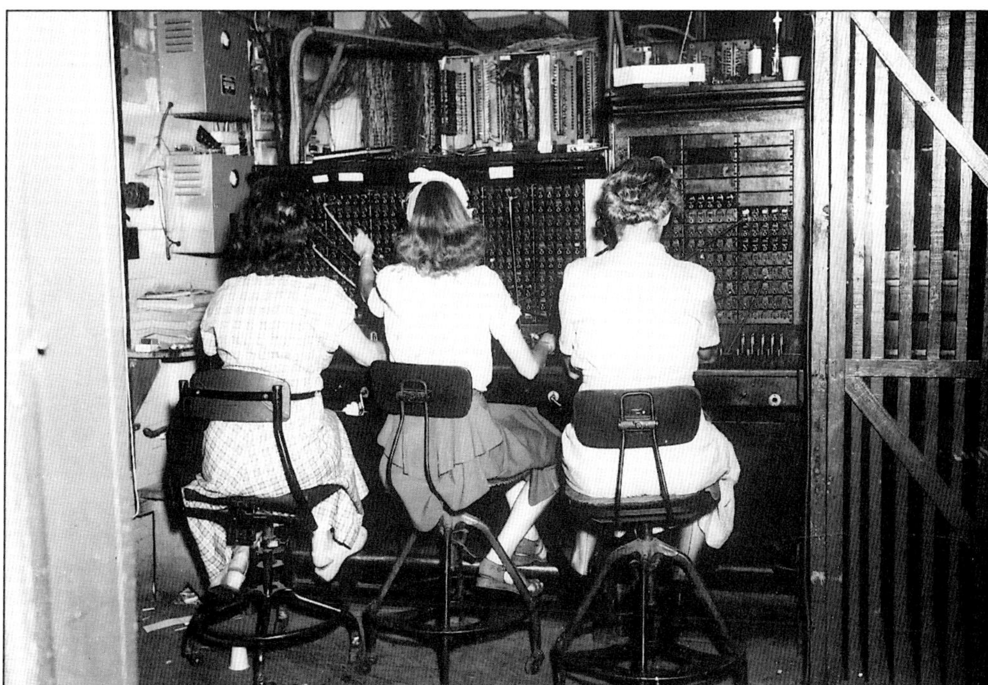

EARLY MONROEVILLE TELEPHONE OPERATORS AT THE MONROEVILLE TELEPHONE COMPANY IN THE EARLY 1940S.

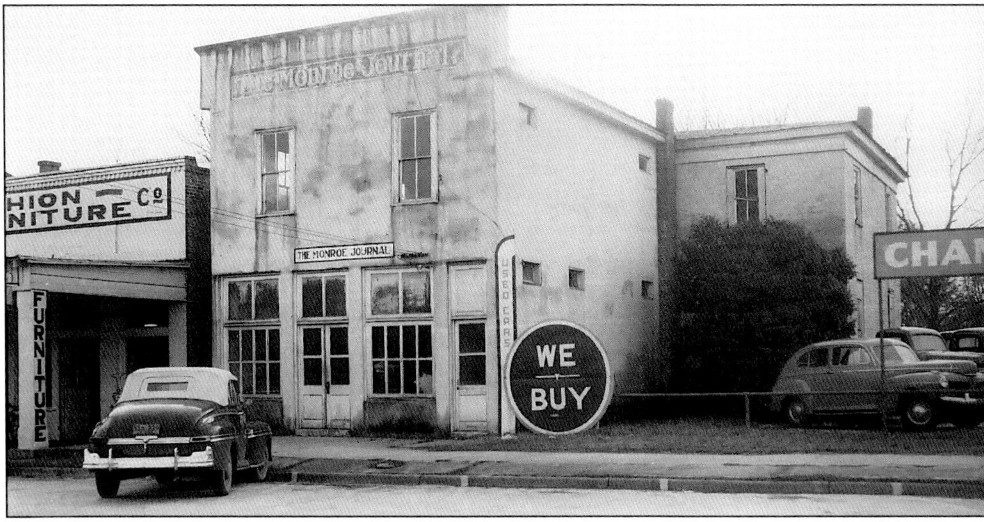

The Monroe Journal, Located on the Square for Many Years. Founded at Claiborne in 1866, *The Monroe Journal* later moved to Monroeville. The Salter family owned the *Journal* for 64 years. A.C. Lee (Harper Lee's father) was the owner and editor of *The Monroe Journal* from 1929 to 1947.

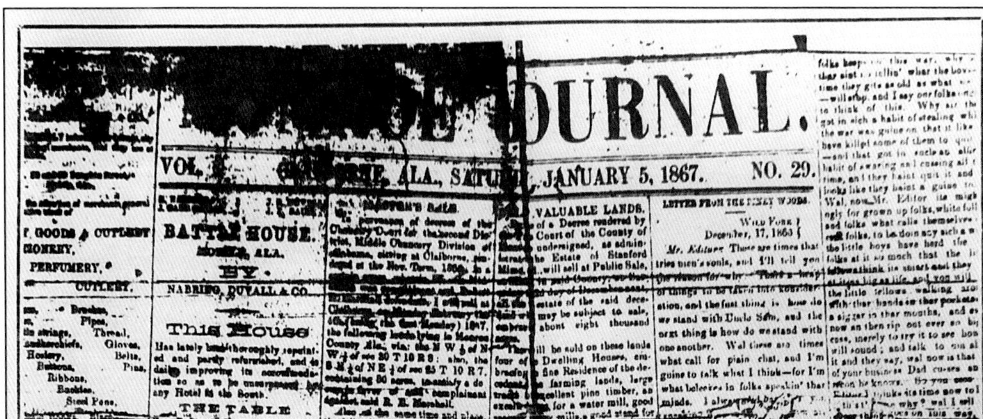

JOURNAL.

VOL. ... ALA., SATURDAY, JANUARY 5, 1867. NO. 29.

VALUABLE LANDS.

This House

WINES AND LIQUORS.

THE MONROE JOURNAL

VOLUME 67—NO. 4. THE MONROE JOURNAL, MONROEVILLE, ALA. THURSDAY, JANUARY 26, 1933. SUBSCRIPTION $1.00 PER YEAR

Roosevelt Plans Industrial Center For The Muscle Shoals District

C. O. Green Died Tuesday Morning

Poll Tax Must Be Paid By February 1

Murderers Of Robert Martin In County Jail

OUR NEXT PRESIDENT'S VIEWPOINT

County Schools

In 1947, Jimmy Faulkner and Bill Stewart bought *The Monroe Journal.* The Stewart family became the owners of the paper for almost 50 years. In 1959, though, the *Journal* stood with other community leaders against "the race hatemongers" of the Ku Klux Klan, who had interfered in plans for a black high school band to march in the Monroeville Christmas parade. A front-page editorial said that whites should not "sit idly by and allow a handful of thoughtless rabble rousers to establish this county as one of bigotry."

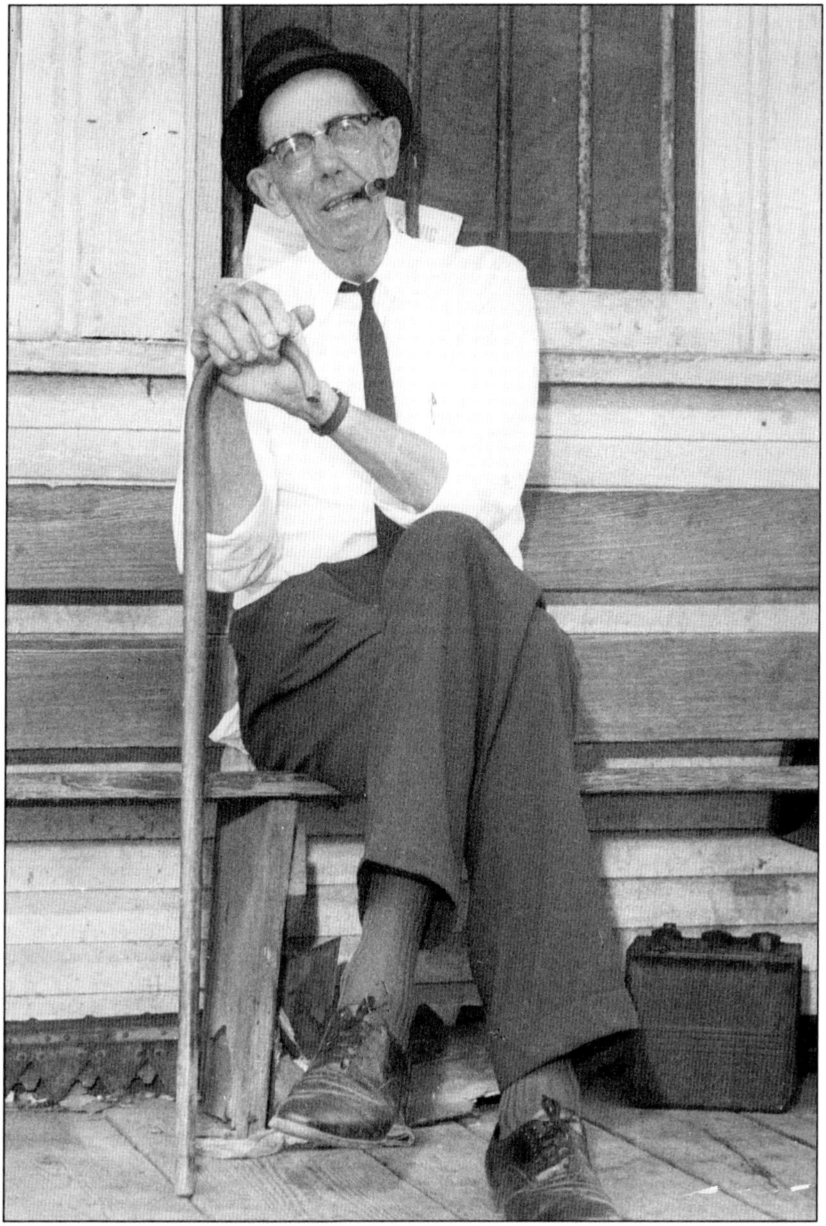

"NEVERMIND WHAT A MAN SAY—WATCH WHAT HE DO."—A.V. "SHORTY" CULPEPPER. "Shorty" Culpepper, the farm agent of Monroe County and a much-beloved character in the hearts and minds of Monroevillians, dispensed his homespun humor in two books, *Poor Kinfolks and Rich Relatives*, and *Taxes and Termites*, published in 1949. These were compilations of columns he had written for the newspapers of his area over the years. Nelle Harper Lee endorsed both of Shorty's books with the following statement: "Shorty Culpepper is an astute and wry observer of the human comedy. He should spend less time fishing and more time writing." In *Taxes and Termites*, the following was written of Shorty: "He put on his first pair of shoes in the early 1920s and went to Auburn for a four-year course in agriculture. By going to summer school and mowing all the professors' lawns free, he finished the course in seven years. He moved to Monroeville in 1928."

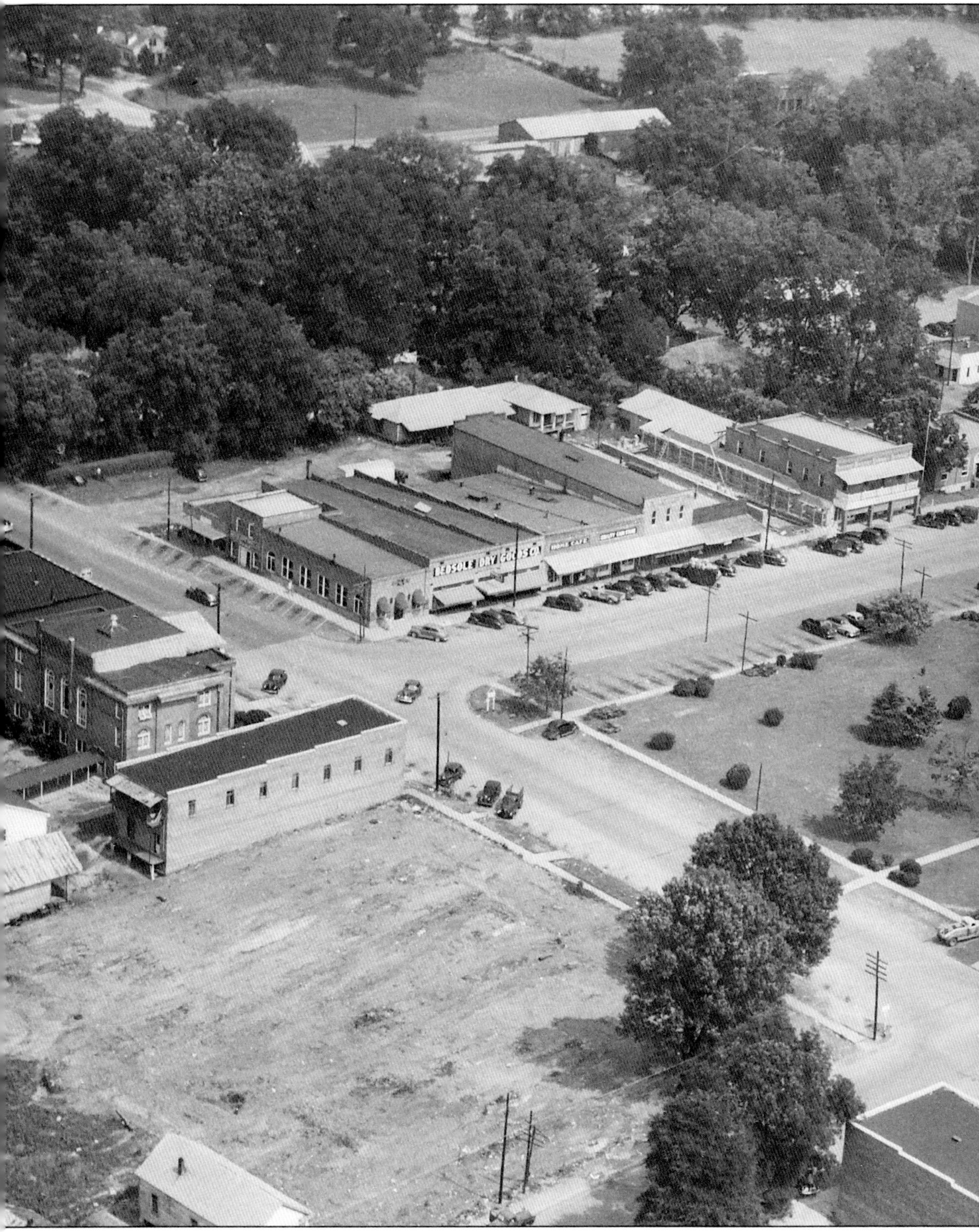

Aerial View of the Courthouse Square in the 1940s. An annex to the old courthouse was added in the late 1940s, creating a vault to store county records. By this time, the old courthouse was crowded, containing the offices of the probate judge along with the probate records and business, county circuit solicitor (district attorney), circuit court judge, circuit court

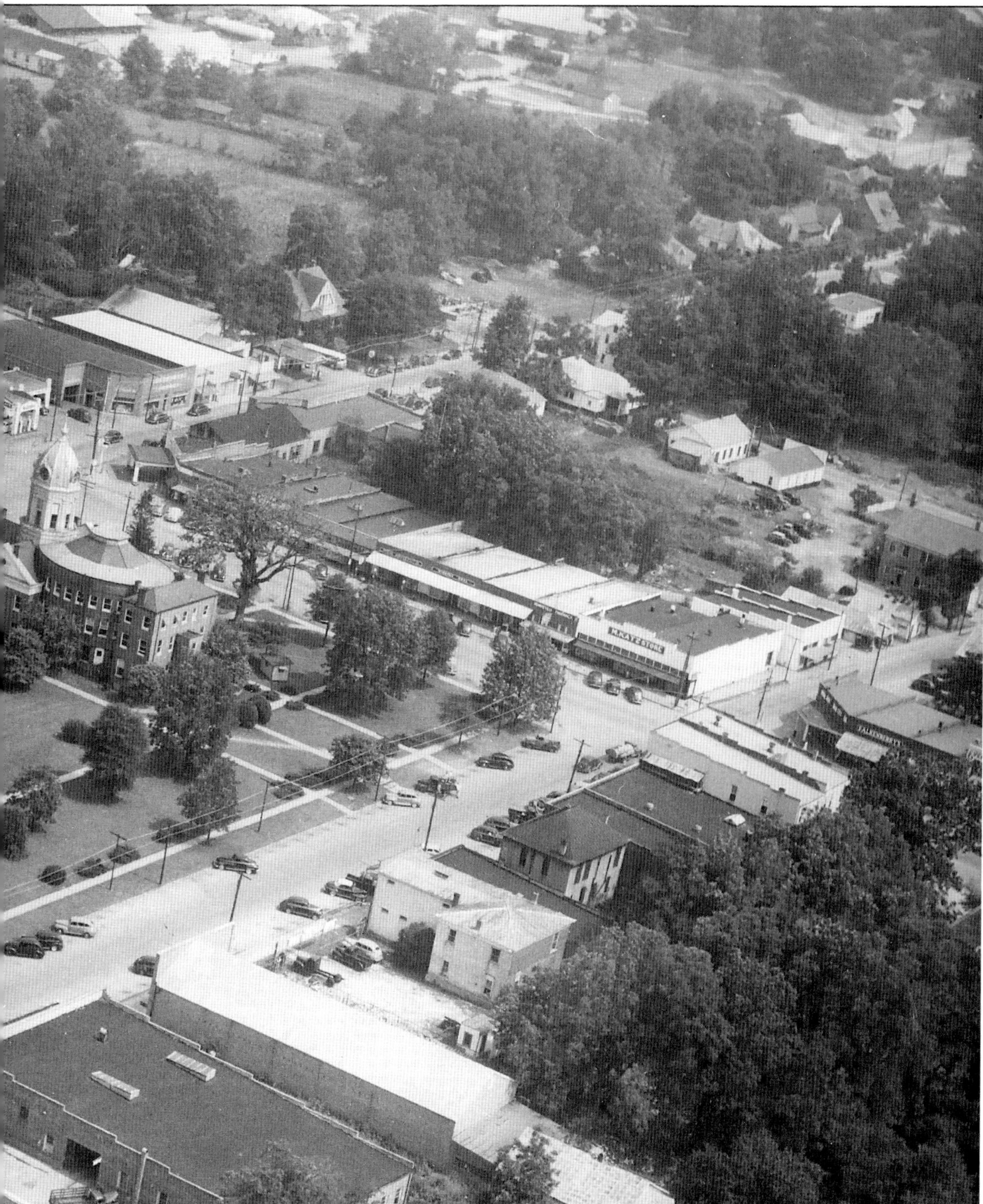

clerk and register, court records and documents, the sheriff's office, county extension agents, tax assessor and collector, and the county commission office. Today the vacant area shown next to the old courthouse is the location of the 1963 courthouse built by Probate Judge Eugene Temple Millsap.

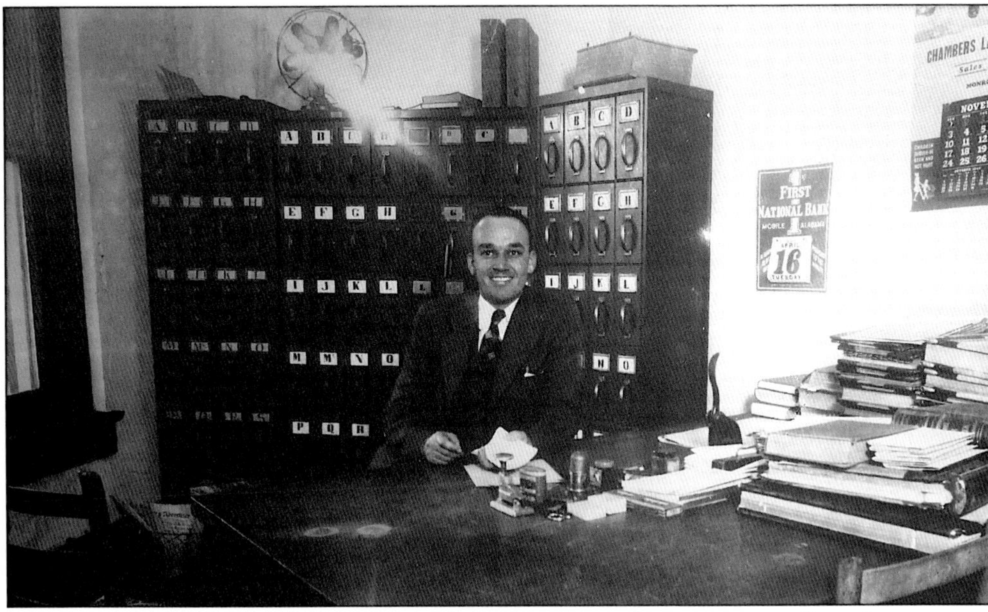

LISTON ALLEN "STRAIGHT-A" HIXON, PICTURED IN HIS OFFICE IN THE OLD COURTHOUSE AROUND 1940. L.A. was called "Straight-A" due to his straight A average at Auburn University. He was the circuit court clerk and registrar for the county.

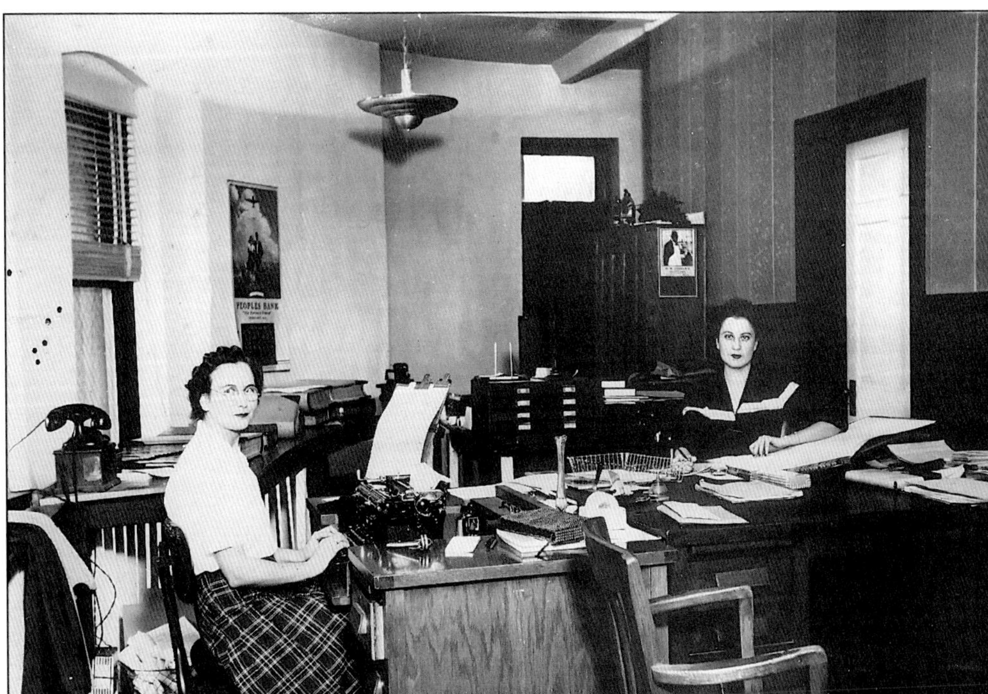

AGNES BIGGS, LEFT, AND KATHERINE LEE IN THE PROBATE OFFICE OF THE OLD COURTHOUSE, LOCATED ON THE FIRST FLOOR IN THE 1940S.

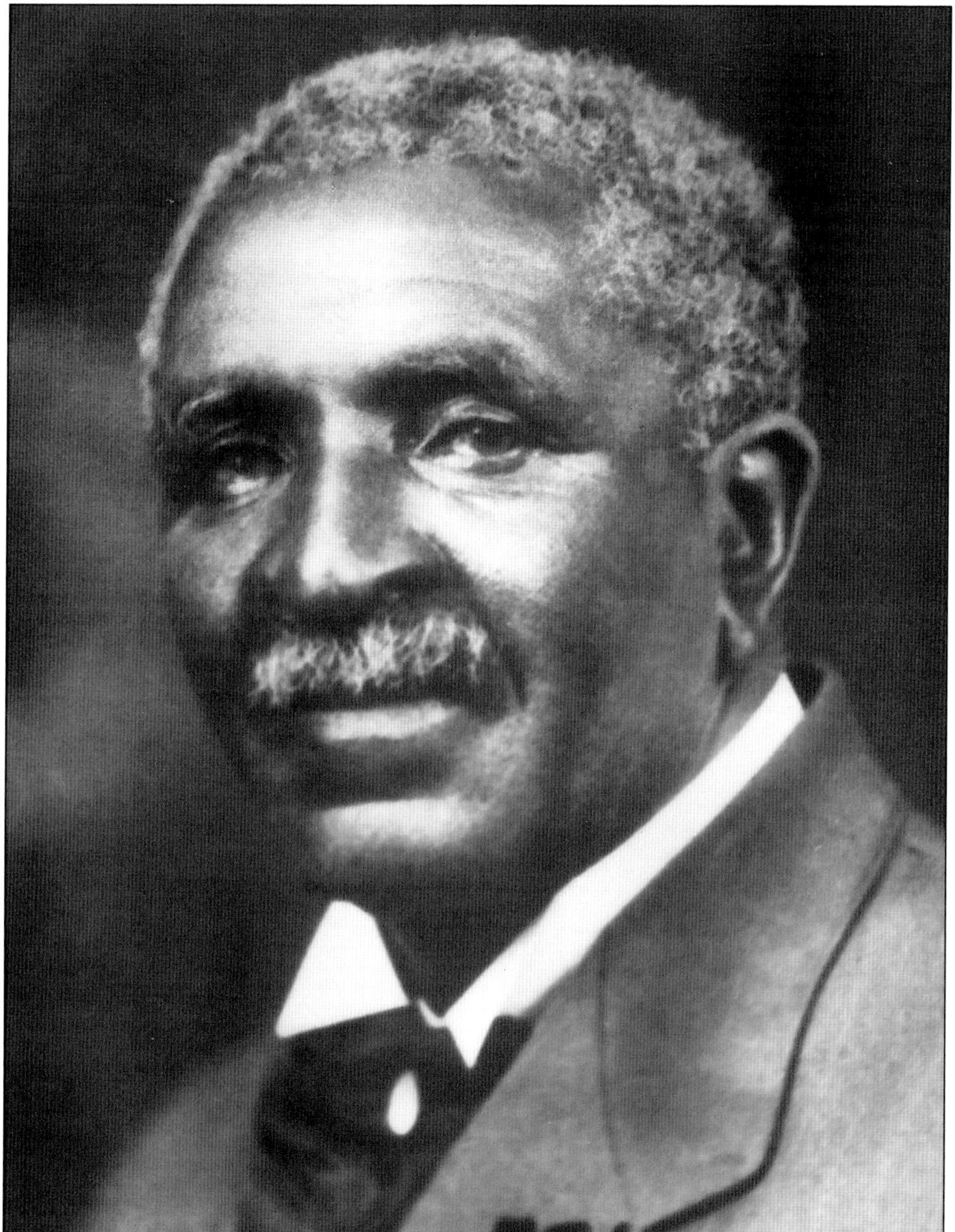

Dr. George Washington Carver of Tuskegee Institute. Dr. Carver, one of the more prominent Alabamians to speak in the old courtroom, spoke to a crowded courtroom on February 14, 1934, after being introduced by Ms. Rosa Lazenby Barnett. Upon the conclusion of her introduction, Dr. Carver arose, faced Ms. Barnett, and said, "I have been introduced before kings and queens of many nations, but this is absolutely the finest introduction that I have ever received."

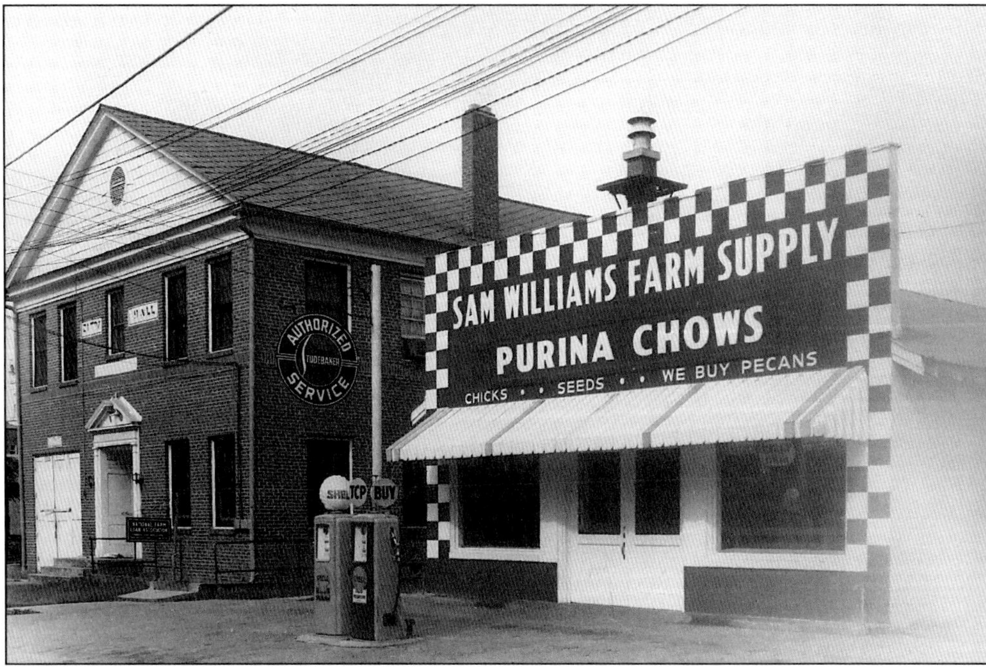

SAM WILLIAMS' FARM SUPPLY, LOCATED NEXT TO CITY HALL IN THE 1950S.

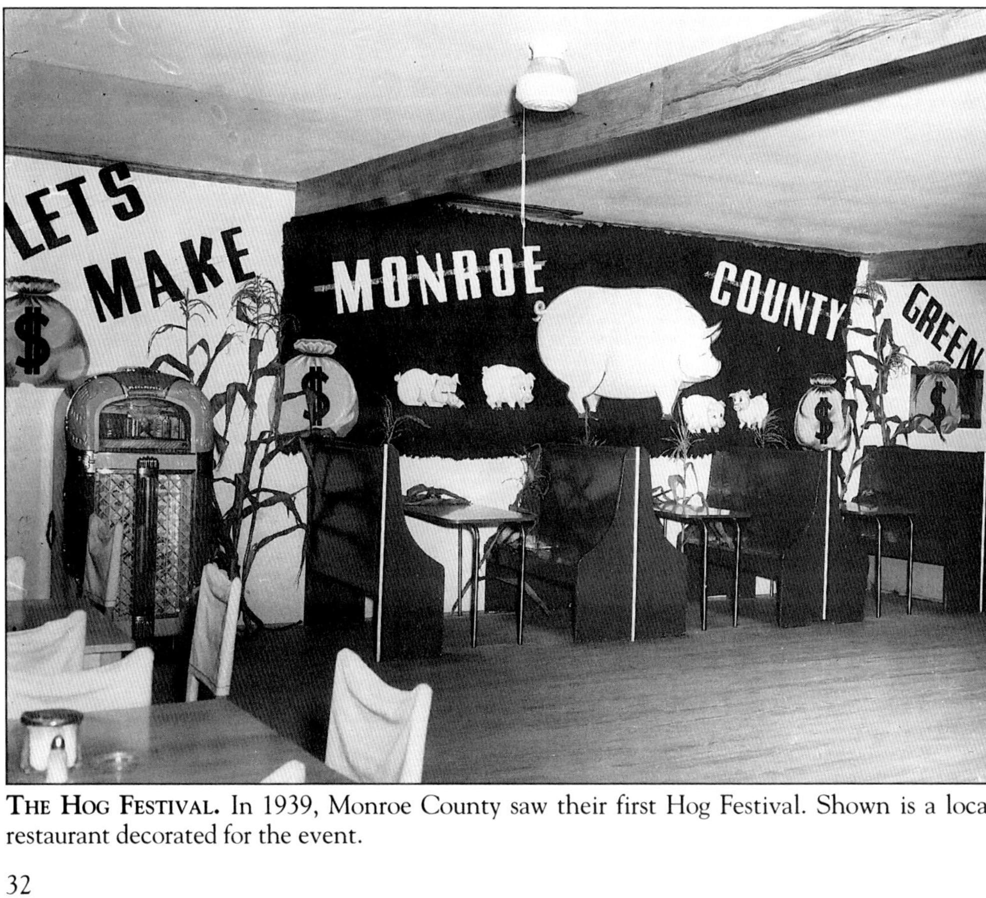

THE HOG FESTIVAL. In 1939, Monroe County saw their first Hog Festival. Shown is a local restaurant decorated for the event.

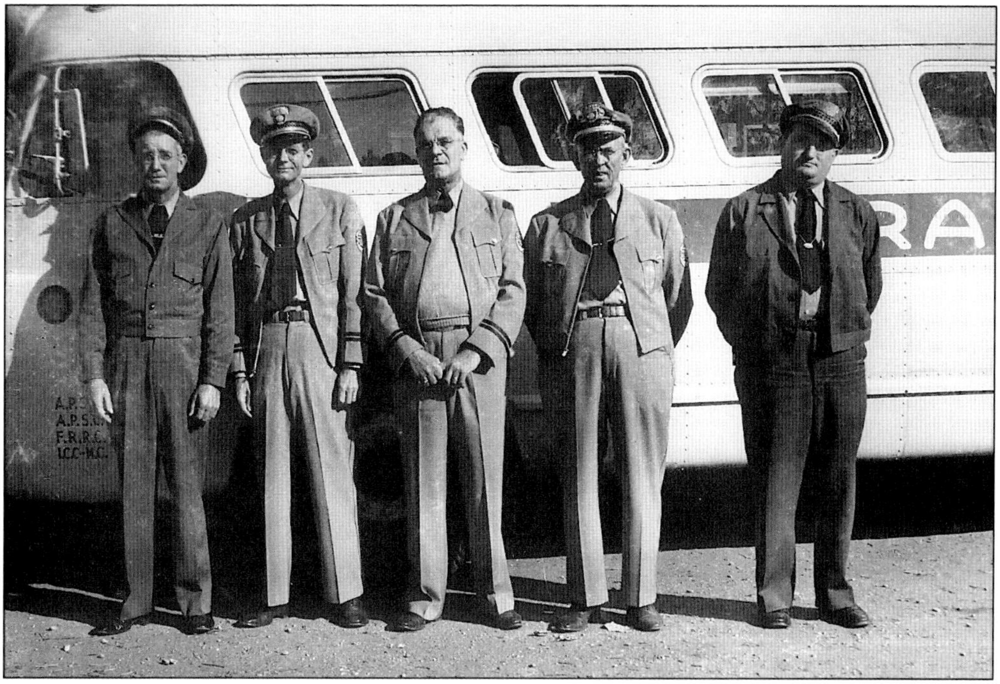

Bus Drivers Standing in front of a Trailway Bus in Monroeville. The buses provided a link to the larger cities of Alabama. Both Harper Lee and Truman Capote talked in their books about people coming and going on the bus lines in Monroeville.

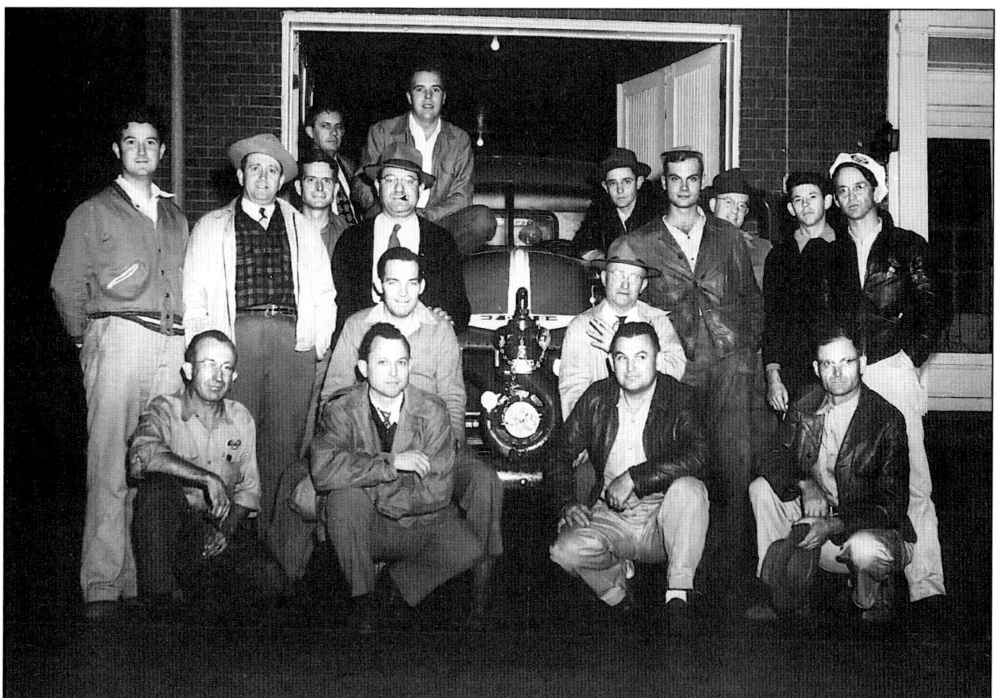

Monroeville Citizens in front of the New Fire Engine at the Monroeville Fire Department, 1950s.

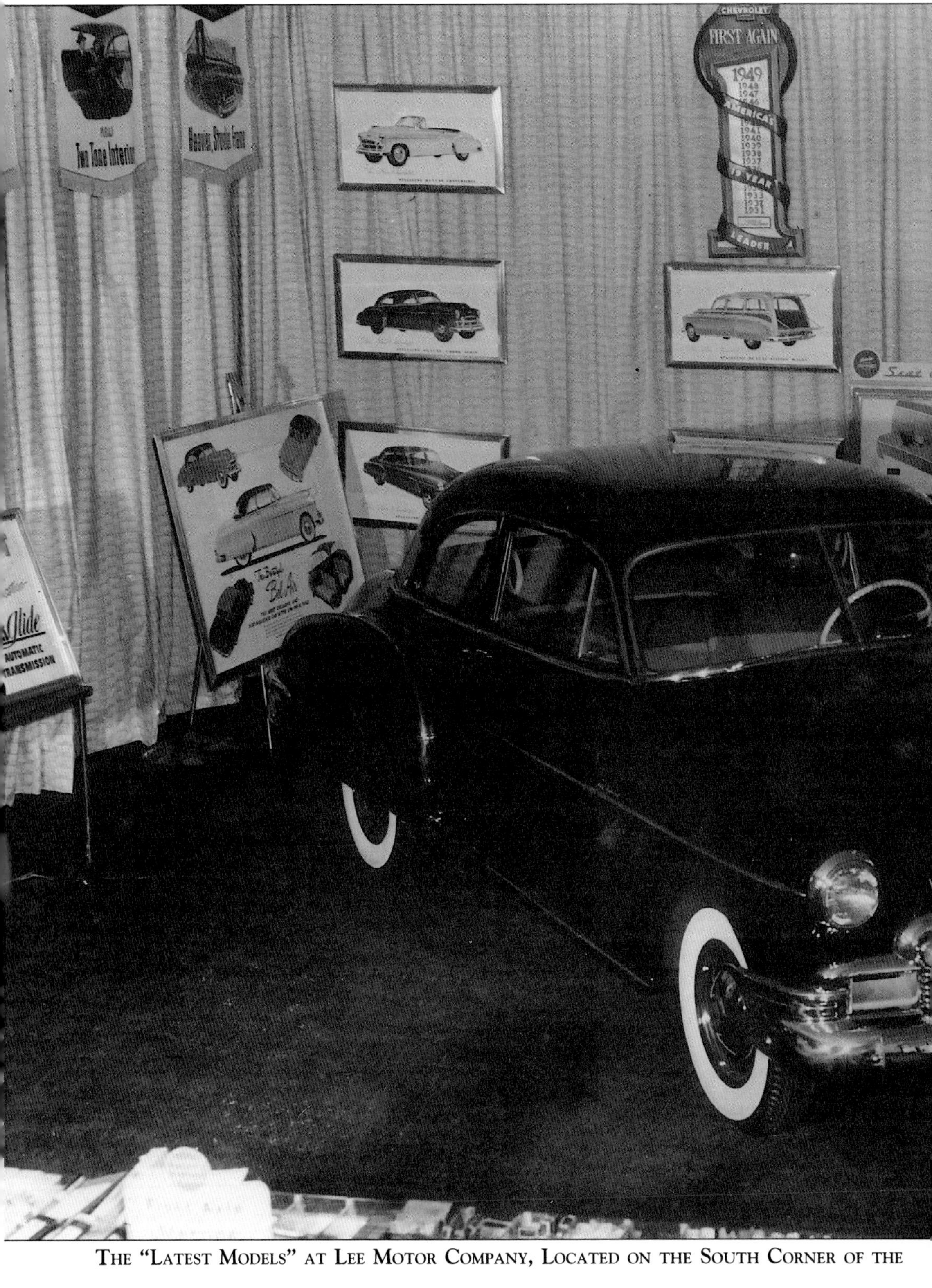

THE "LATEST MODELS" AT LEE MOTOR COMPANY, LOCATED ON THE SOUTH CORNER OF THE

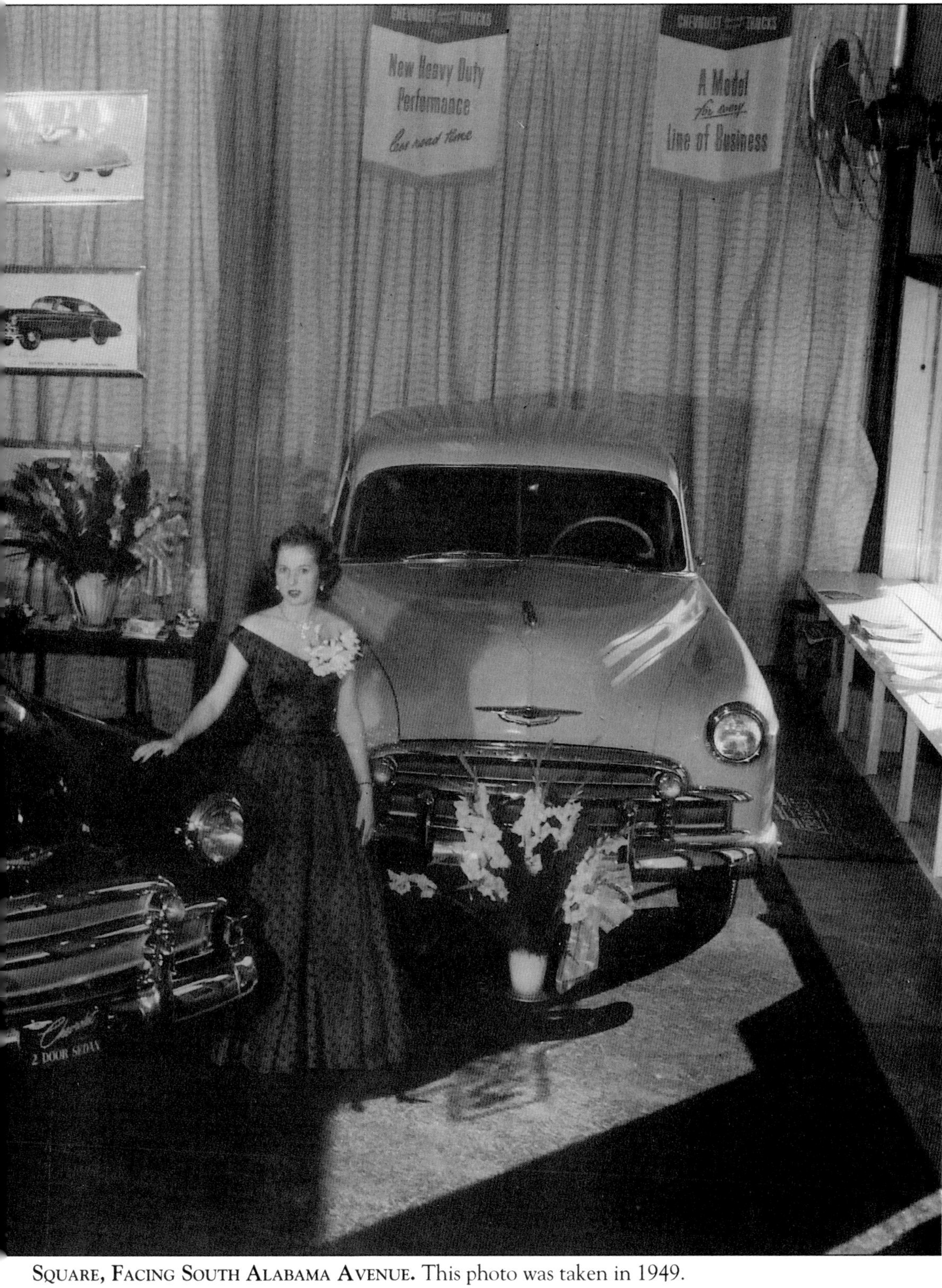

SQUARE, FACING SOUTH ALABAMA AVENUE. This photo was taken in 1949.

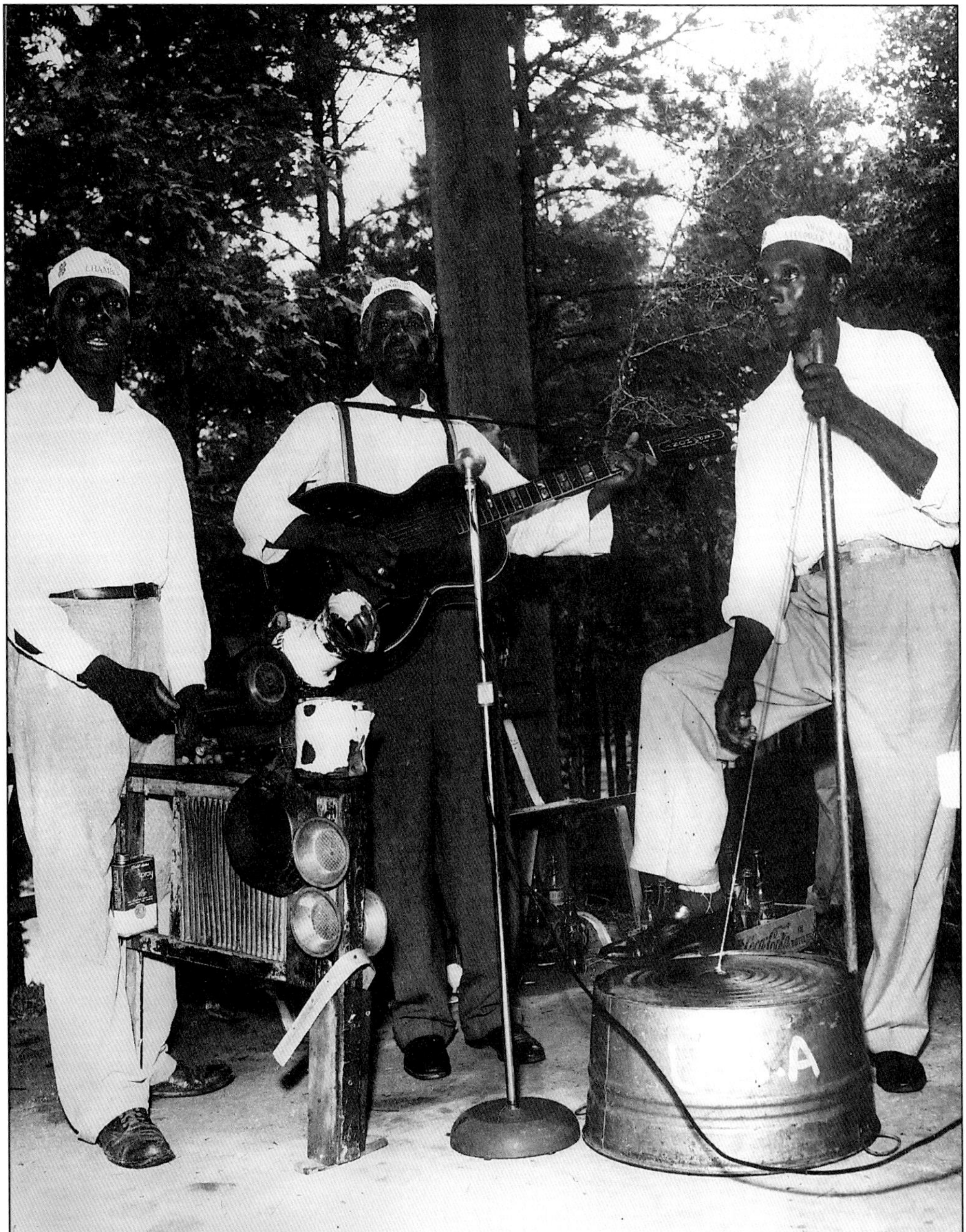

LOCAL BAND. The photograph is believed to have been taken by Max McAliley in the late 1940s. All band members are wearing Chamber of Commerce hats.

Three

Diversions

"The South has never been a placid place."
—Cynthia Tucker
Editor of the *Atlanta Constitution* editorial page, and native of Monroeville

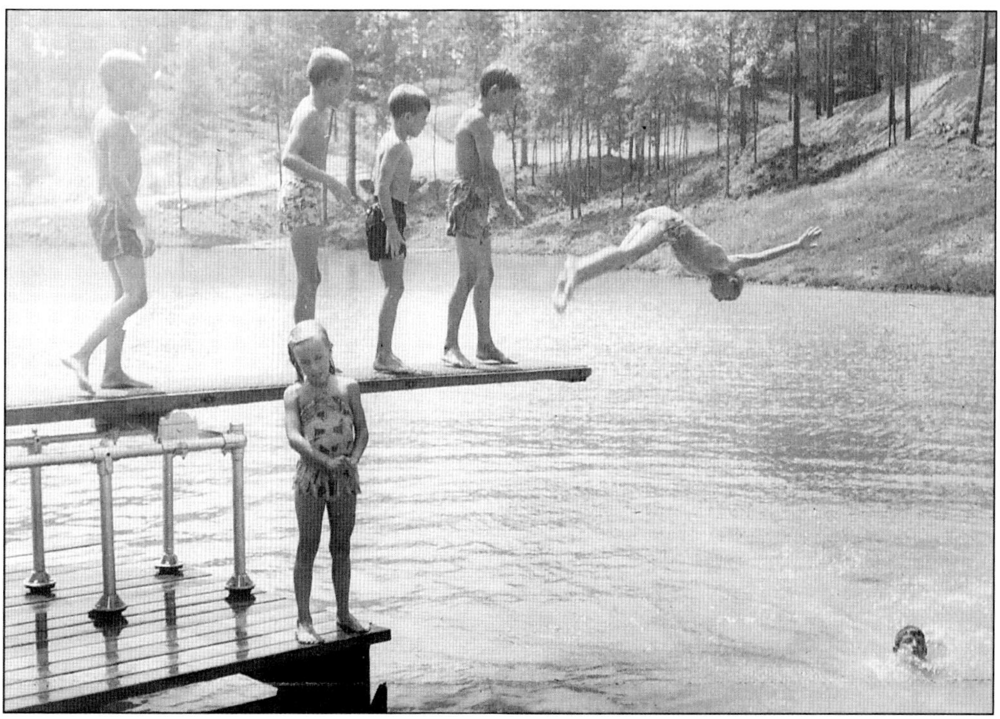

Children's Day Camp in the Early 1950s at Whitey Lee Park, Built by Vanity Fair Corporation. Vanity Fair came to Monroeville in 1937.

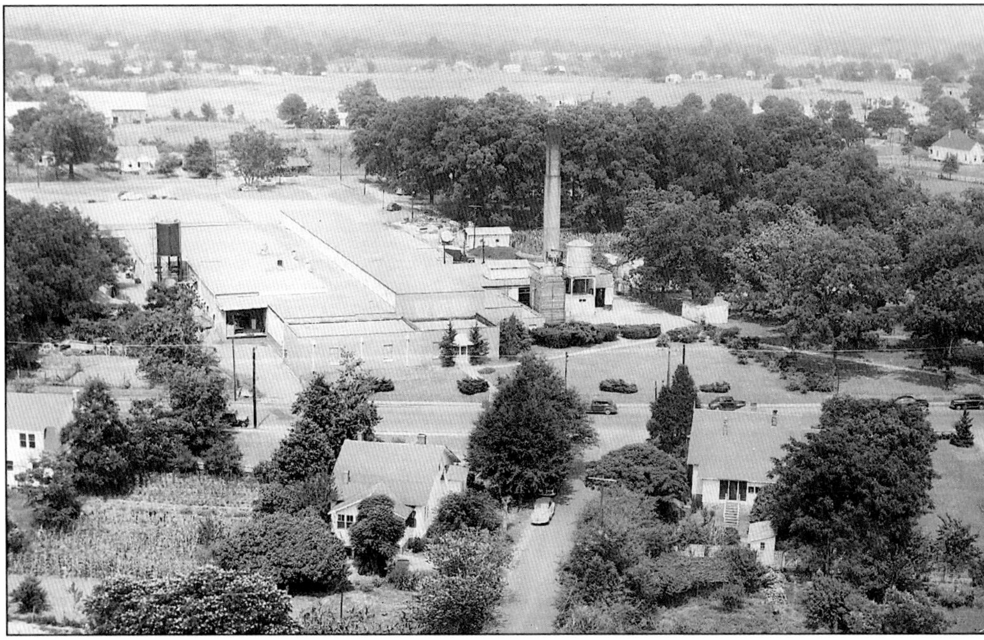

Aerial View of Vanity Fair Corporation in the 1940s. Vanity Fair Corporation was the beginning of outside cultural and economic influences for Monroe County. It employed women who had never worked before as seamstresses, and was the largest corporate employer in the county for many years.

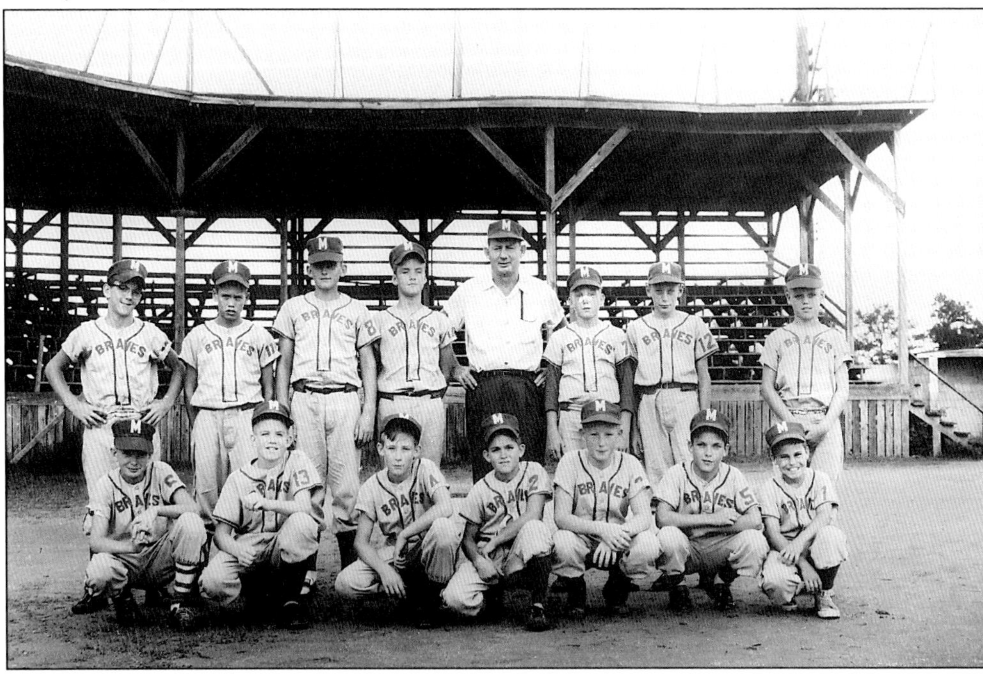

Little League Baseball Team at Vanity Fair Ball Park. From left to right are: (front row) Mickey Blanton, Jerry Jackson, Robin Sanderson, unknown, Jack Kelly, unknown, and unknown; (back row) Louie Hayles, Guy Sawyer, Mike Lawrence, Tim Jones, Pete Kelly, Joe Kelly, Joe Tucker, and unknown.

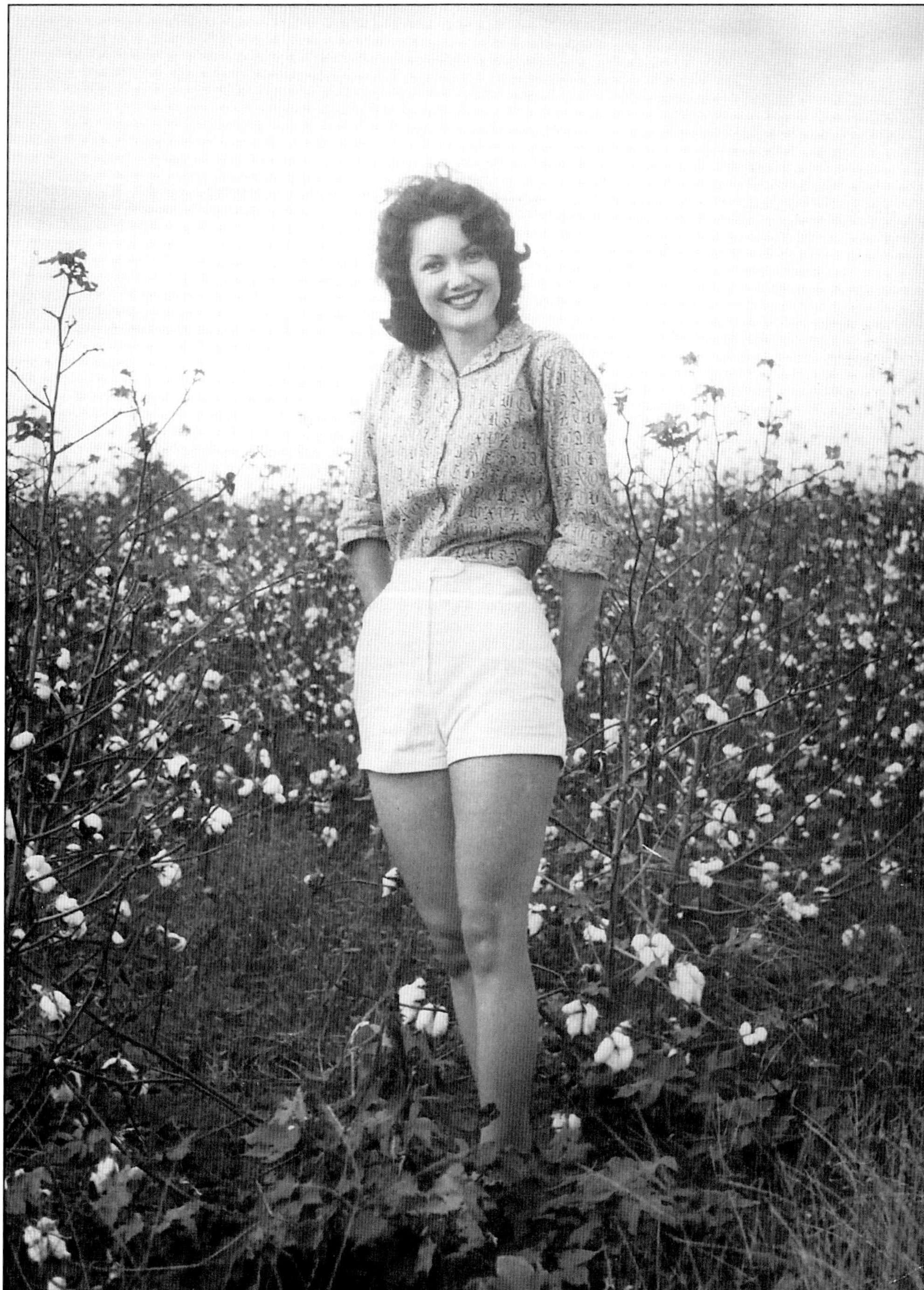

Ga Nell Dennis Posing in a Field of Cotton South of Monroeville. This photograph was taken by Max McAliley in the 1950s. Cotton continues to play a major role in the industry of Monroe County, making the county one of the top cotton-producing counties in the state.

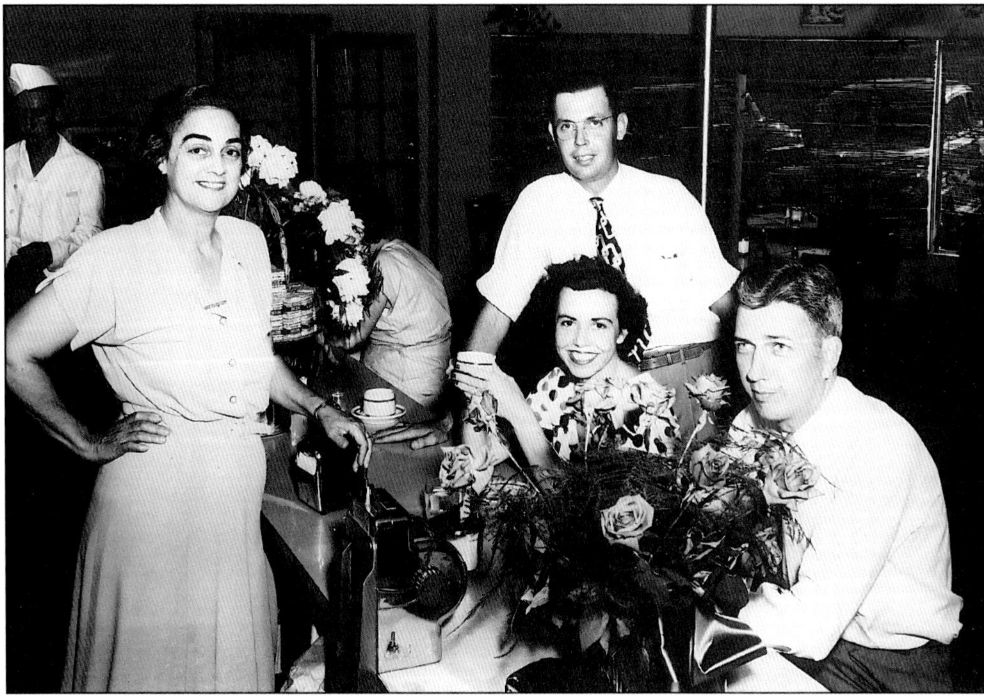

Hi Ho Restaurant, Located on Pineville Road. The Hi Ho, owned by Miss Emma Yarlborough (pictured at left), was the social gathering point during the late 1940s and 1950s. Dances were held in the back of the restaurant. Truman Capote was spotted here more than once.

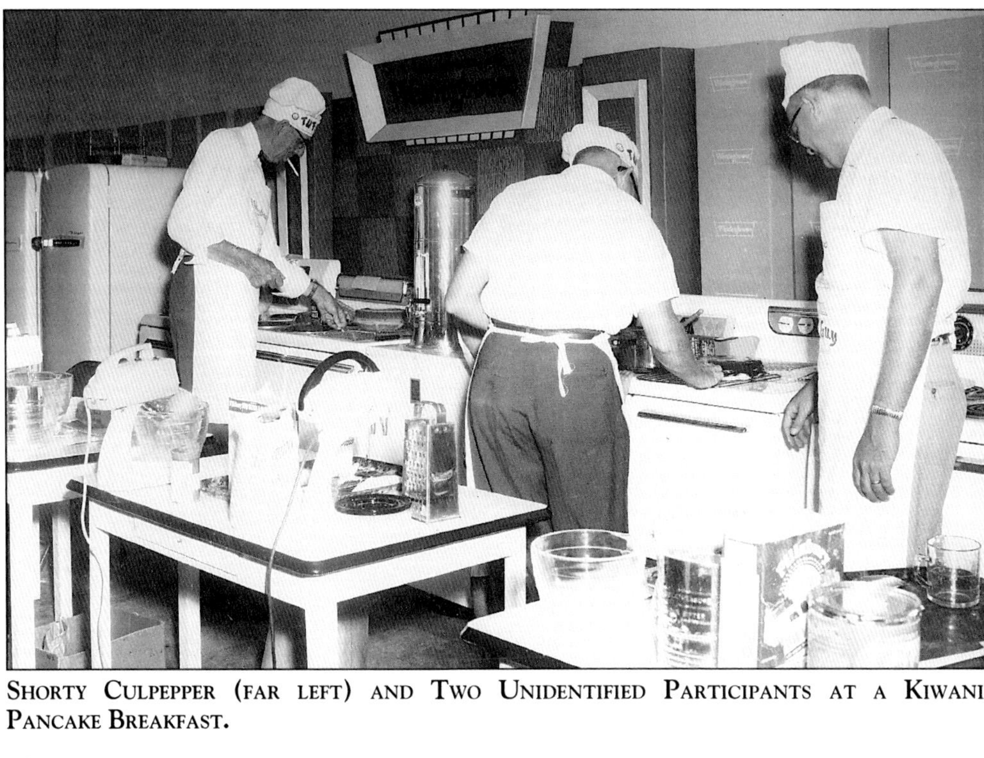

Shorty Culpepper (far left) and Two Unidentified Participants at a Kiwanis Pancake Breakfast.

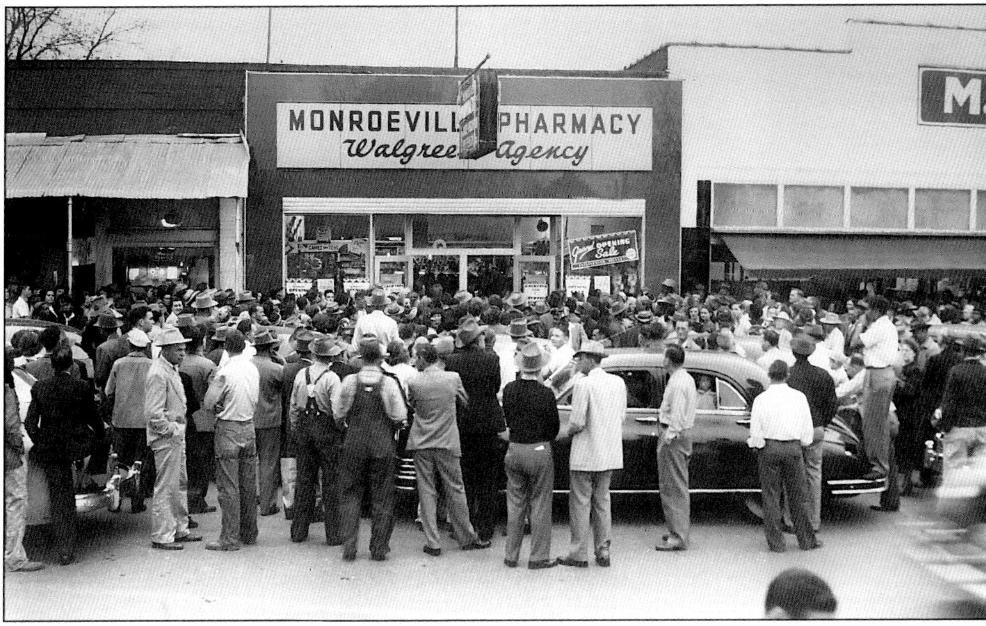

The Grand Opening of the Monroeville Pharmacy, Located on the South Side of the Square. As a child, Truman Capote used to take friends to the pharmacy and charge fountain drinks and milkshakes.

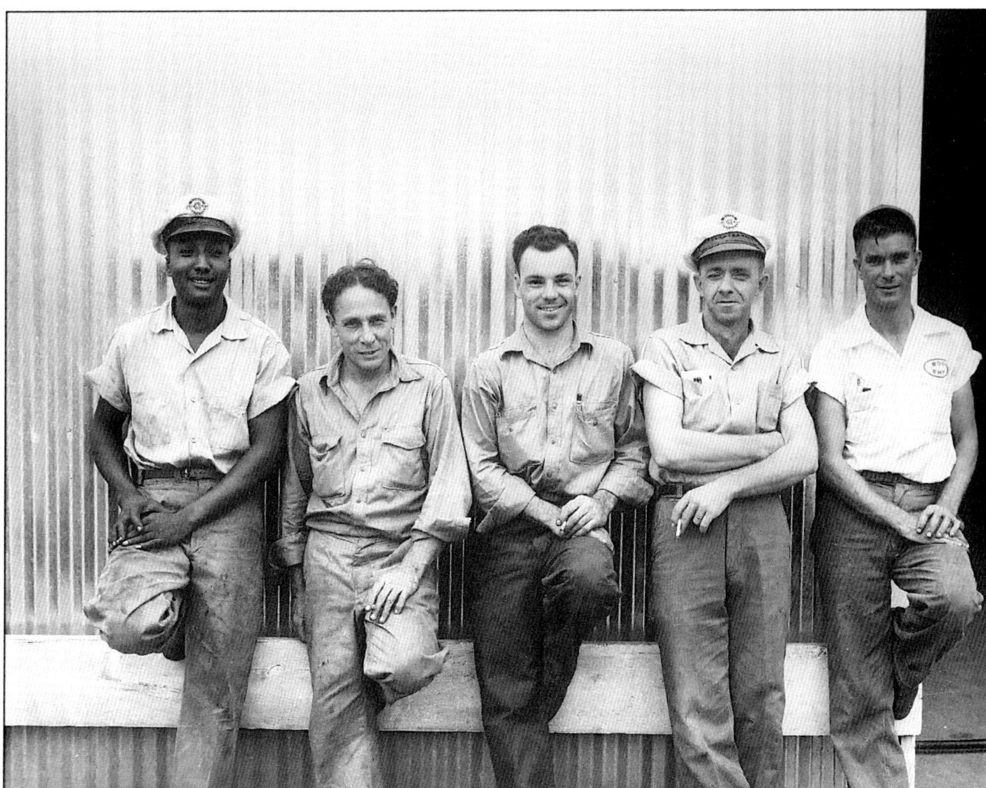

Lee Motor Company Employees Taking a Break in the 1950s.

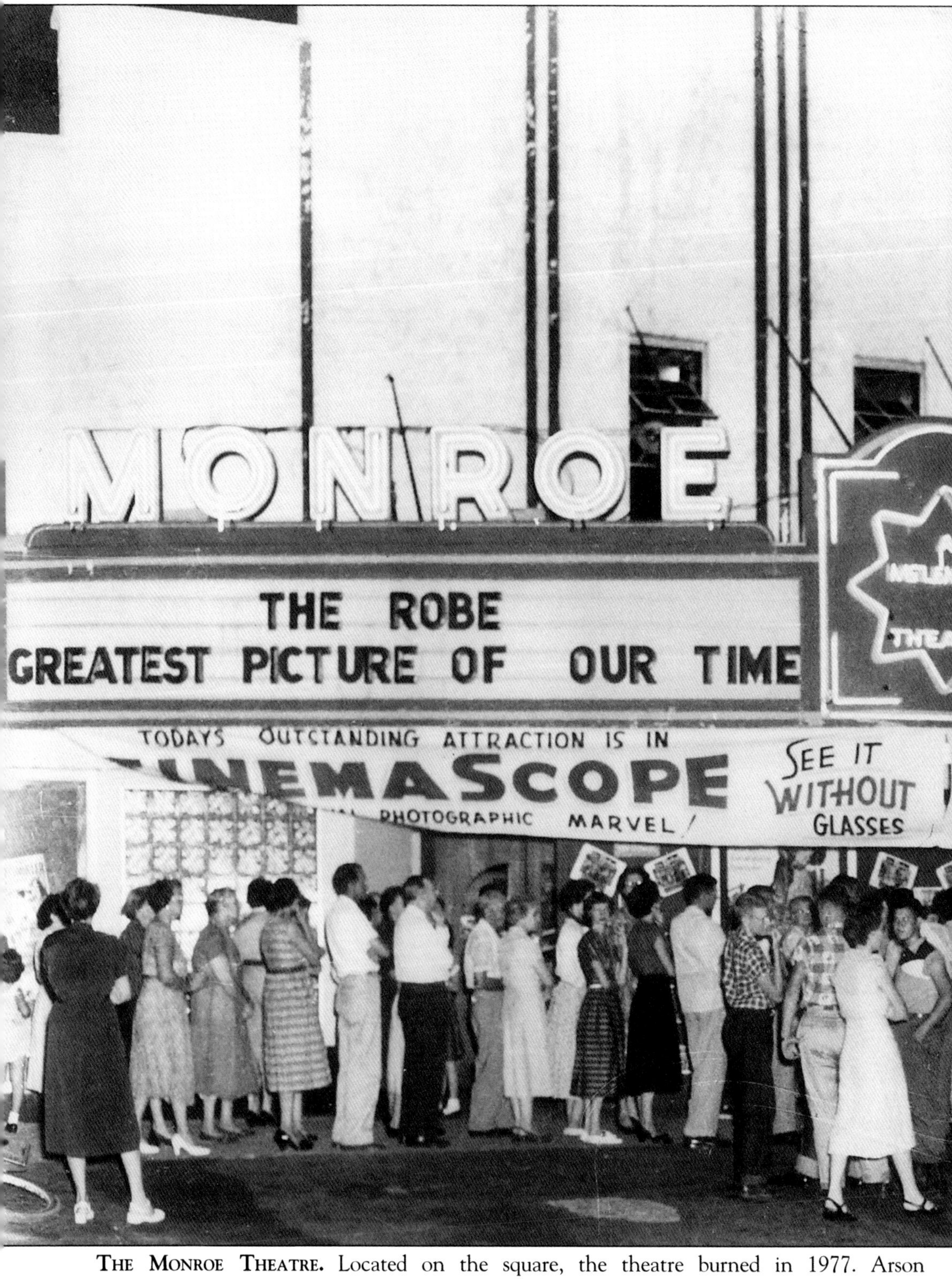

The Monroe Theatre. Located on the square, the theatre burned in 1977. Arson

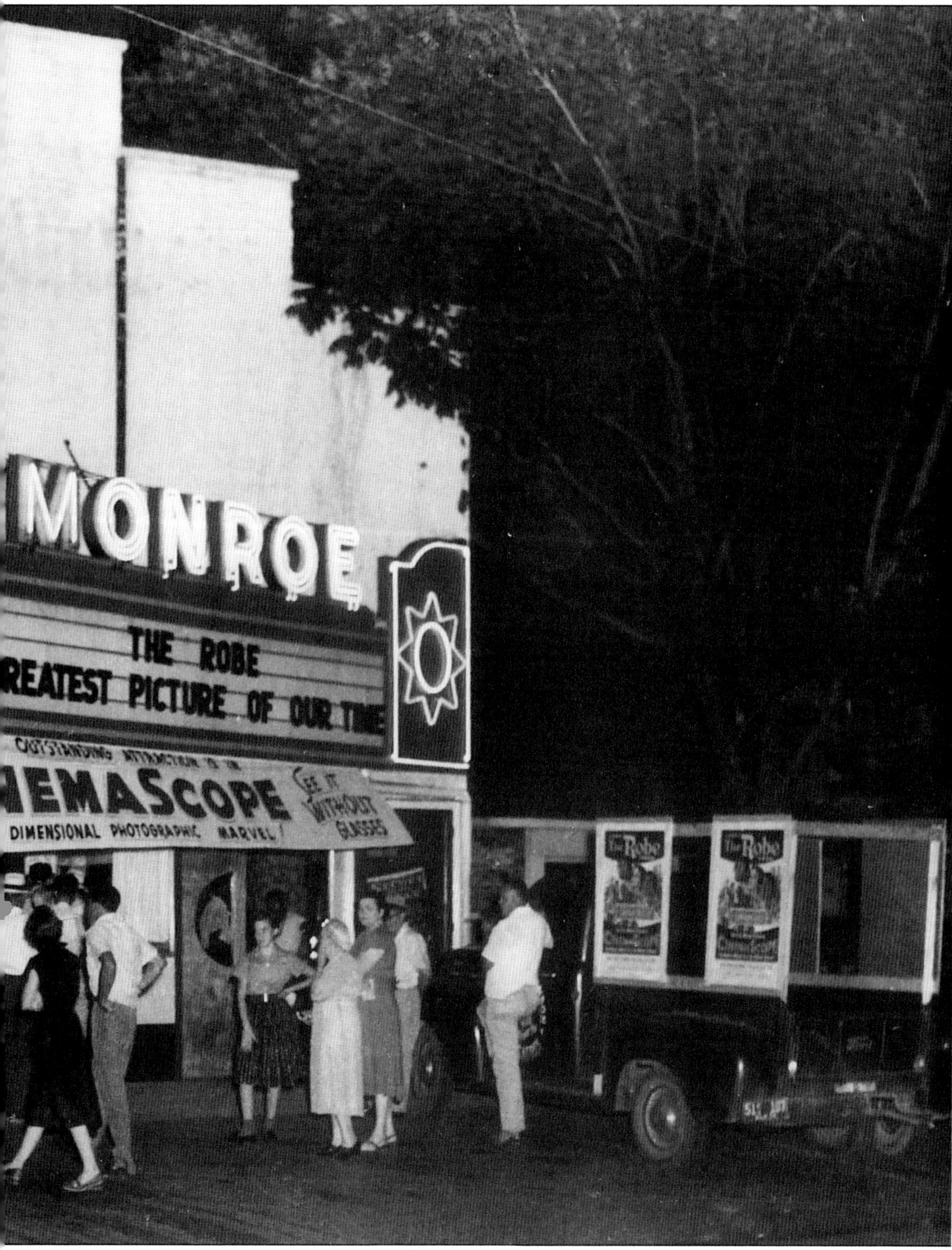

was suspected.

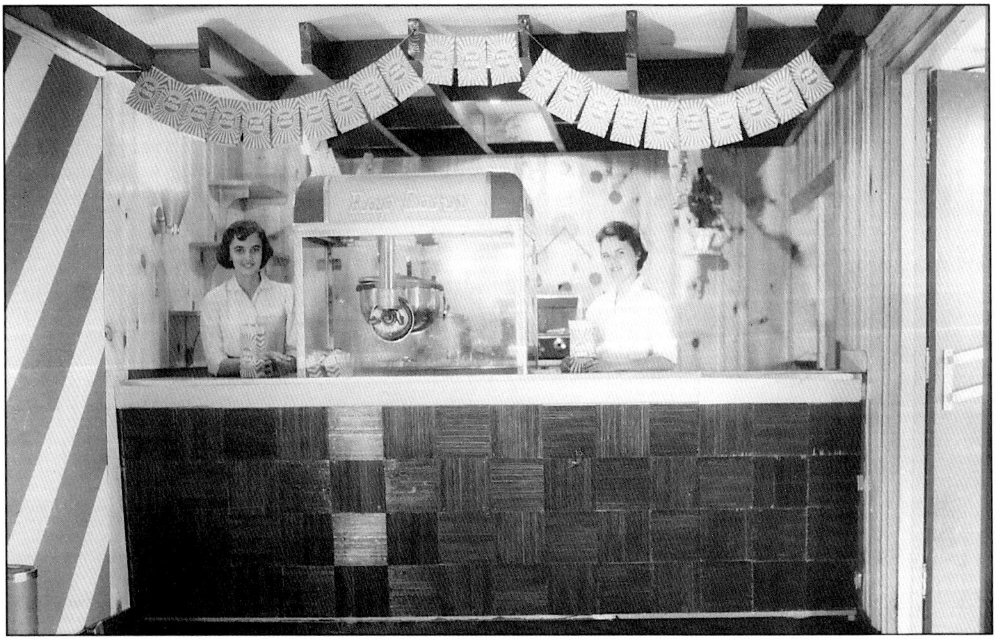

THE MONROE THEATRE CONCESSION STAND IN THE 1950s.

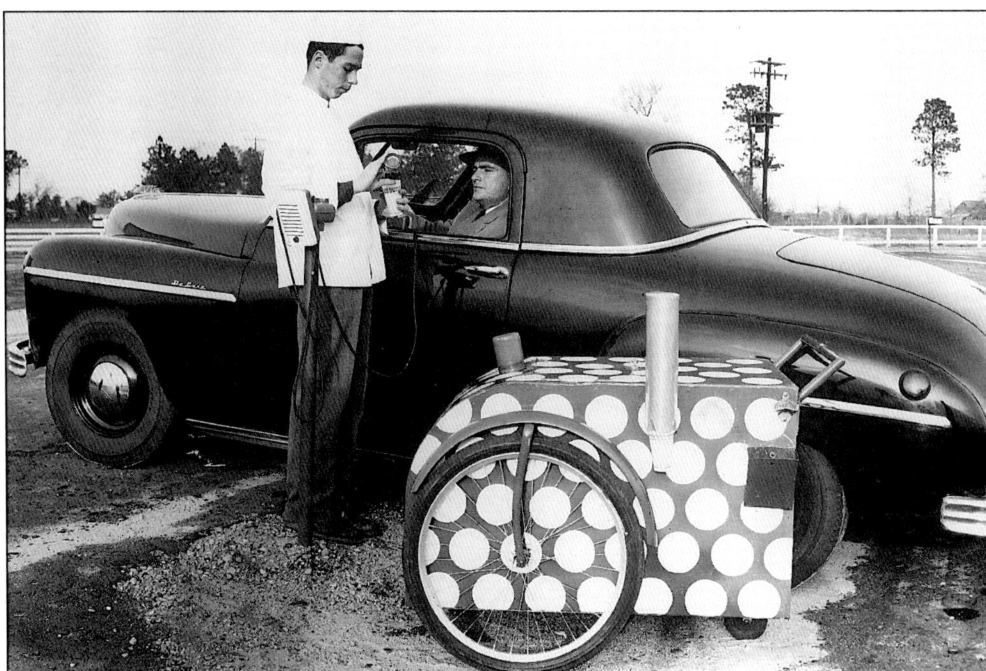

THE MONROEVILLE DRIVE-IN MOVIE THEATRE IN THE EARLY 1950s.

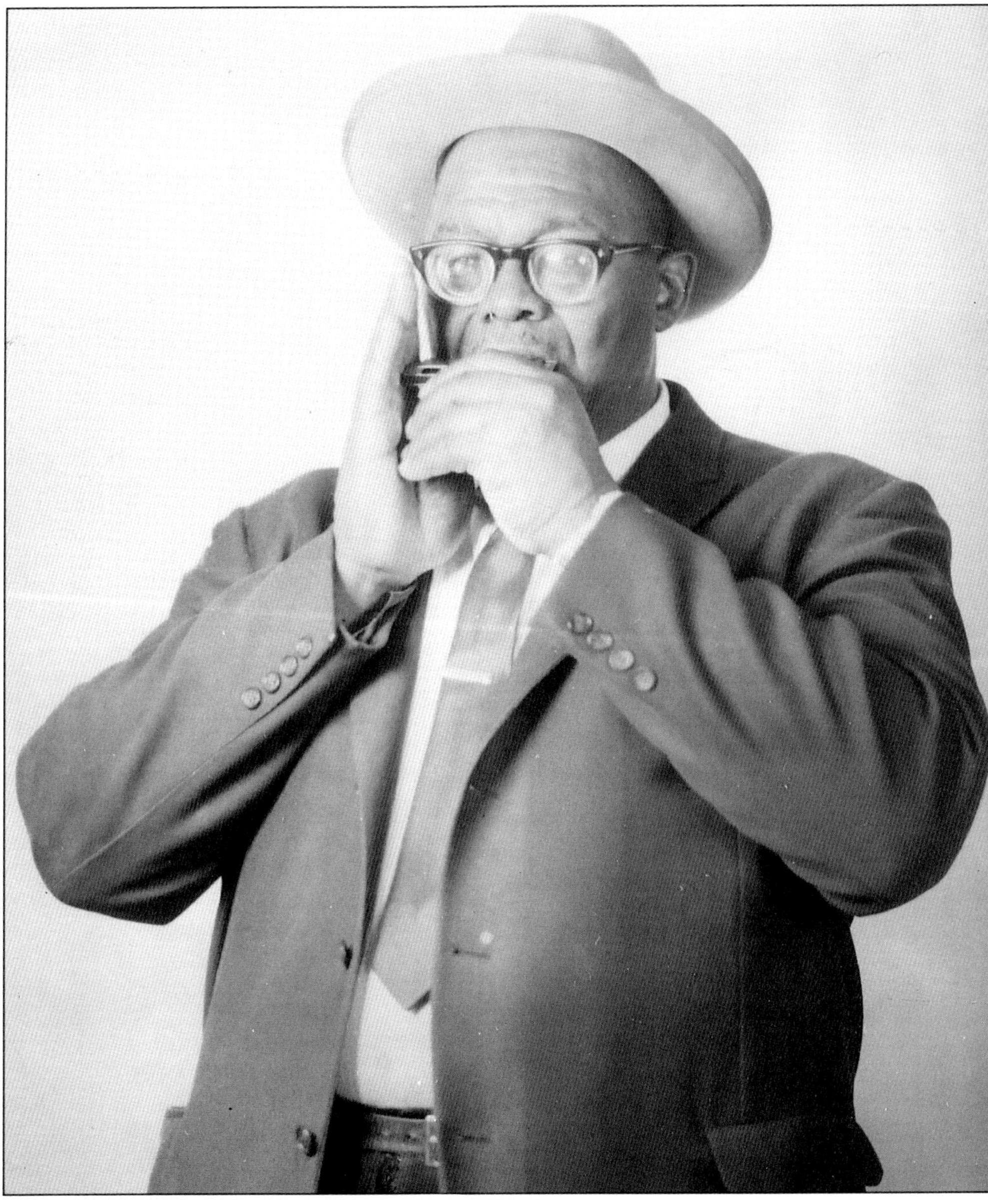

Folk and Gospel Singer Dan J. Smith. Smith, who grew up outside Monroeville on the road toward Perdue Hill, taught himself to play harmonica as a child, then gave up his music-making for many years until he was discovered by Pete Seeger. Smith played with Seeger's "Hudson River Sloop Band."

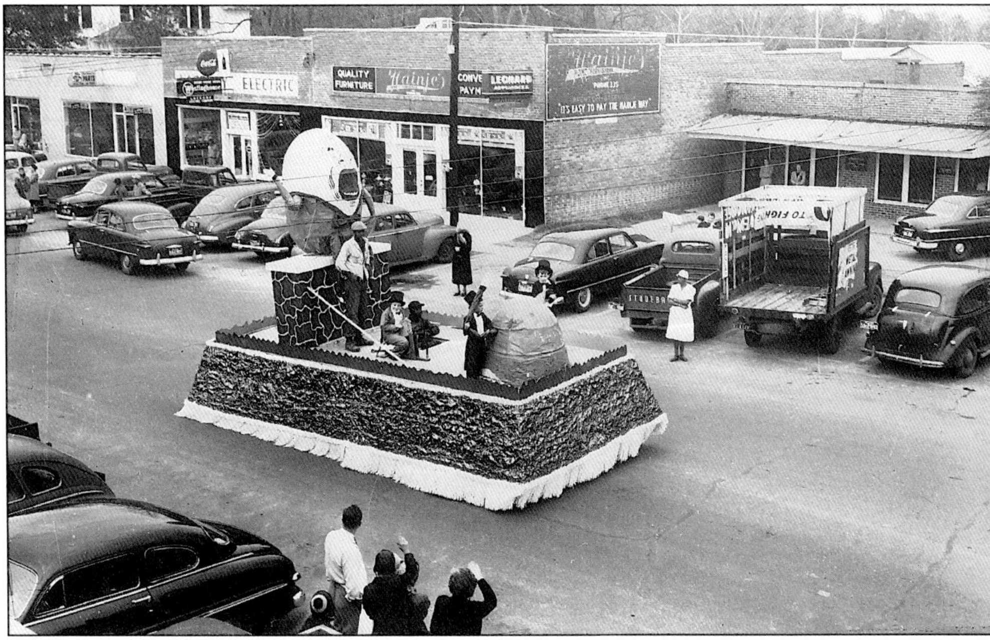

THE 1950S ANNUAL MONROEVILLE CHRISTMAS PARADE ON WEST CLAIBORNE STREET. The offices next to Hainje's Furniture were those of Dr. Woodrow Eddins, who practiced medicine in Monroe County for over 50 years.

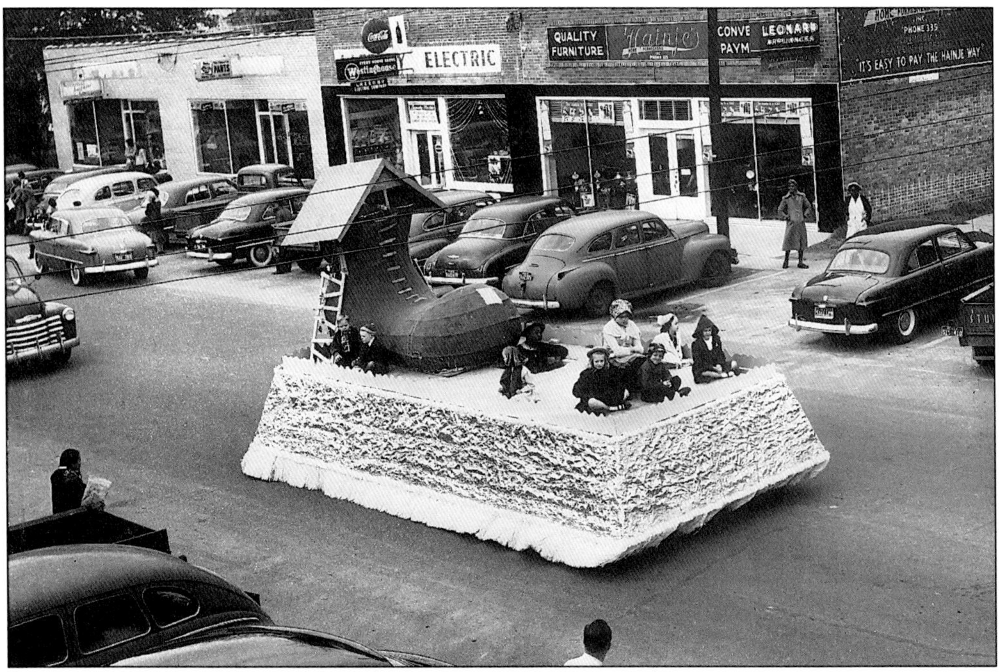

1959 CHRISTMAS PARADE. The parade that year was threatened by the Ku Klux Klan because of the participation of the marching band of Union High School in Clausell. Tempers ran high as the heads of the Kiwanis and Civitan Clubs fought the KKK to hold the parade with the traditional black band. When the KKK threatened violence at the parade, the parade was cancelled that year.

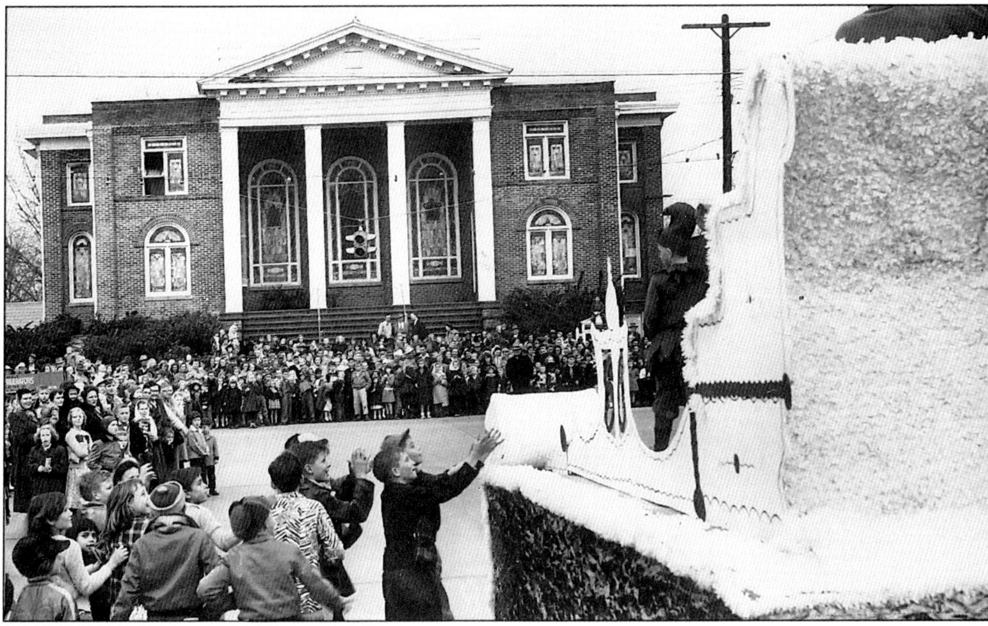

The North Side of the Square and the First Baptist Church. The First Baptist Church housed a red, white, and blue stained-glass memorial to World War veterans. Unfortunately, the church building was demolished in the early 1970s. The new church was built on Pineville Road.

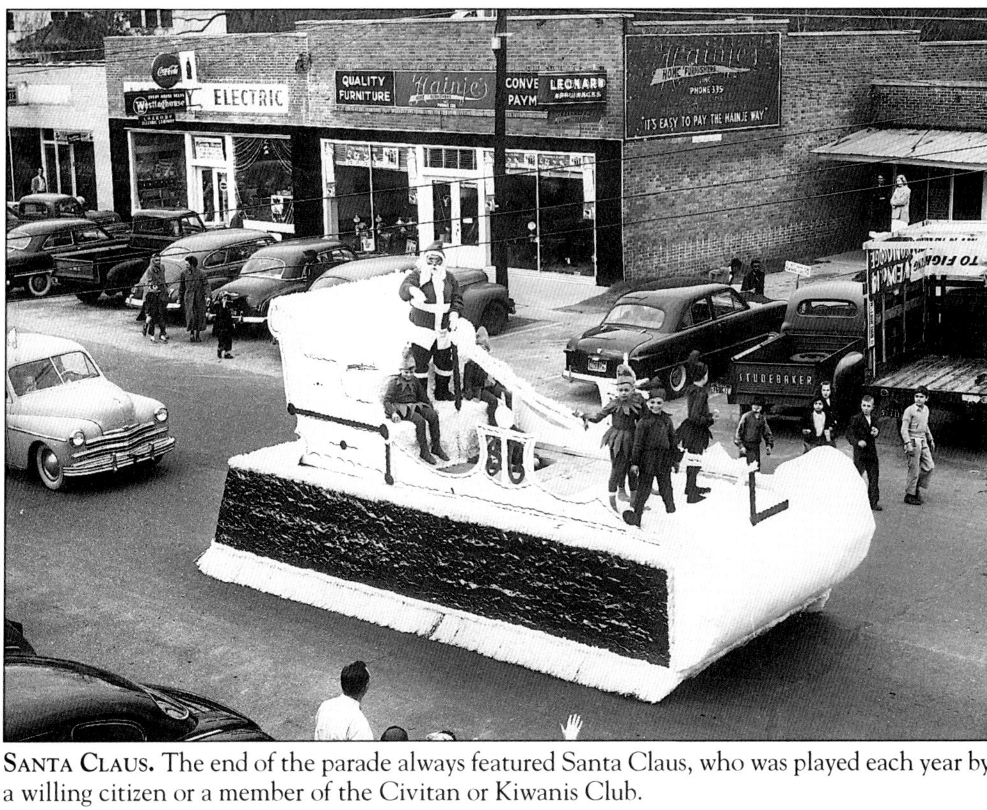

Santa Claus. The end of the parade always featured Santa Claus, who was played each year by a willing citizen or a member of the Civitan or Kiwanis Club.

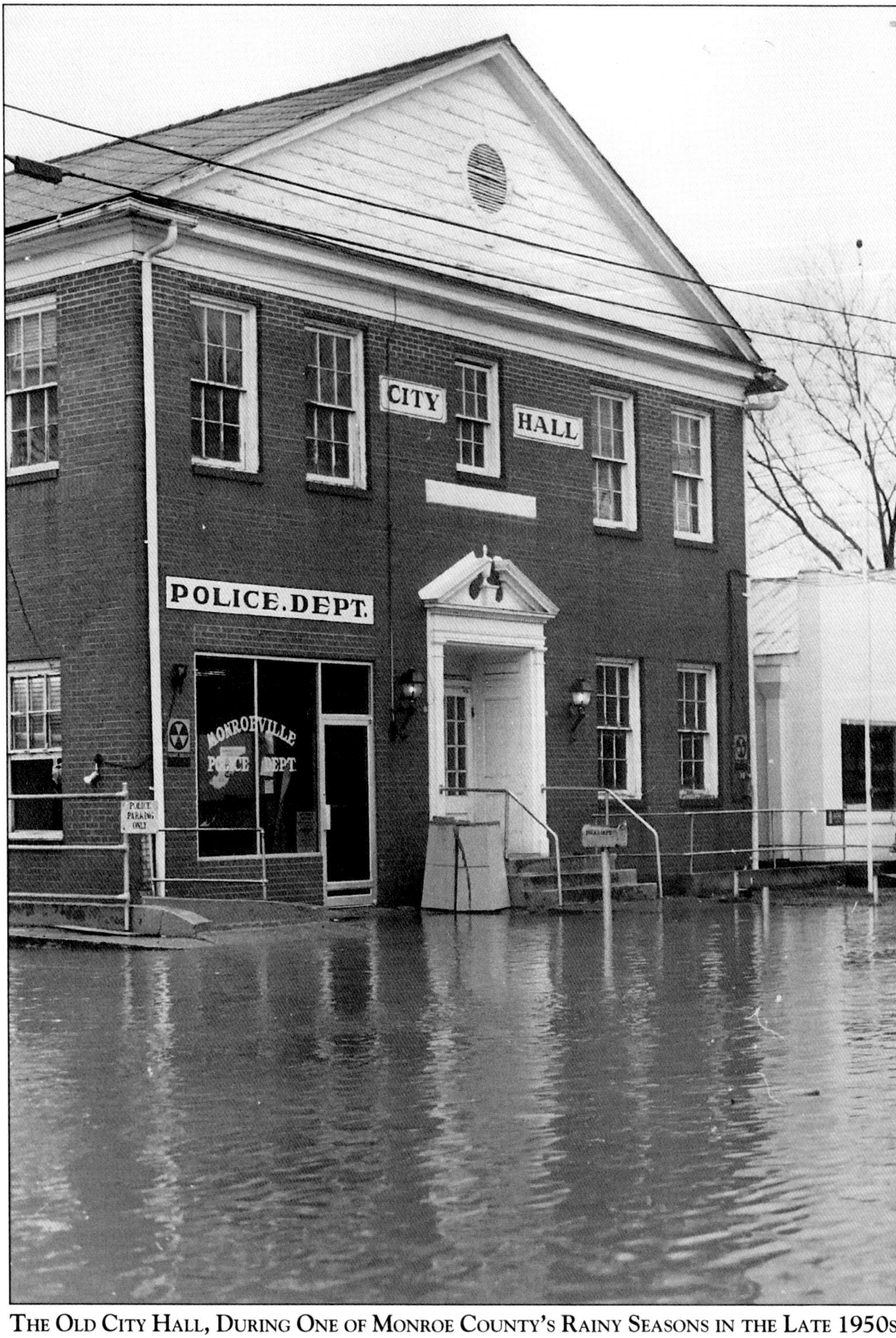

THE OLD CITY HALL, DURING ONE OF MONROE COUNTY'S RAINY SEASONS IN THE LATE 1950S, EARLY 1960S.

Four

POLITICS

"Everything is made for love."
—U.S. Congressman Frank Boykin

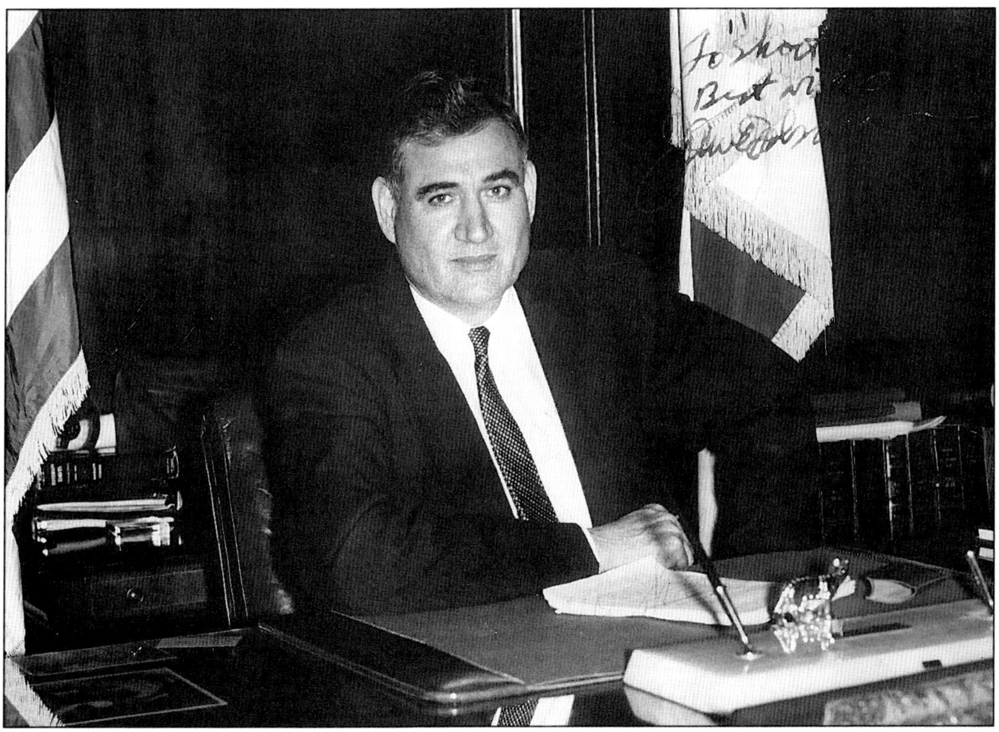

"BIG JIM" FOLSOM, GOVERNOR OF THE STATE OF ALABAMA FROM 1947 TO 1951 AND 1955 TO 1959. Big Jim was a regular visitor to the old courthouse in Monroeville. During his campaign for the office of governor, he would bring his "Pea-Pickers" band and sit in the judge's chair in the old courtroom visiting with Monroe Countians or campaigning outside on the square.

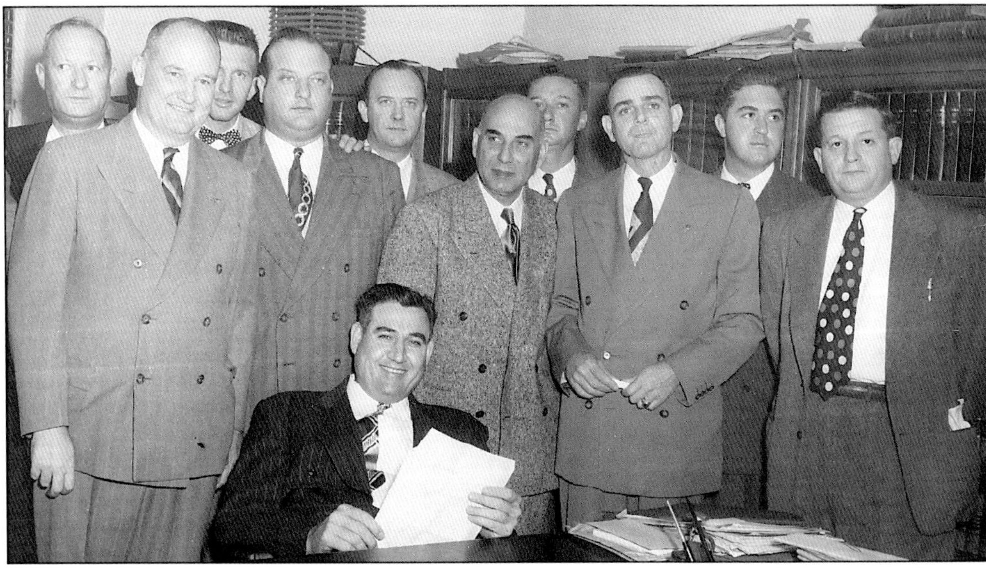

BIG JIM FOLSOM. Although Probate Judge Millsap did not support Folsom's first run for governor, the two became good friends after his election. Millsap became part of the "Folsom Chosen," and his close relationship with the governor brought many good things to Monroe County, including something desperately needed—roads.

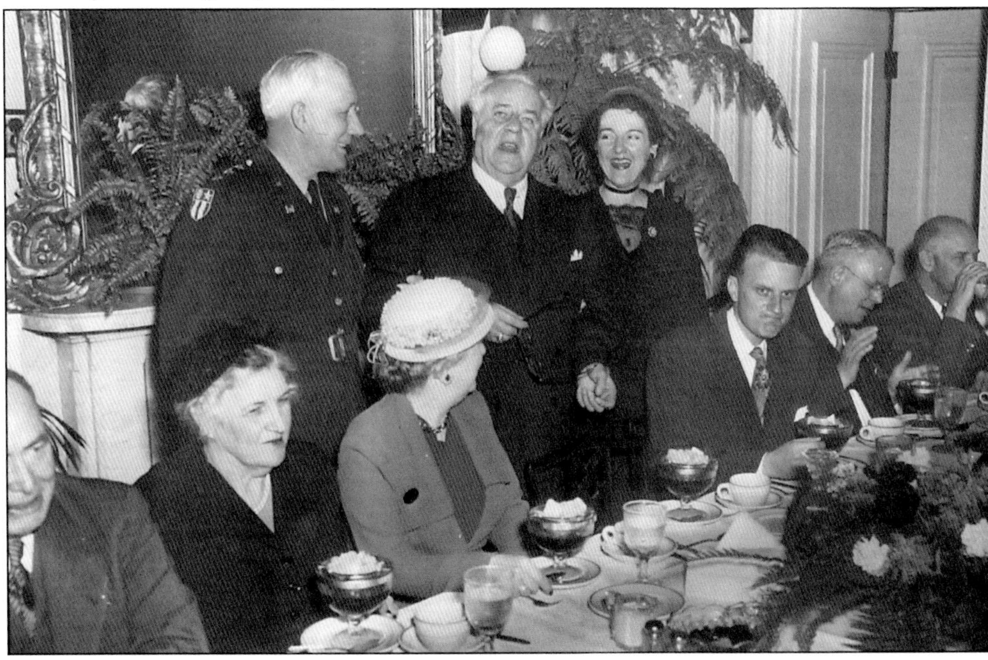

U.S. CONGRESSMAN FRANK BOYKIN (CENTER, STANDING) OF WASHINGTON COUNTY. Boykin, representative for Monroe County, was another politician who had close ties to Monroe County. This photo was taken at a Washington State dinner during the Eisenhower years. Shown are Hon. Joseph Martin, Mrs. Frank Boykin, Lt. Gen. Lewis A. Pick, Mrs. Pete Jarman, Hon. Frank Boykin, Mrs. Lewis A. Pick, Rev. Billy Graham, Hon. Pete Jarman, and Hon. Lister Hill (senator from Montgomery). (Hill and Sen. John Sparkman were leaders in a Democrats for Eisenhower movement.)

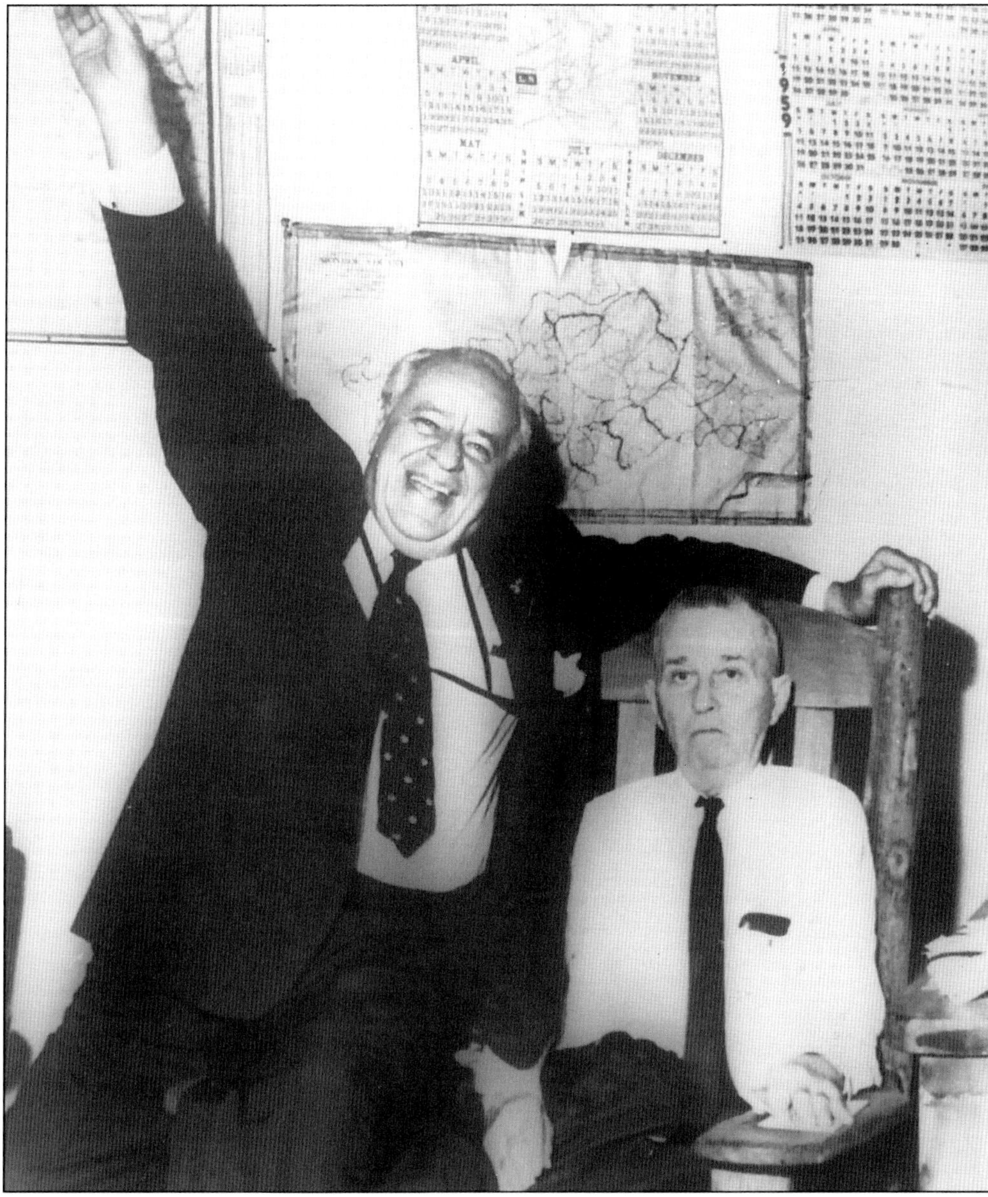

U.S. SENATOR FRANK BOYKIN WITH HIS LONGTIME FRIEND JUDGE MILLSAP. This photograph was taken during the last years of the judge's life. During the Millsap administration, Monroe County was named the Million-Dollar County. The county jail, county coliseum, and county garage were built. The new half-million-dollar courthouse was built and paid for, with well over a million dollars in the county coffers. The National Guard Armory, named in his honor, was also built. Monroe County became and still is one of the most financially stable counties in the state. "Shorty" Millsap was a quiet man who never expressed his opinions loudly or publicly. He had his own ideas about "states-righters" and was a thinker who assessed the situation and acted accordingly, maybe months later, working behind the scenes. A patient man, he had grown up poor and had made his way into the world on his own ability. Millsap was accused by many people of using "strong arm tactics." Nevertheless, he brought Monroe County into the 20th century.

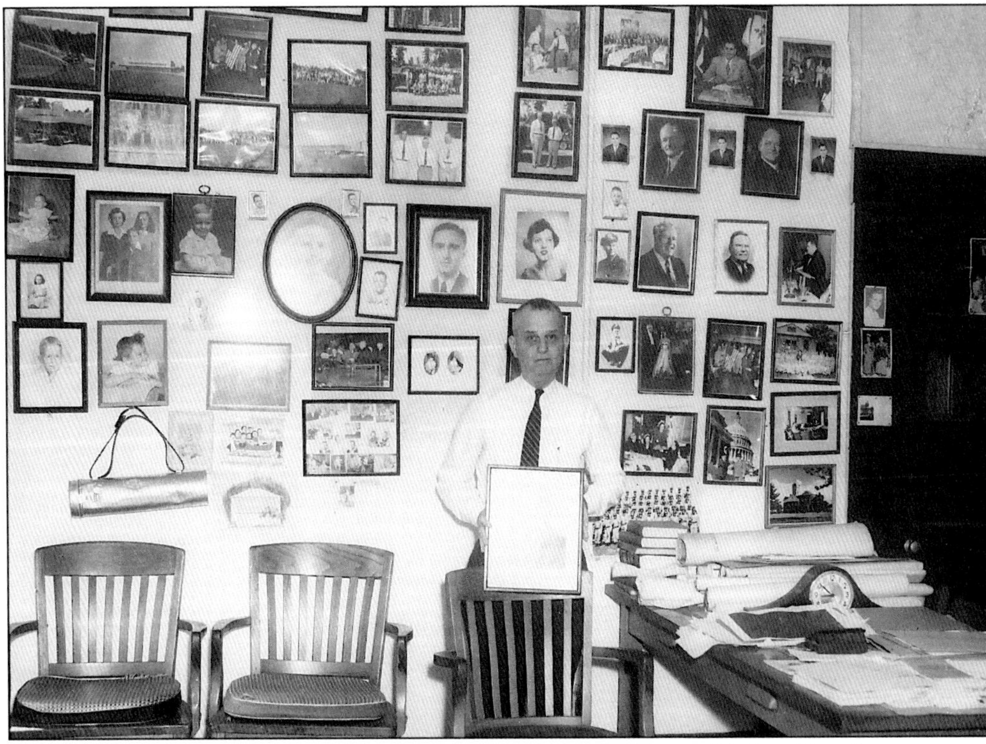

JUDGE MILLSAP IN HIS OFFICE IN THE OLD COURTHOUSE. On the wall behind him hung pictures of friends and relatives, from President Harry Truman to Federal Judge John McDuffie (who served in the U.S. Congress during the Roosevelt administration), to Truman Capote.

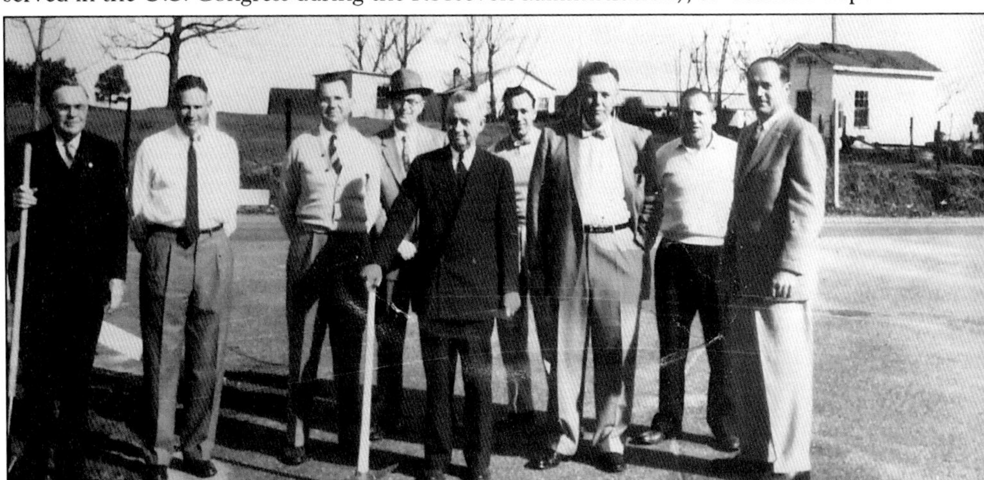

GROUNDBREAKING FOR THE VANITY FAIR TEXTILE MILL DURING THE 1960S. From left to right are: A.C. Lee (Harper Lee's father), Ed Michaels (vice-president of Vanity Fair), Moses Katz, John Barnett Jr., E.T. Millsap, Don Cox, Ward Ostberg, Dan Brown, and Brook Adams. Millsap passed away in 1963 while still in office, missing perhaps the most turbulent times in Alabama history since the War Between the States. A *Montgomery Advertiser* article in October 1963 stated, "His passing marked the end of an era." This influencial era depended on strong political sections of the state.

FORREST HOOD (FOB) JAMES JR., DEMOCRAT, CAMPAIGNING IN 1978 FOR THE GUBERNATORIAL RACE. James won the race, taking office in 1979. Gov. James, from Opelika, Alabama, served his first term as a Democratic governor, and his second as a Republican governor in 1994. He is a self-made man, becoming a millionaire in business. When faced with the impossible task of paying the tremendous medical bills of a terminally-ill son, James came up with the money by developing a better barbell which he began mass-producing on a one-man assembly line, which turned into a national manufacturing company. A graduate of Auburn University, the late coach "Shug" Jordan described him as "the greatest broken field runner" he ever coached, and a man who does not know the meaning of the word "quit."

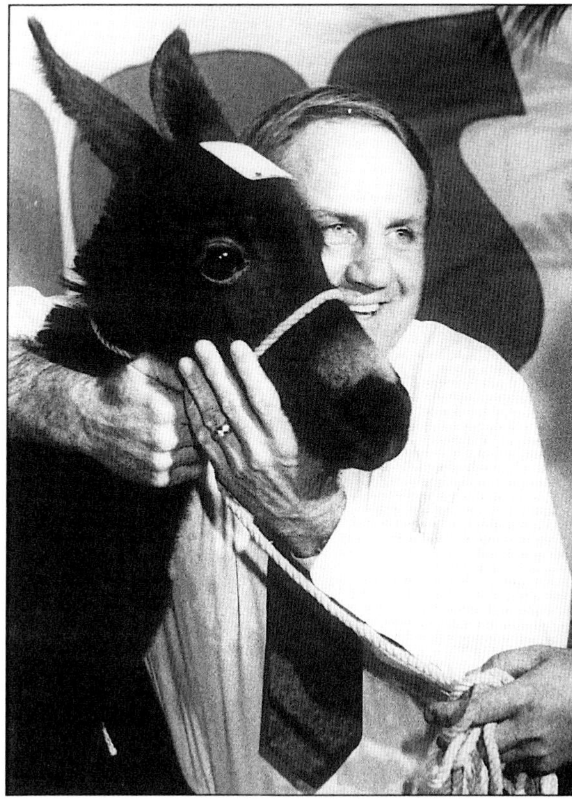

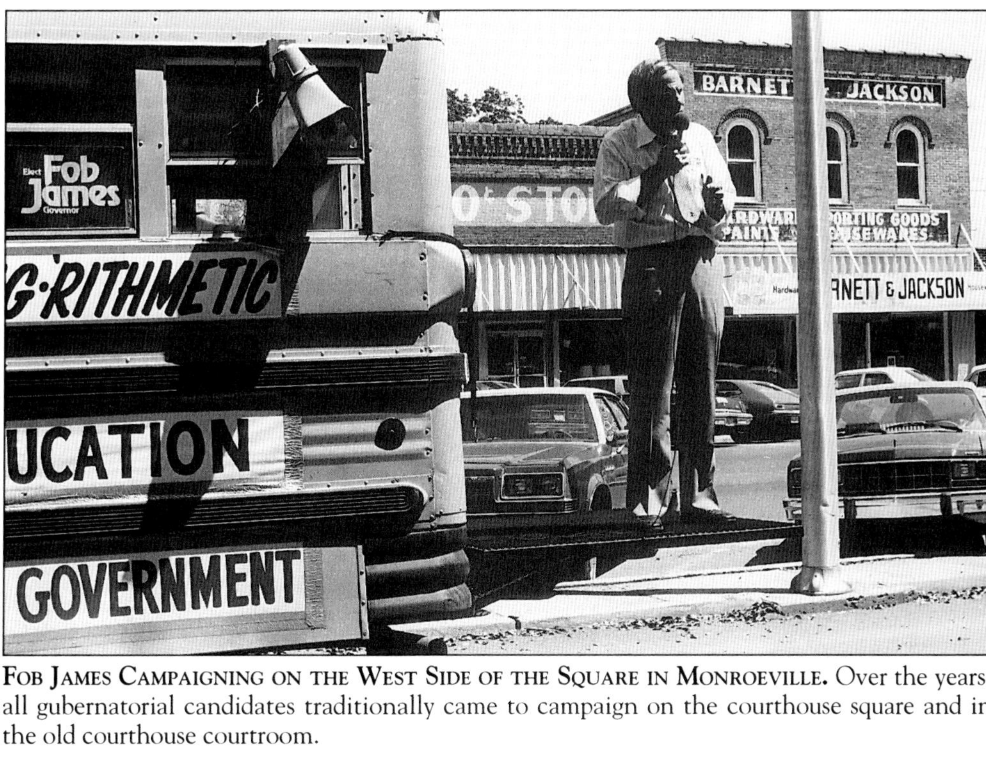

FOB JAMES CAMPAIGNING ON THE WEST SIDE OF THE SQUARE IN MONROEVILLE. Over the years, all gubernatorial candidates traditionally came to campaign on the courthouse square and in the old courthouse courtroom.

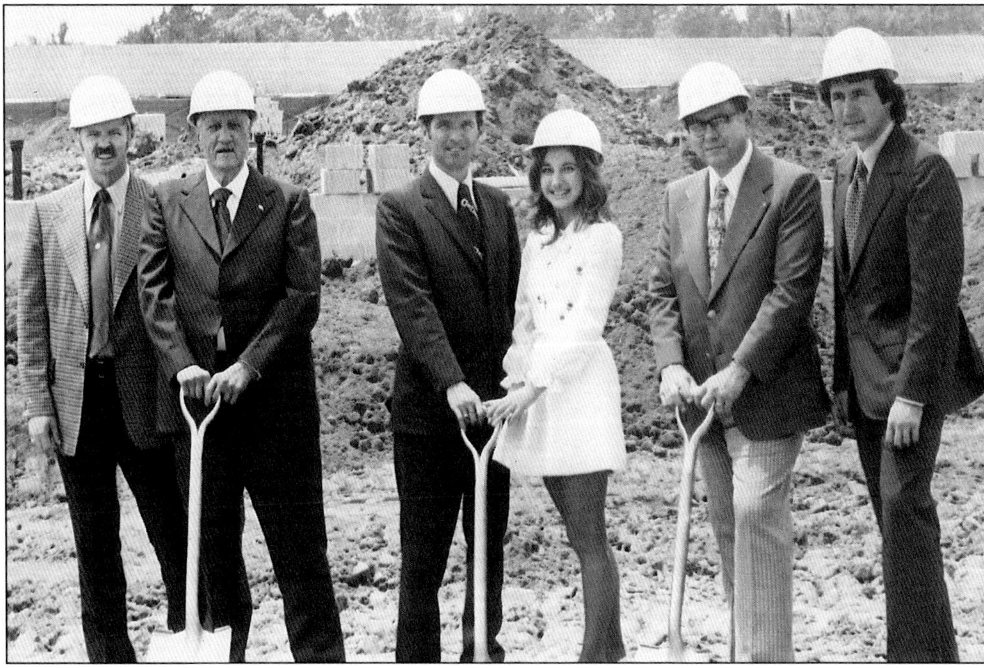

Dr. Jack Hines, Former Mayor of Monroeville (second from left), Probate Judge Otha Lee Biggs and Miss Jaye (center). They are breaking ground for Monroe Shopping Center in the 1970s.

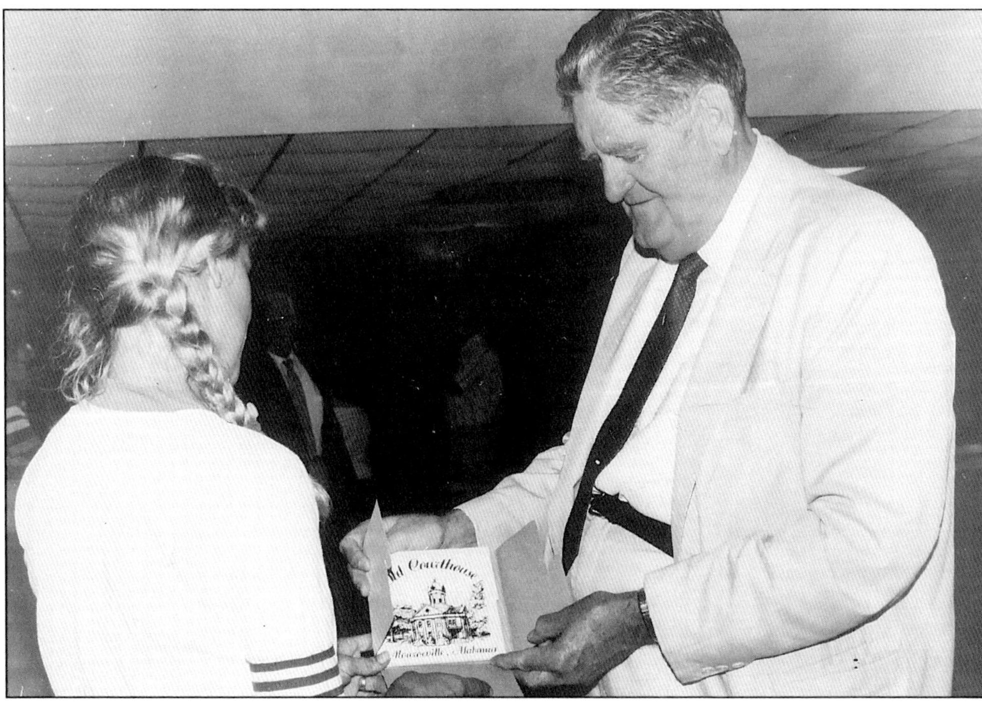

U.S. Senator Howell Heflin of Alabama, Receiving an Old Courthouse Plaque from Dawn Crook, Museum Staff. Heflin visited the Old Courthouse and Museum during his last term in office. After retiring, his seat was won by Jeff Sessions of Monroe County.

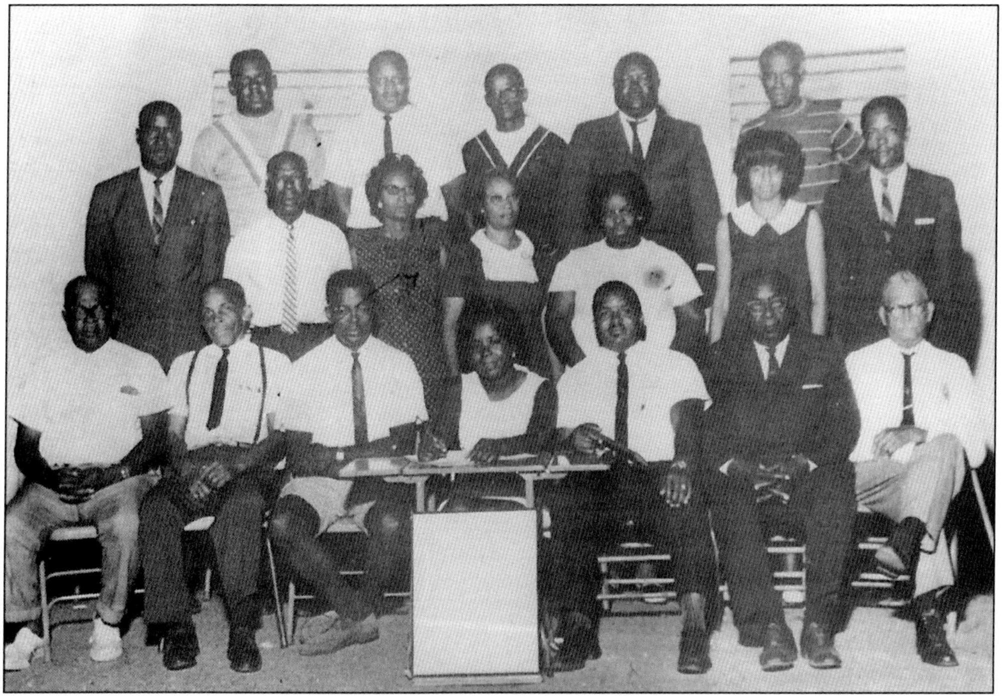

The First Organized NAACP in Monroe County in 1963. The first president was Willie Frank Marshall (seated third from right) from Tunnel Springs; vice-president was H.B. Williams (third from left) from Packer's Bend. Because the State of Alabama outlawed the NAACP in the 1950s, it was not until the 1960s that the NAACP became prominent. During this time, there were leadership action committees which acted as think-tanks for courses of action to take on issues facing the African-American population in Monroe County. As black voting rights became an issue in Alabama and in the nation, some county officials quietly stressed black voter registration, not out of a civil rights liberalism, but to avoid federally enforced registration in the future. This brought horrific results in other parts of the state and in Mississippi. Although black voter registration was not widespread in Monroe County, there were 800 to 900 blacks on voting rolls in the early 1960s, while in many counties in Alabama the numbers were considerably smaller. Amidst the small turnout for registration, the NAACP filed a suit for redistricting. The lawsuit was in litigation for eight years. At the end, a compromise was made with the county commission, which made two districts out of four with black majority voters. Alex Roberts became the first black county commissioner of Monroe County. Charlie McCorvey Jr. became the second. Willie Frank Marshall stated that a compromise was reached because "the black and white leaders were more shrewd and progressive in Monroe County than in many other counties."

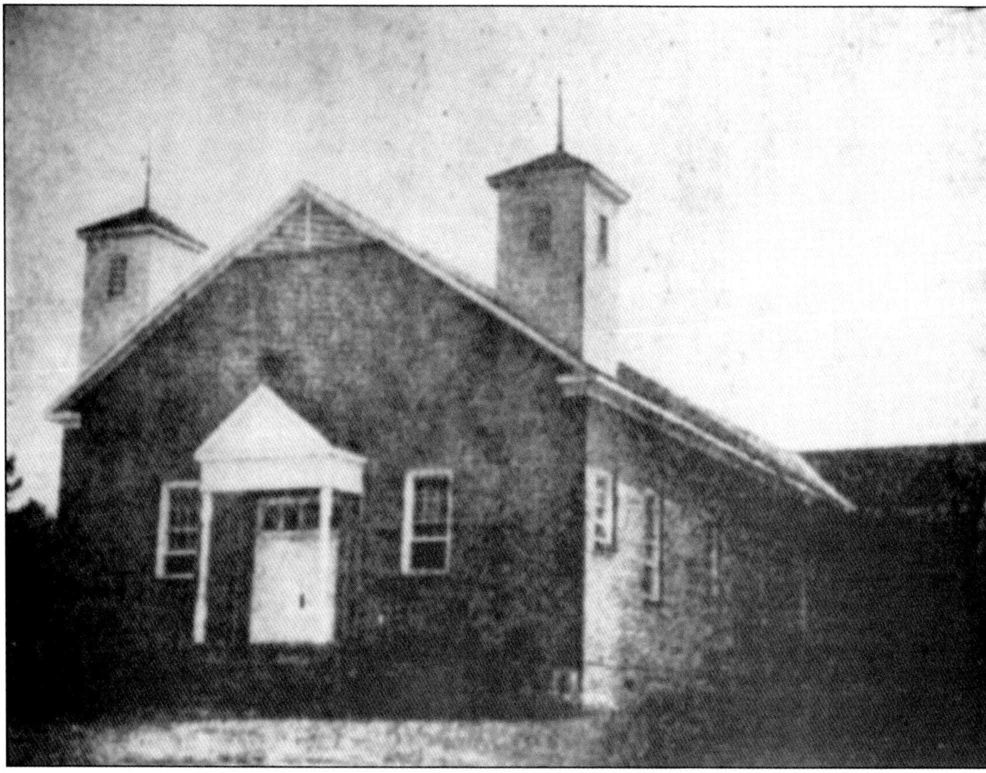

ANTIOCH CHURCH IN TUNNEL SPRINGS, WHERE THE NAACP MET ON A REGULAR BASIS.

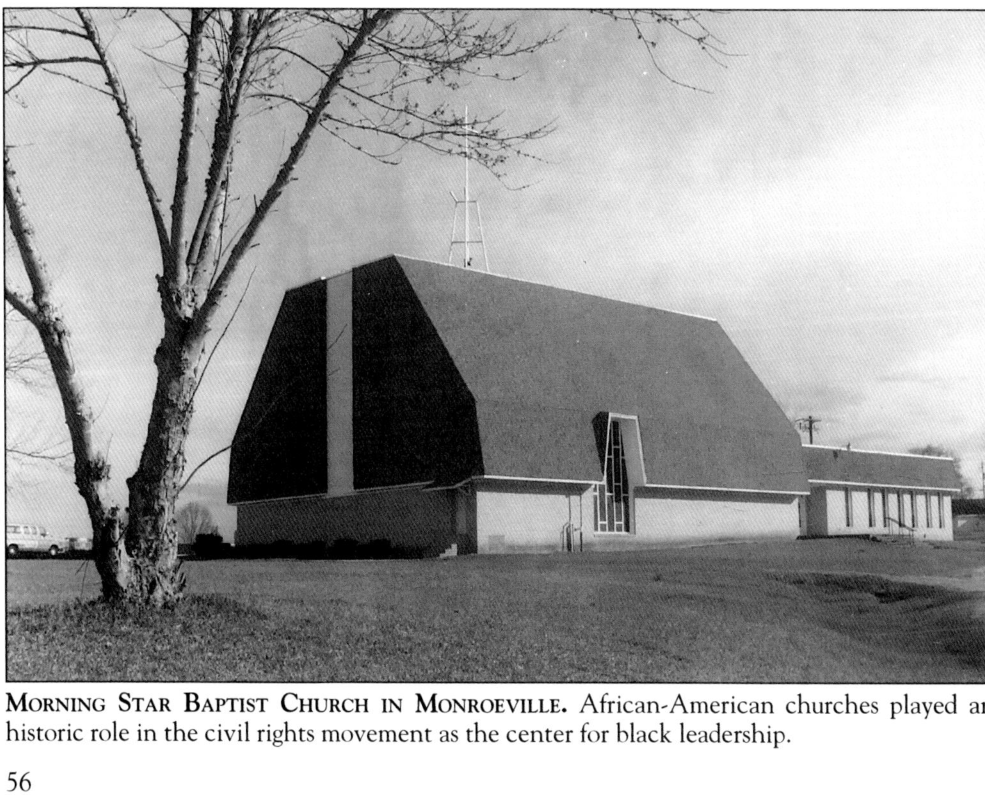

MORNING STAR BAPTIST CHURCH IN MONROEVILLE. African-American churches played an historic role in the civil rights movement as the center for black leadership.

Five

WALLACE

"Monroeville was a night town—where you had so many people you could hardly see the end of them."
—George C. Wallace

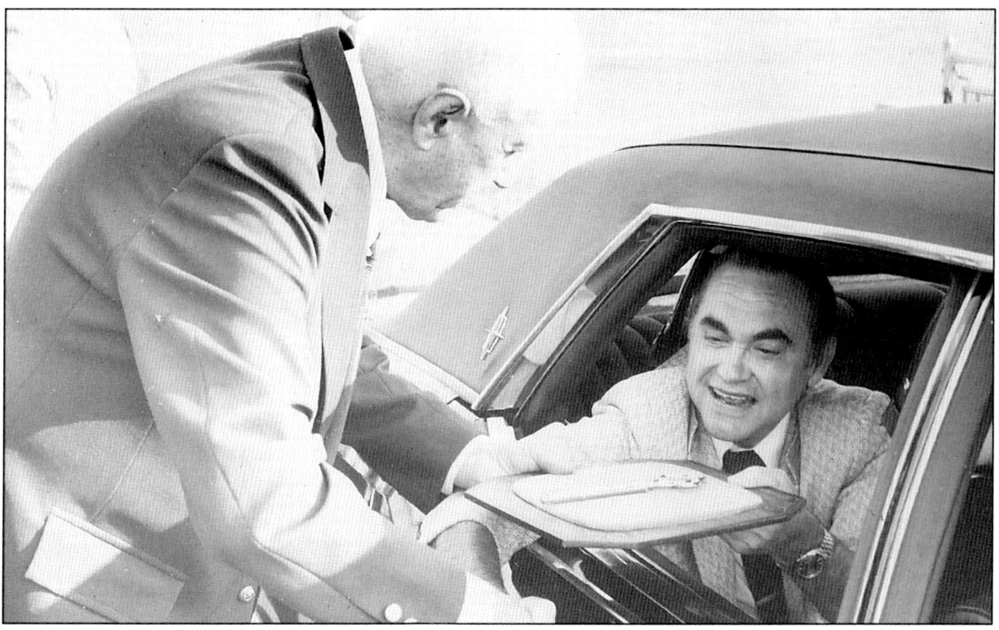

DR. JACK HINES, MAYOR OF MONROEVILLE, PRESENTING A KEY TO THE CITY TO GOVERNOR GEORGE WALLACE IN OCTOBER OF 1973. Wallace was in Monroeville campaigning for the next gubernatorial election. He was also in Monroeville for a double ceremony: to dedicate the new Central Cutting Plant at Vanity Fair Mills, and to participate in a Chamber of Commerce banquet honoring M.O. (Whitey) Lee, chairman and president of Vanity Fair Corporation. Wallace had been shot at a 1972 rally in a Maryland shopping center while running for President of the United States.

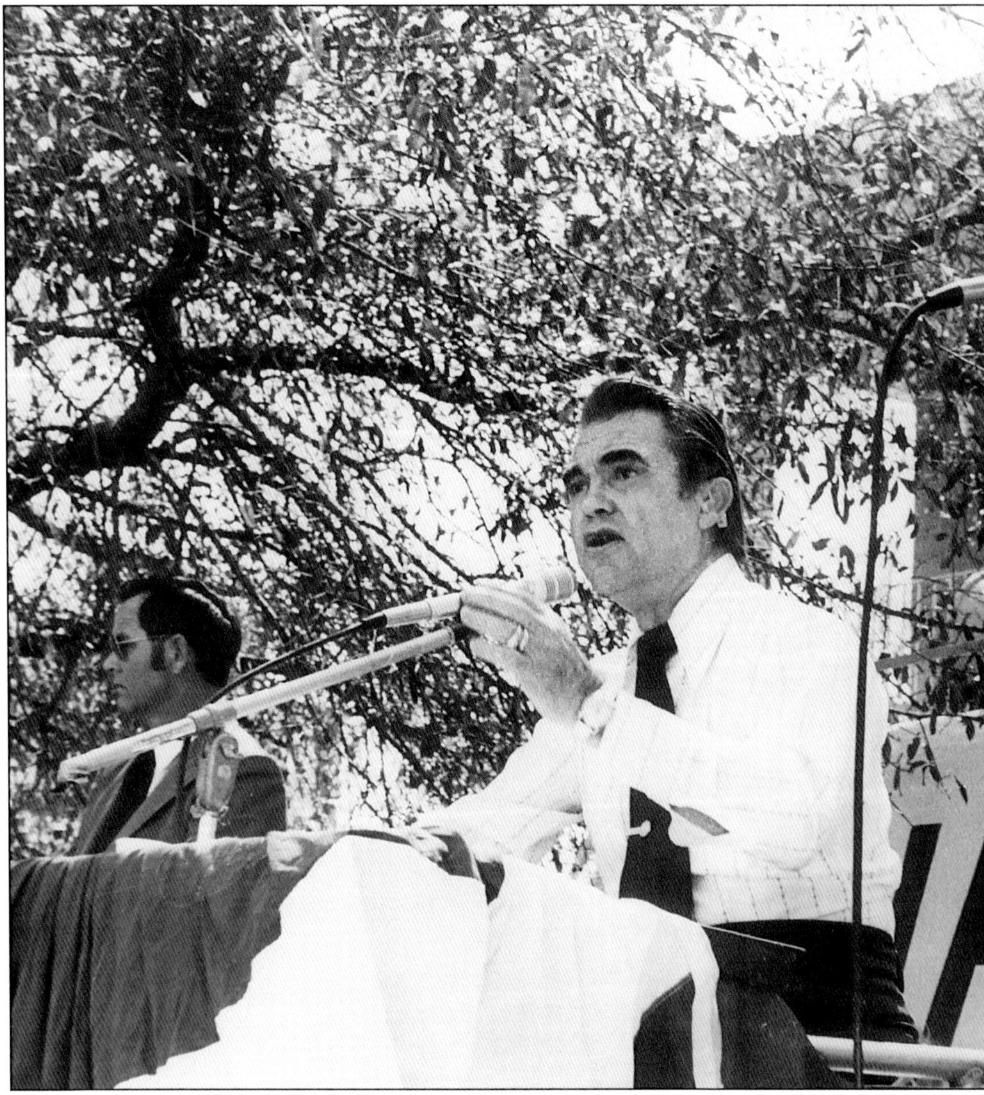

GOVERNOR GEORGE WALLACE CAMPAIGNING FOR RE-ELECTION IN FRONT OF THE NEW MONROE COUNTY COURTHOUSE IN 1973. George Wallace and Monroe County Probate Judge Shorty Millsap first met in Montgomery in 1946 or 1947, at the Jeff Davis Hotel (specifically, its Mirror Lounge). This was, according to Stephan Lesher (author of the biography *George Wallace*), the place where the "Folson Chosen" met. Wallace was eager to meet the "political mainstays"

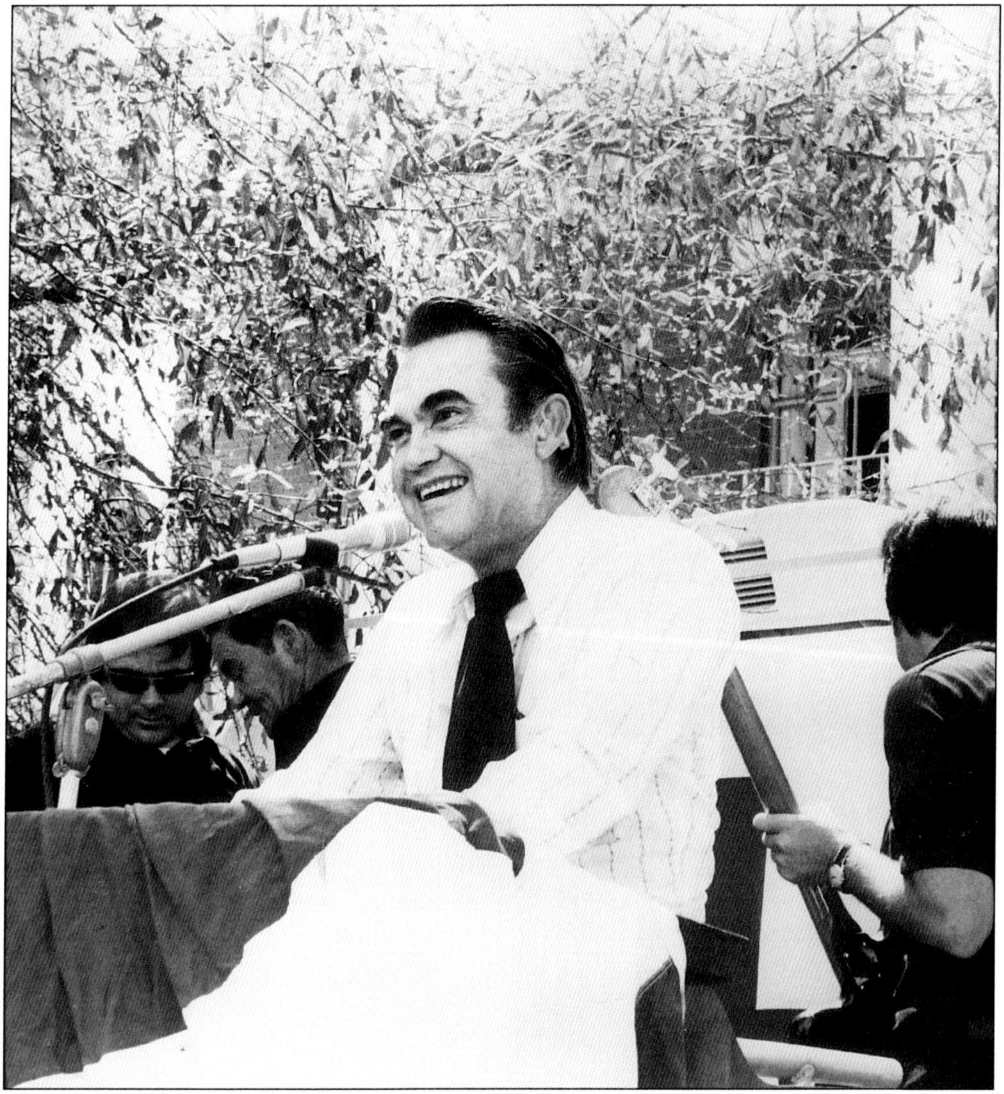

of the party and was introduced to "Shorty" Millsap of Monroeville, who was considered a "political boss" in southwest Alabama.

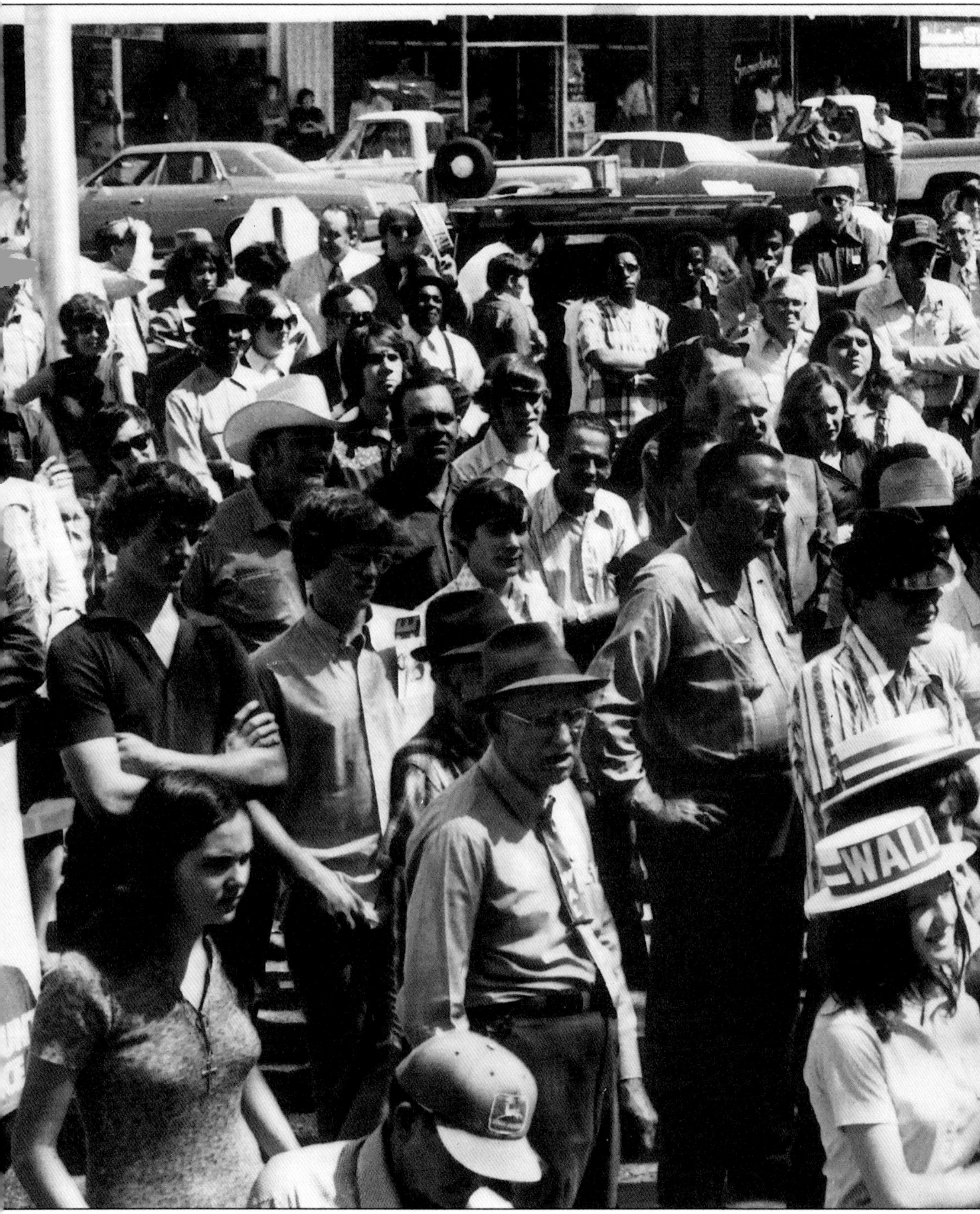

WALLACE POLITICAL RALLY ON COURTHOUSE SQUARE. Wallace would visit the judge and the old courthouse in his bid for election in 1958. According to the biography, Wallace learned the community customs of towns relating to when residents would leave their jobs and homes to congregate at the center of town for shopping or socializing. Wallace called Monroeville "a night town—where you had so many people you could hardly see the end of them." He

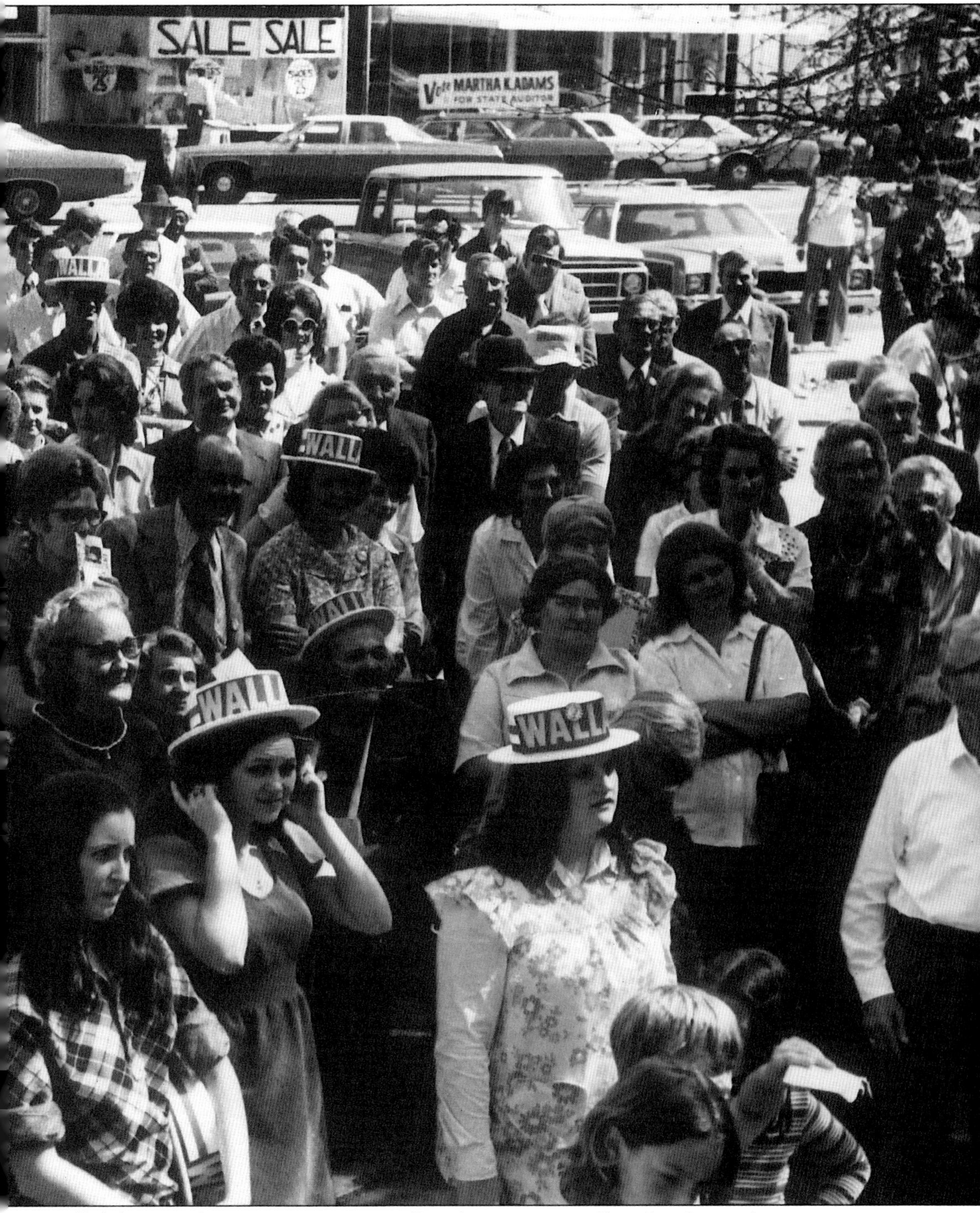

recalled that people were in a "party mood" and receptive to rallies that featured country music. A former judge (Wallace was a circuit judge and his grandfather was a probate judge, both of Barbour County), Wallace was always out in the public eye seeking attention. He was an avid "states' rights" man.

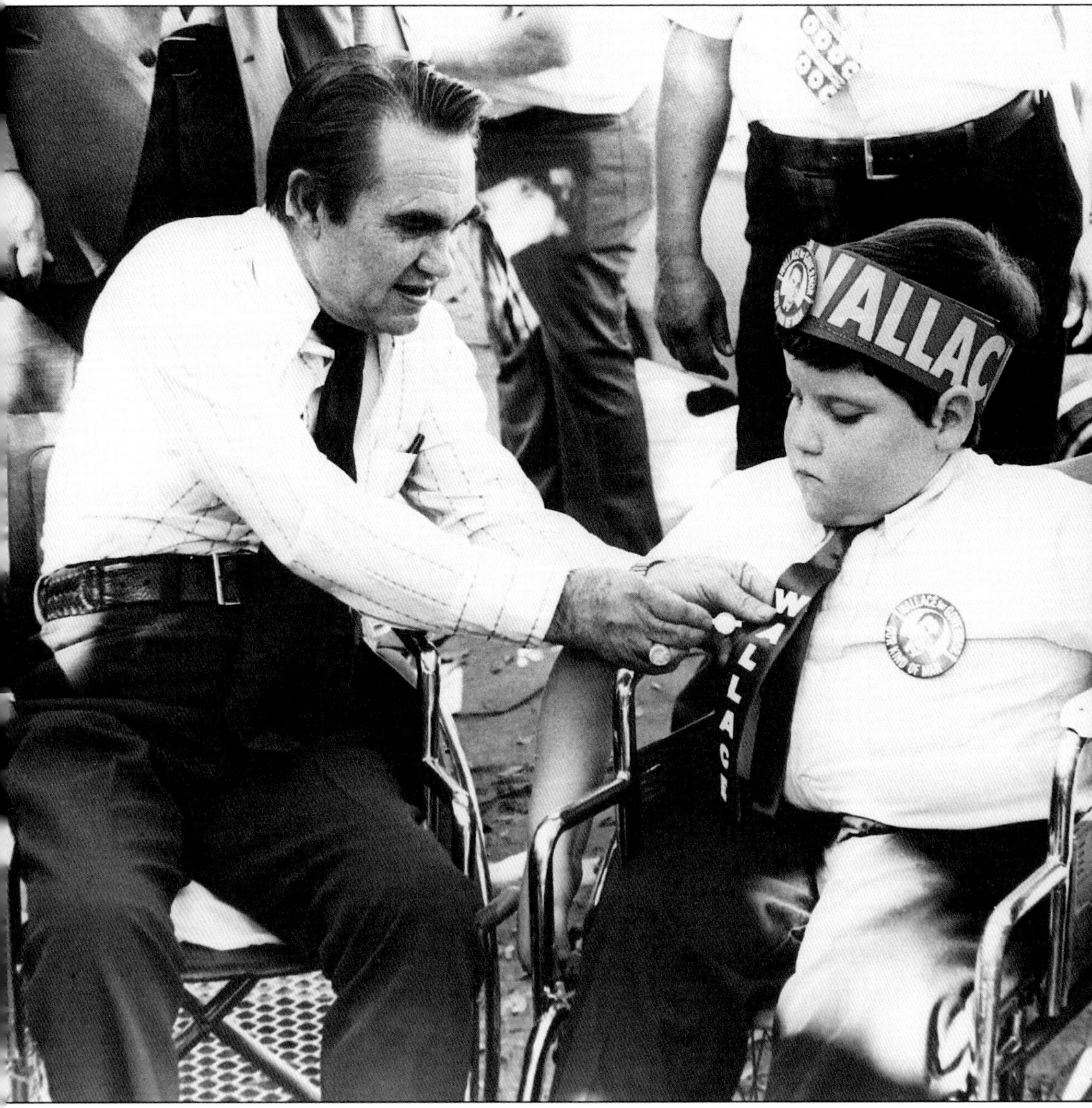

George Wallace. Wallace's political career began in 1946 when he ran for the state legislature. He would become a familiar figure to the town of Monroeville, seeking support of Monroe Countians. In his first bid for governor, Wallace did not have the support of Probate Judge Millsap. Wallace lost to John Patterson in 1958. In his second run for office, he was victorious,

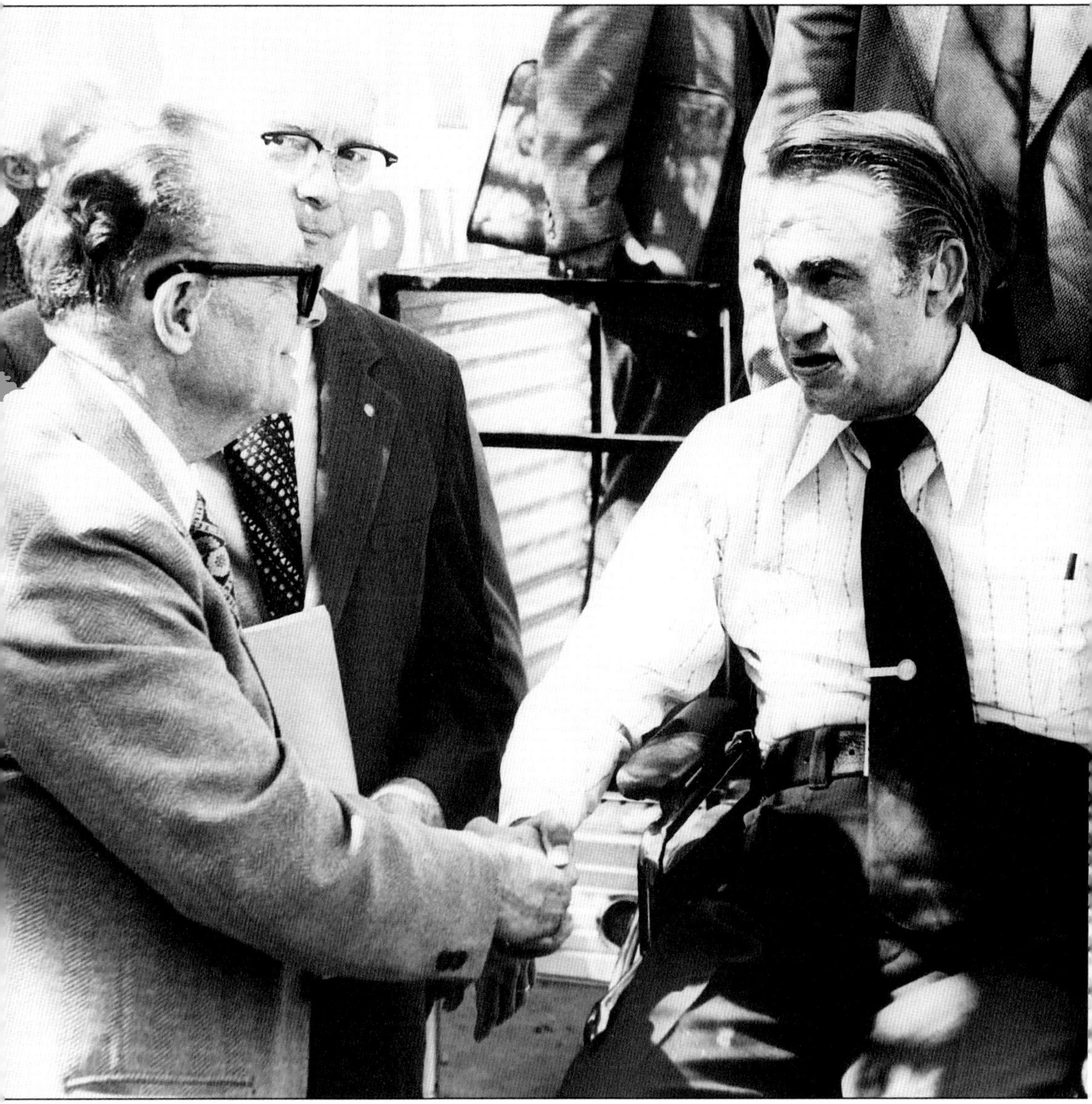

leading Alabama into the civil rights movement. The 1960s would bring the black vote and a "states' rights" attitude, which Wallace fathered. State politicians would defy the central federal government. The liberalism of the Folsom era was dead, and conservatism would rule the State House for many years.

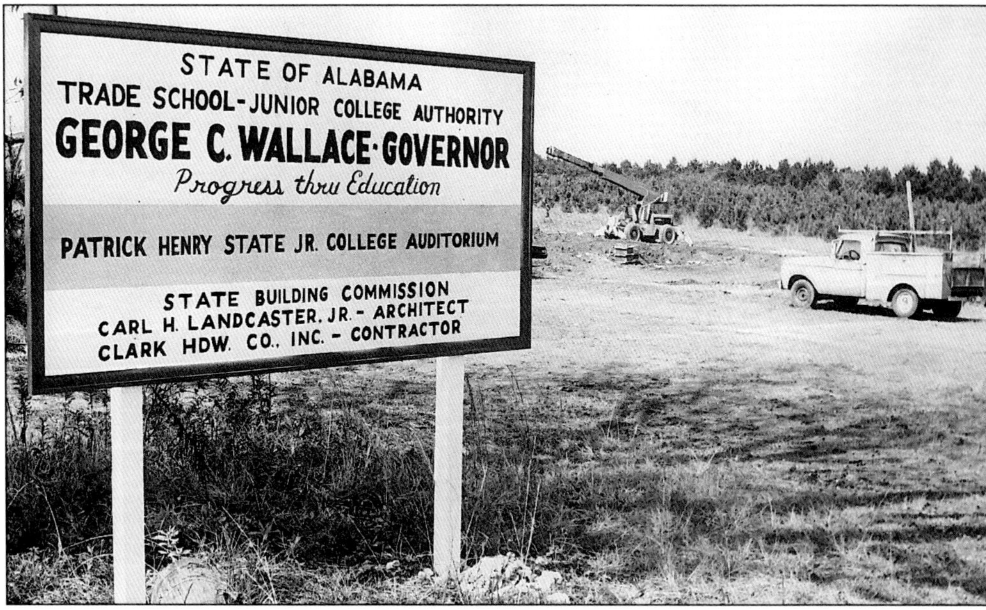

THE SITE WHERE THE PATRICK HENRY STATE JUNIOR COLLEGE AUDITORIUM WAS TO BE BUILT IN 1965. Under George Wallace's governorship, the junior college and trade school program was initiated. In 1965, Patrick Henry State Junior College was established in Monroeville. The college, now Alabama Southern Community College, is still a vital part of this community.

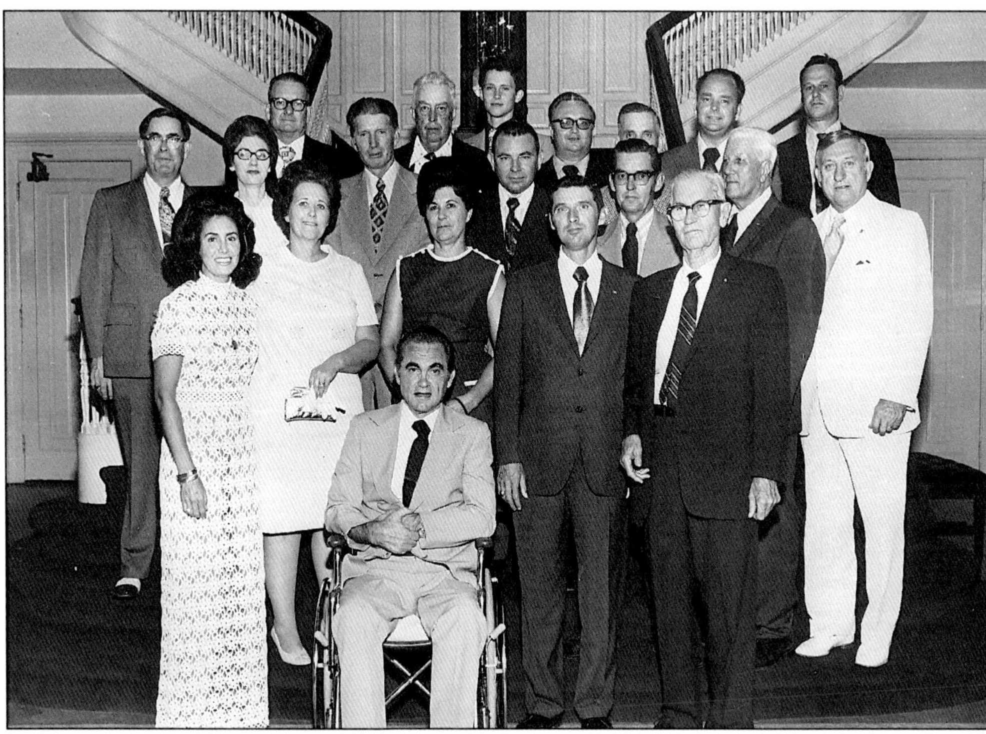
WALLACE WITH HIS SECOND WIFE, CORNELIA, AT THE STATE HOUSE IN MONTGOMERY. Monroe County Probate Judge Otha Lee Biggs is pictured on his right.

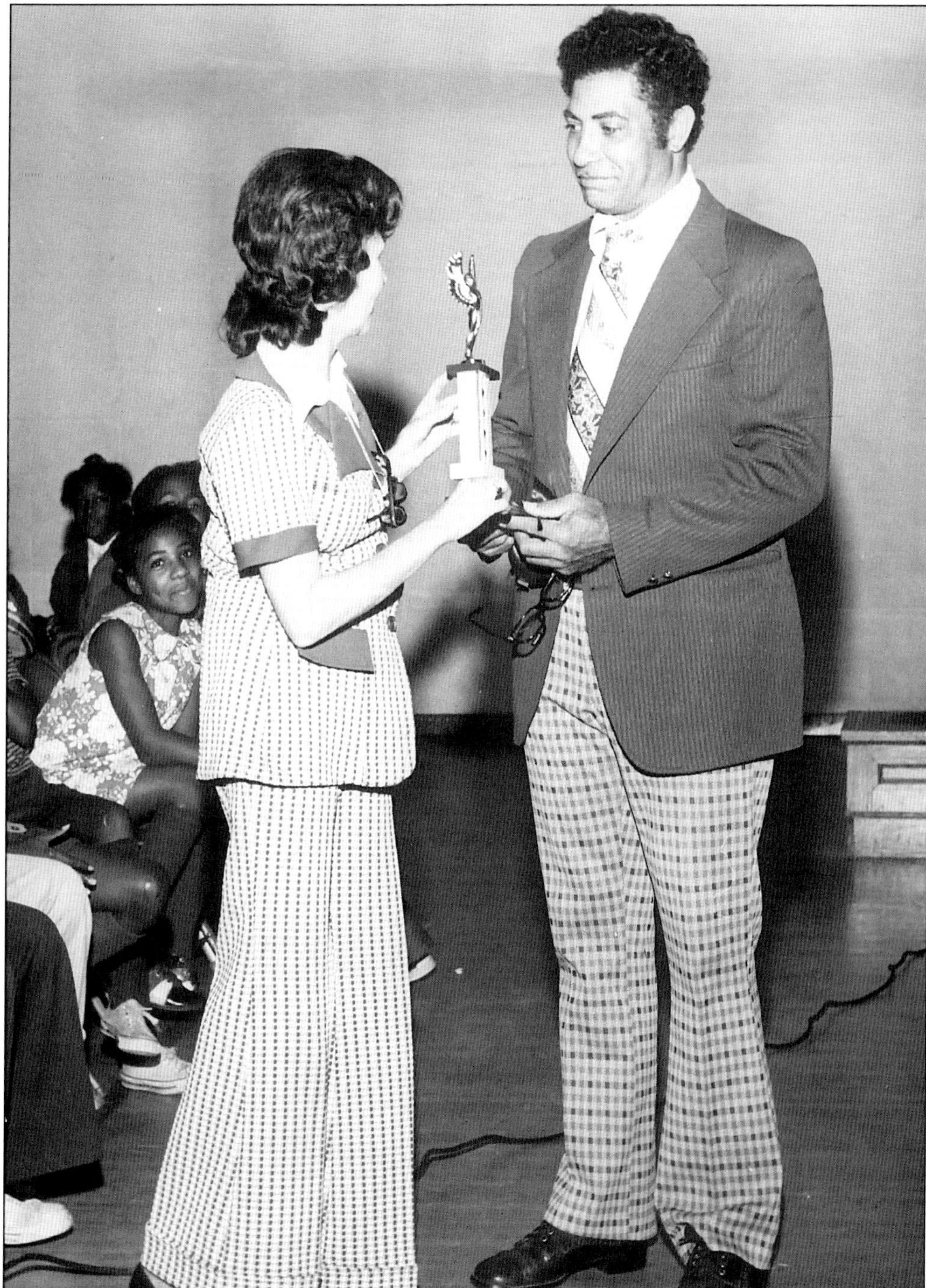

JOHN A. TUCKER. In the 1970s, despite the racial campaigns run during the 1960s, George Wallace began to depend on black support. Blacks were making many gains in Monroe County. John A. Tucker became one of the first principals of integrated schools in Monroeville. He was principal in 1970 of the middle school, and later became principal of the junior high school. Robert McMillan became assistant principal of the high school.

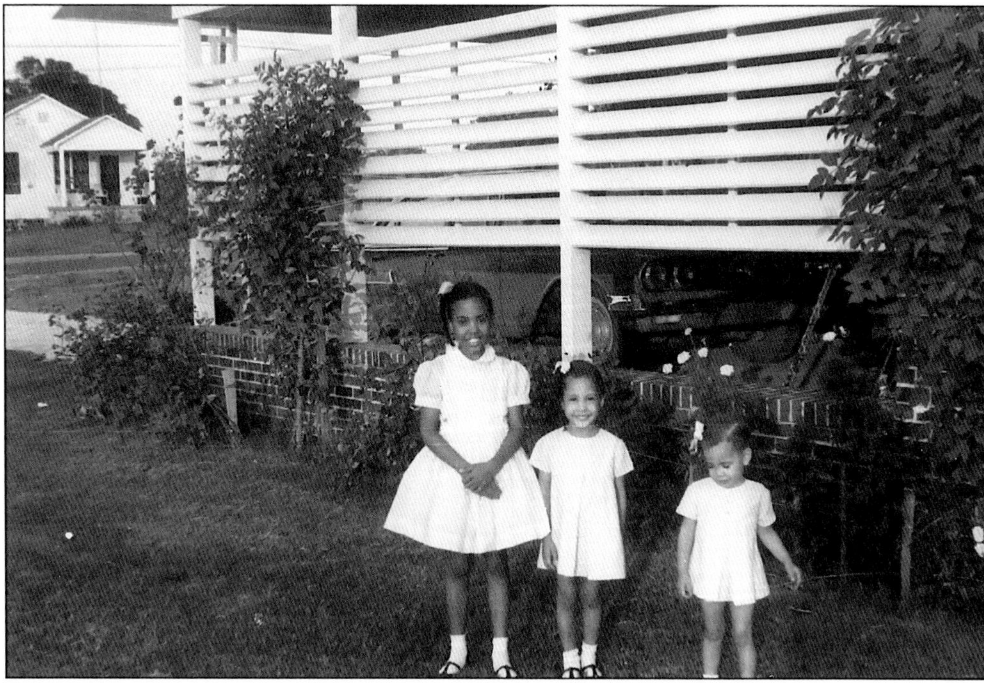

CYNTHIA, KAREN, AND SHERYL TUCKER IN 1964. The Tucker family was a typical middle-class black family in Monroeville. Both parents, John and Mary, were educators—first in the segregated school district, and then in the integrated schools. Their children, Cynthia, Karen, Sheryl, and John, all excelled in academia, each earning college degrees and succeeding in their respective careers.

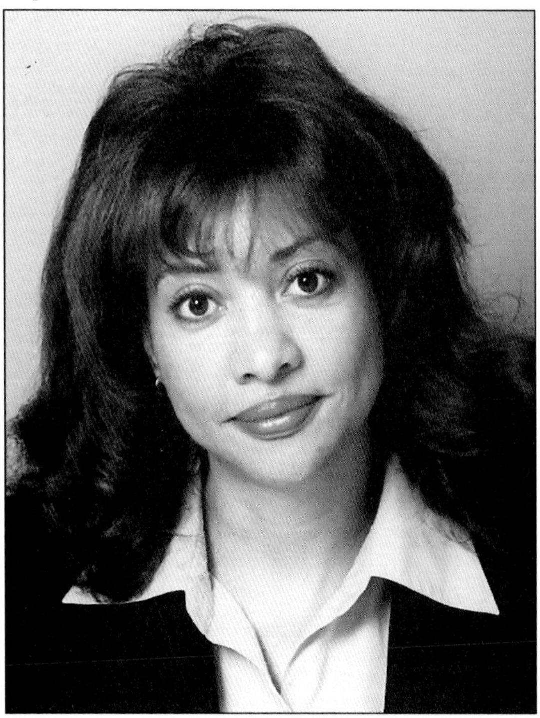

CYNTHIA TUCKER, EDITOR OF THE *ATLANTA CONSTITUTION* EDITORIAL PAGE, SYNDICATED COLUMNIST, AND TELEVISION COMMENTATOR. In one of her columns, she writes: " . . . The segregated South is now the stuff of textbook history. Everybody knows that tale. What of the history less remembered, the poverty that was endemic to the South, a fact of life for many whites as well as blacks?"

Six

CAPOTE

"The courthouse bell sounded so cold and clear. And there were no birds singing: they're gone to warmer country, yes indeed. Oh, Buddy, stop stuffing biscuits and fetch our buggy. Help me find my hat. We've thirty cakes to bake."
—*A Christmas Memory* by Truman Capote

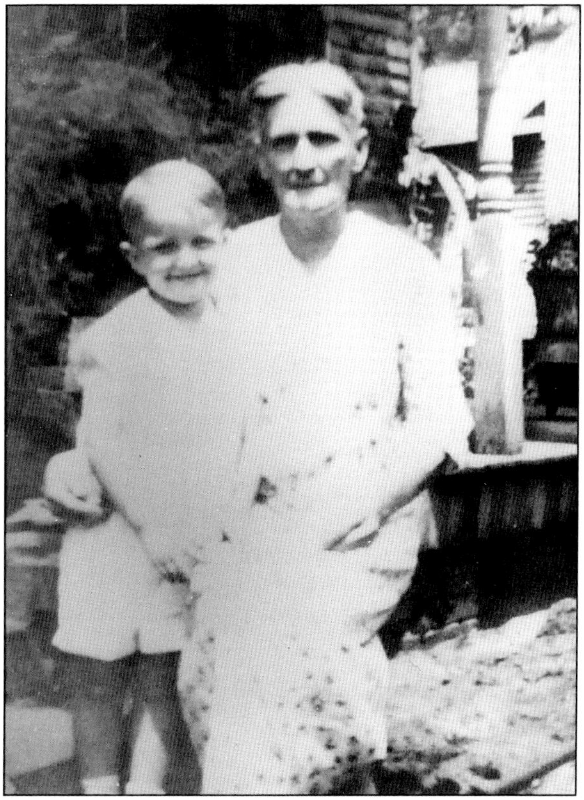

NANCY RUMBLEY FAULK ("SOOK"), AND TRUMAN CAPOTE ("BUDDY"). Truman Capote spent five years in the Faulk household in Monroeville living with his cousins. "Sook" became his favorite.

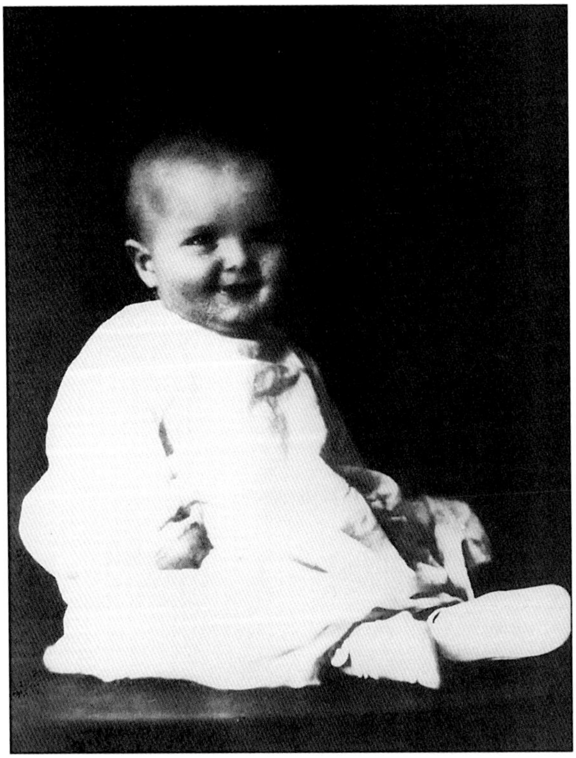

Truman Streckfus Persons, Born on the Afternoon of Sept. 30, 1924, in the Touro Infirmary of New Orleans. The Persons family also made frequent visits to their relatives in Monroeville, and it is possible that Jennie was responsible for Truman's release from the hospital. According to Truman's first cousin, Jennings Carter, Jennie sent the money down to get him out of the hospital, as the custom was for the hospital to keep the baby until the bill was paid.

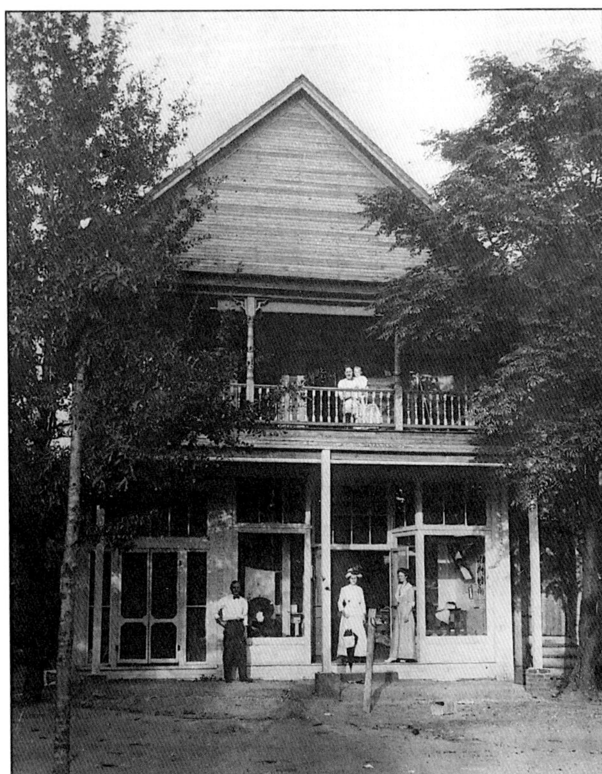

The Faulk Millinery Shop, c. 1900. The shop was owned by Jenny Faulk, who helped raise Truman in Monroeville. The store was located on the east side of the square, across from the courthouse. Mr. Smith (shown lower left) was the barber who operated his business downstairs. He and his wife lived upstairs (wife and infant shown upstairs). The two women pictured are Jennie and Callie Faulk.

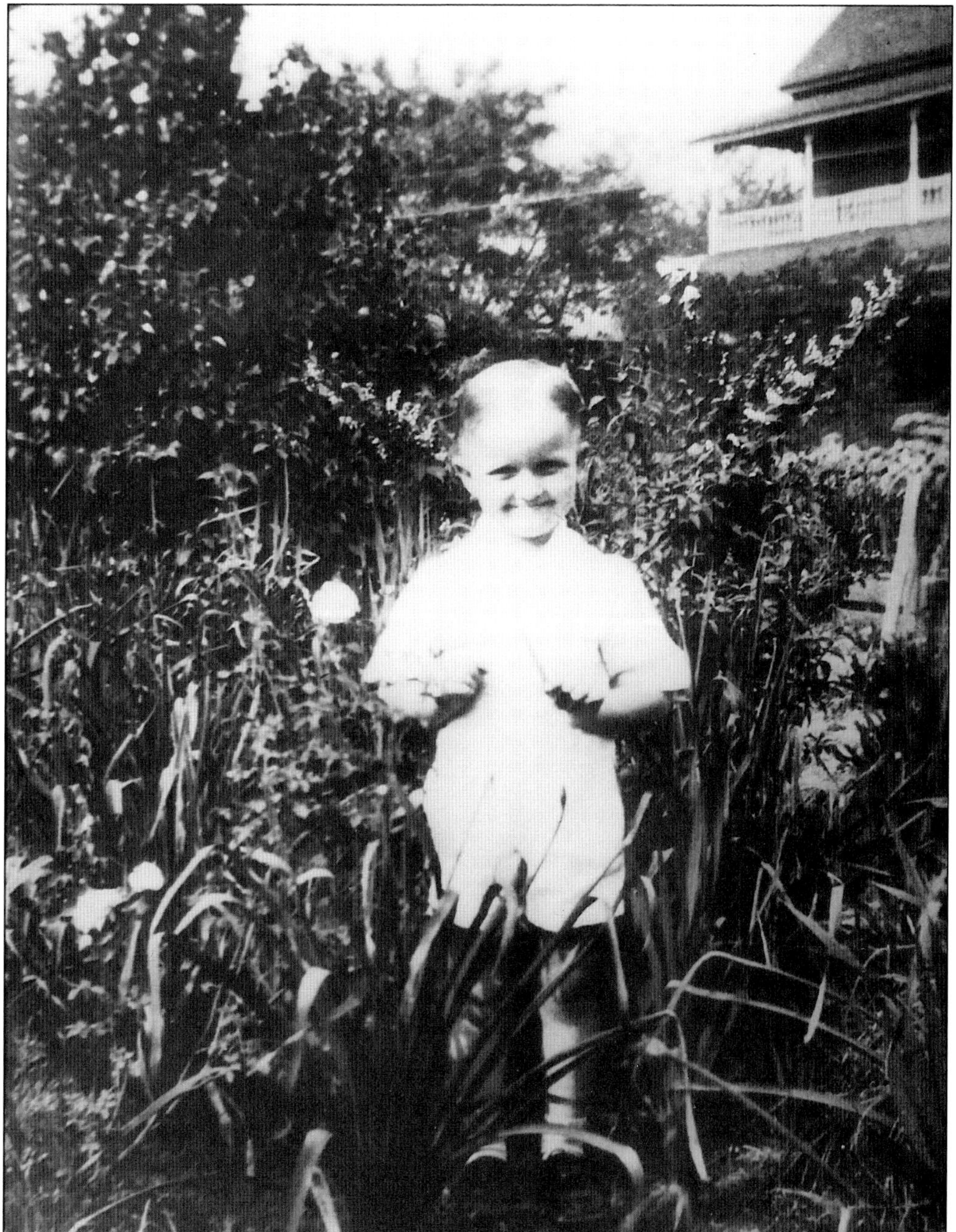

TRUMAN. Truman's first extended visit to Monroeville occurred when Lillie Mae, his mother, left him in the care of Jennie and her two sisters. He immediately became attached to his cousin "Sook." The two remained close throughout the remainder of her life, and she always referred to him with great affection as her "Buddy."

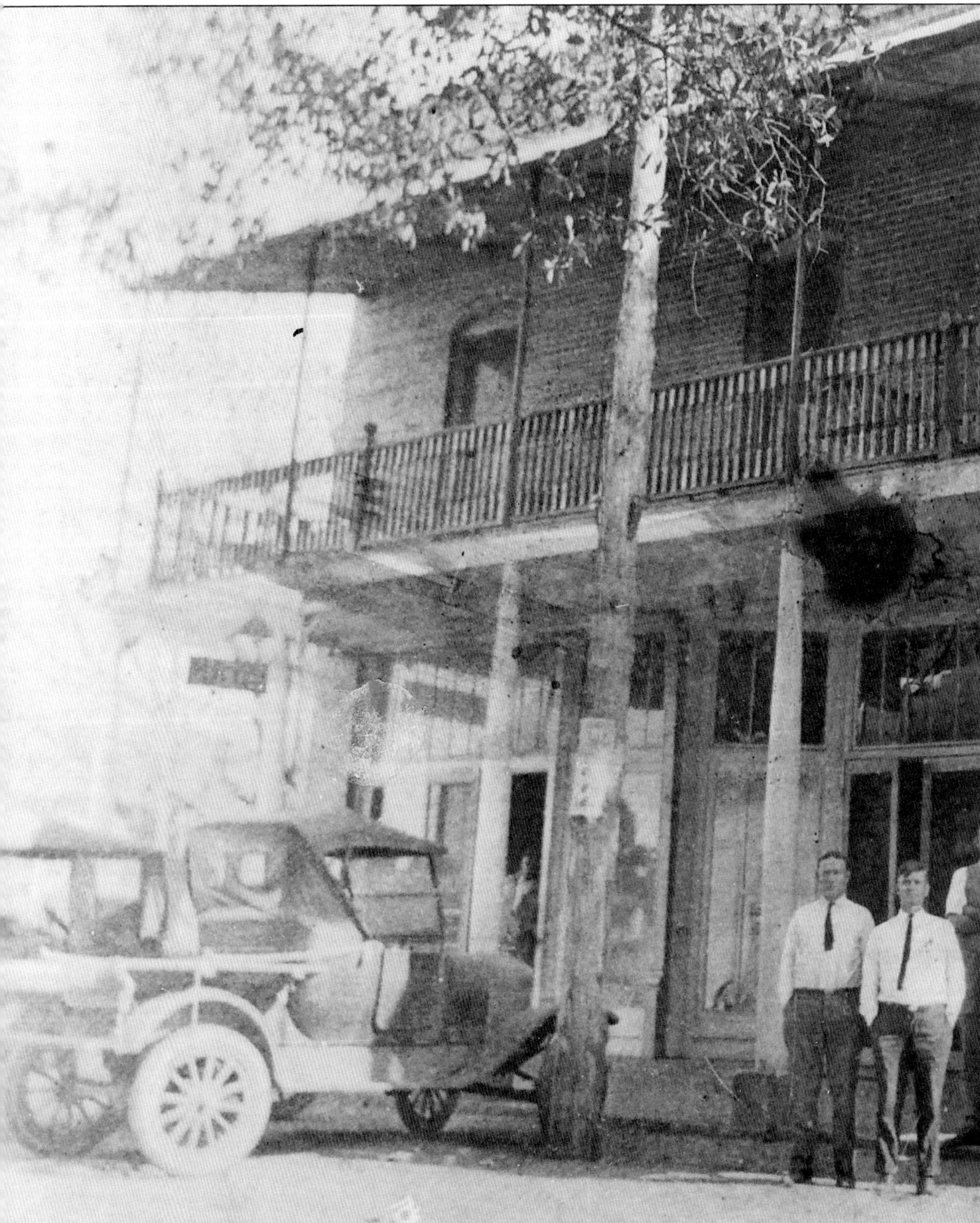

The Faulk Millinery Shop, Monroeville Town Square, c. 1920s. From left to right are: Mr. Griffin, Jeff Smith (barber), Bill Falkenberry, unknown, Jennie Faulk, Callie Faulk, J.J. Hestle (Dr., DDT), Mr. Holliway, Mable Holliway, Nanny Swanson, Mrs. Roberts, Mrs. Sam Tucker, and Miss Riley. (Names provided by Jennings F. Carter.) Jennie Faulk was

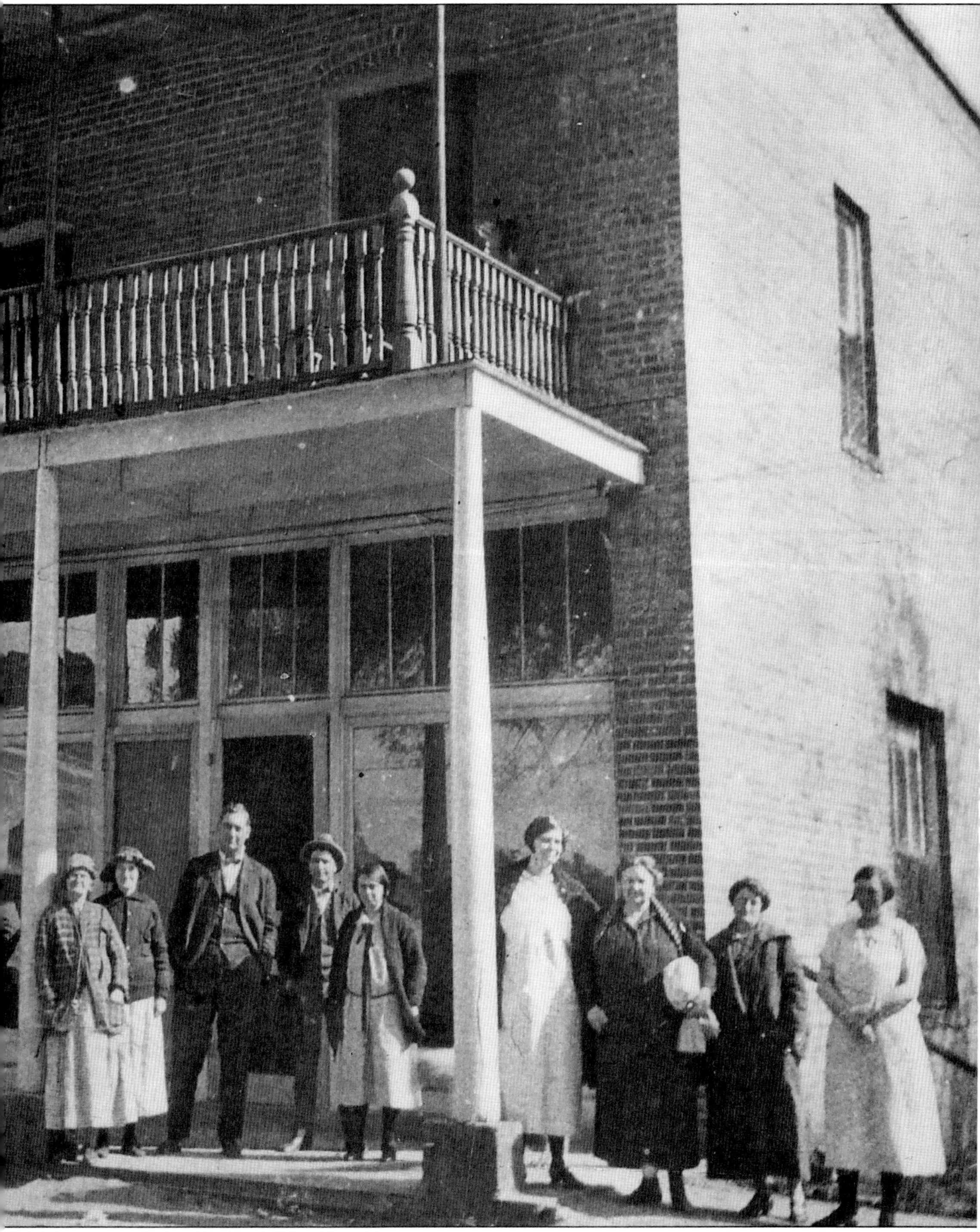

the matriarch of the Faulk household. Her business, which drew customers from as far away as Pensacola and New Orleans, eventually became so successful that it was necessary for one of her sisters, Caroline Elizabeth Faulk ("Callie"), to join the enterprise as bookkeeper and business partner.

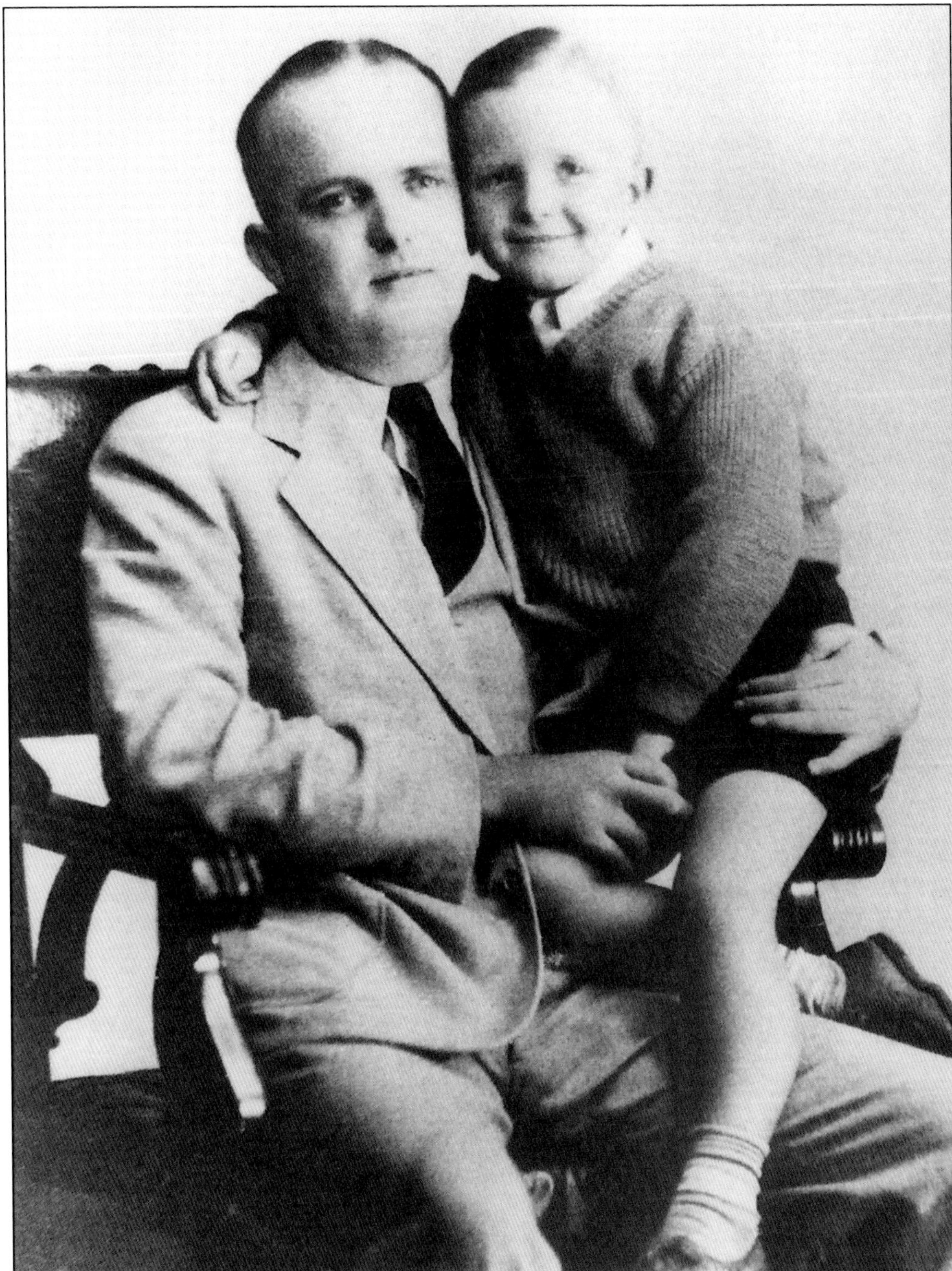

Julian Archilus Persons (Truman's father) and Truman. Julian was an employee of the Streckfus Shipping Line in New Orleans in 1923. He and Lillie Mae Faulk, Truman's mother, began a whirlwind courtship, and the romancing continued by mail during the summer of that same year, while he was tending to several business ventures in New Orleans and Colorado. Arch and Lillie Mae, having secured a marriage license from Probate Judge M.M. Fountain on August 14, 1923, were married the next day in the Faulk home on South Alabama Avenue.

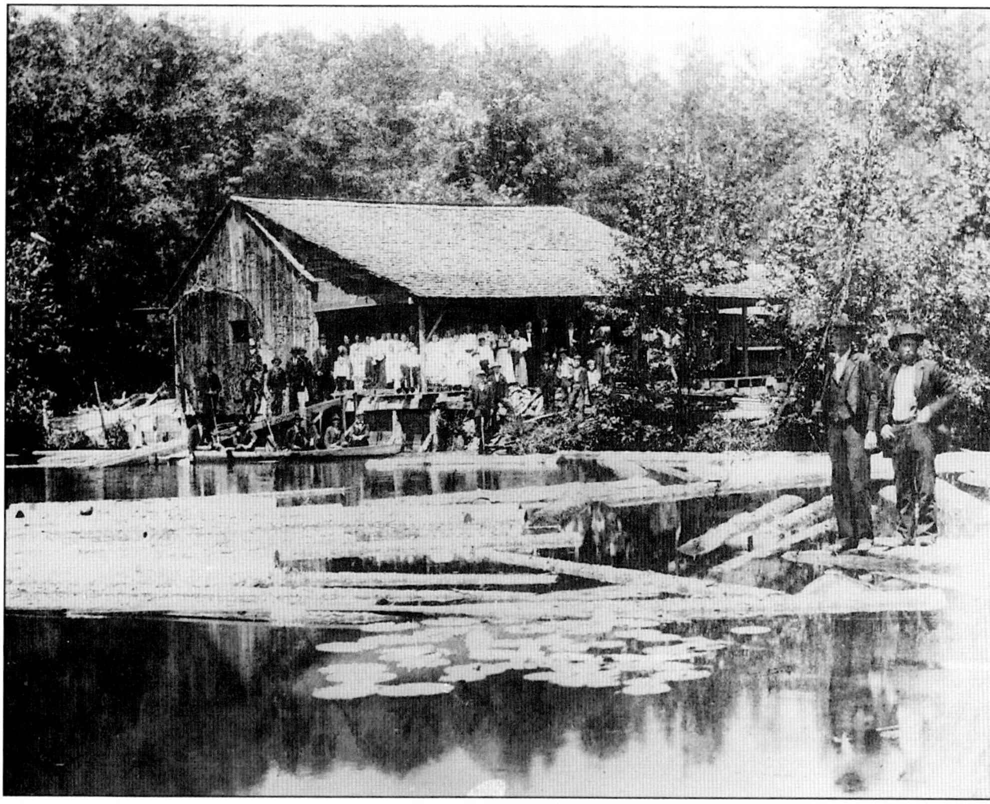

HATTER'S MILL, LOCATED OFF DREWRY ROAD, A FAVORITE SWIMMING HOLE.

Truman and his cousins swam at Hatter's Mill often. Jennings Carter, son of Lillie Mae's sister, Mary Ida Carter, was also a childhood companion, and undoubtedly many happy summer afternoons passed while they played on South Alabama Avenue and swam at the popular swimming hole on Hatter's Mill Creek. In September 1930, Truman was enrolled at Monroeville Elementary School. This was to be the only complete school year which he would attend here as a student. In July of 1931, his mother picked him up on her way to meet with Arch in Pensacola. Apparently, during Truman's stay with his relatives, the relationship between Arch and Lillie Mae became strained to the point that the only logical solution was a divorce. This was granted four months later, and in the divorce settlement, custody of Truman was a major point of discussion. It was eventually agreed that Lillie Mae would have custody from September 1 through May 31 each year, and Arch the remainder of the year. Unfortunately, neither parent upheld the agreement, and Truman returned to Monroeville. A continuing sense of abandonment haunted him throughout much of his life, and the only individual that he felt he could count on during his childhood was his beloved "Sook." Many years later, she would become the model for the kindly old lady in several of his books and short stories, most notably *The Grass Harp* and *A Christmas Memory*.

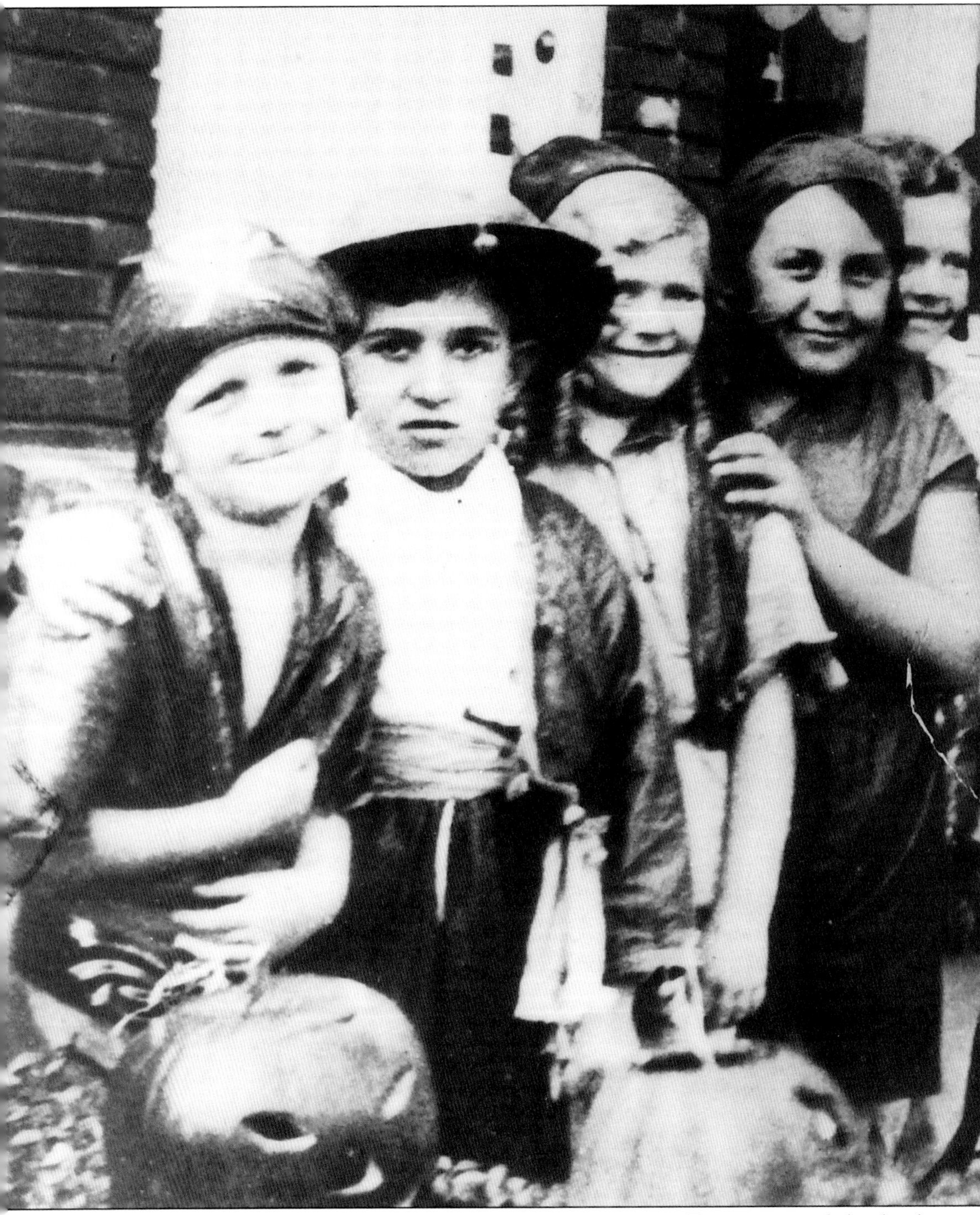

Truman (far left) with Schoolmates in Monroeville. Truman attended school in Monroeville for two more partial terms, but generally would only return for summer visits in the Faulk home—all the while dreaming of one day becoming an accomplished writer. His next-door neighbor and best friend, Nelle Harper Lee, also held the same aspirations. On March 24, 1932, Lillie Mae remarried, this time to businessman Joe Capote, a Cuban immigrant who

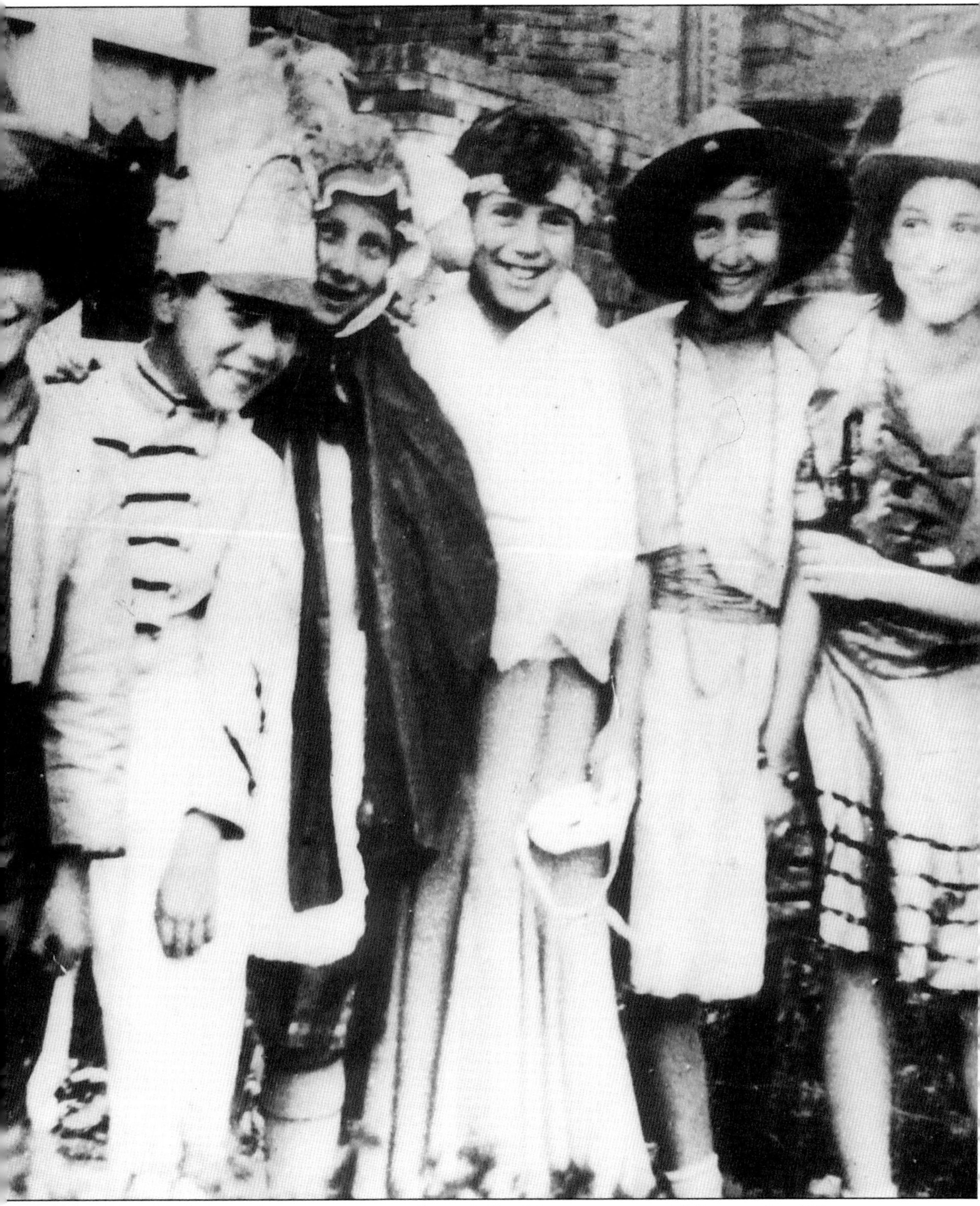

lived in New York City. Just over one year later, Lillie Mae was granted full custody of Truman. However, Truman's summer visits to Monroeville continued for two more years, until he was adopted by Joe and given the name Truman Garcia Capote. In February 1935, just after the completion of adoption proceedings, Truman returned to New York with his parents, ending his final extended visit to the Faulk household.

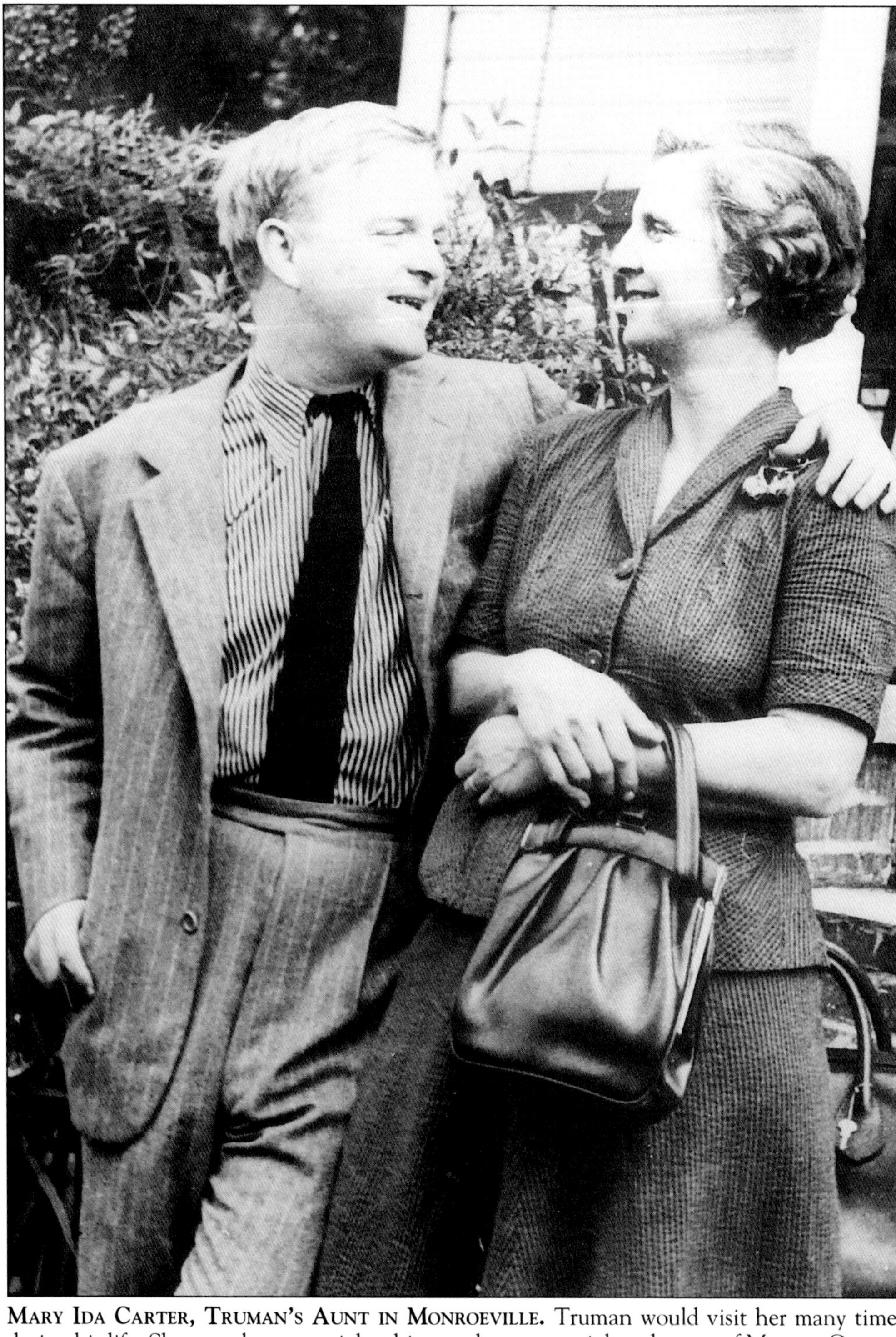

Mary Ida Carter, Truman's Aunt in Monroeville. Truman would visit her many times during his life. She was always special to him, as she was special to the rest of Monroe County. Mrs. Carter was the first curator of the Old Courthouse Museum in the 1960s, and spent many hours in the old courtroom. Mrs. Carter passed away on October 25, 1995.

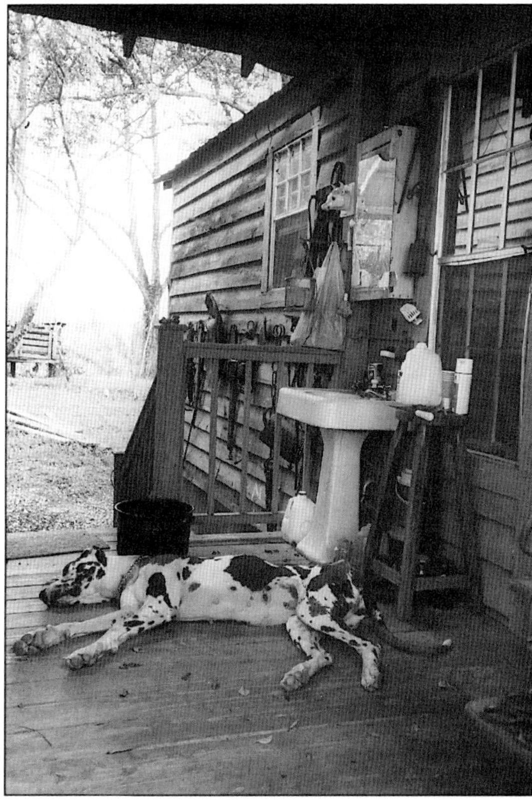

THE CARTER HOUSE, LOCATED OFF DREWRY ROAD. Truman visited Mary Ida after his success. She was his "local publicity agent" and always made sure everyone knew of Truman's latest successes. In April 1963, just back in America after a visit to Switzerland, Truman took a break from the writing of *In Cold Blood* and paid a visit to his family in Monroeville, reportedly his first visit with them since 1955. A reception was held on April 13 at the home of his aunt Mary Ida and was attended by many of his relatives and longtime friends. *The Monroe Journal* reported that 40 individuals visited with Truman during the course of the afternoon, including Nelle Harper Lee, who had recently received the Pulitzer Prize for her own work, *To Kill a Mockingbird*.

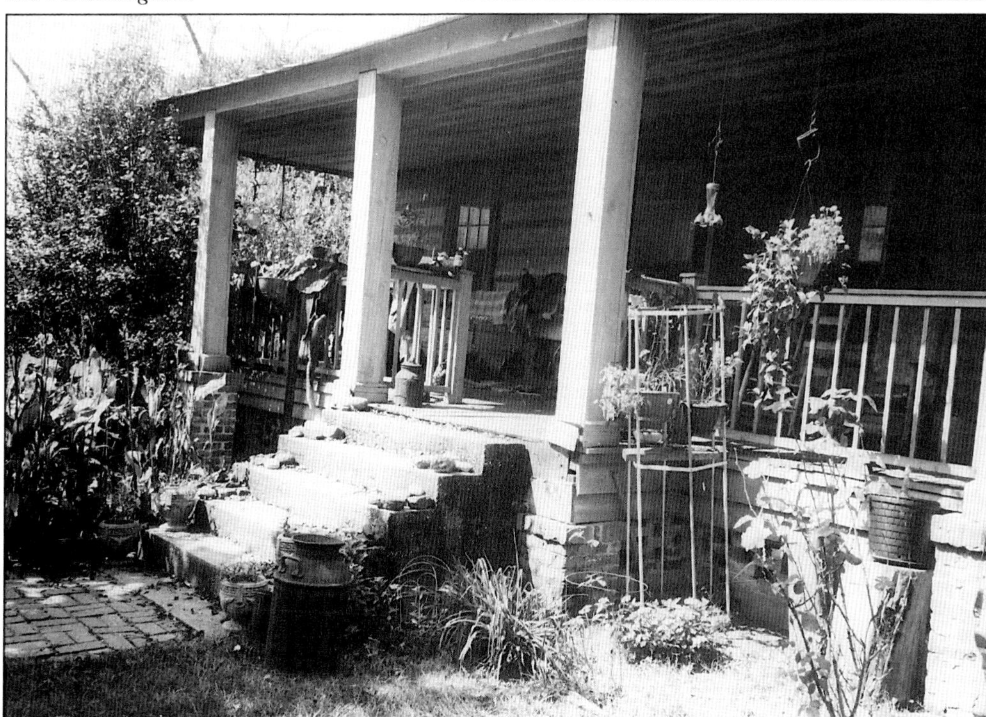

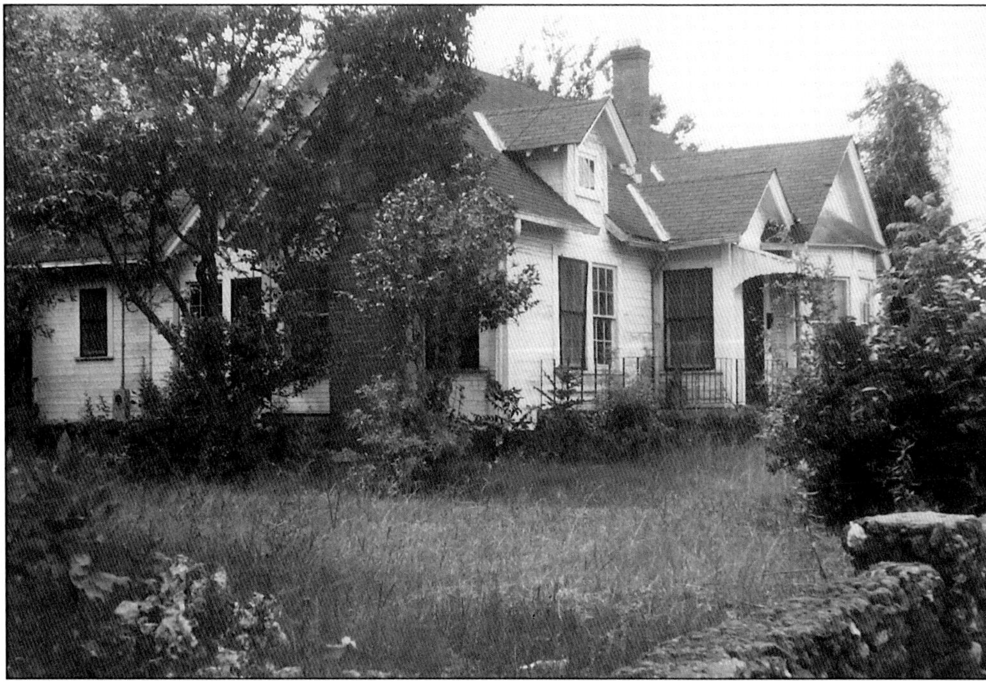

THE SECOND FAULK HOME ON SOUTH ALABAMA AVENUE WITH "THE STONE WALL" RUNNING IN FRONT OF THE HOUSE. The house itself (the second on the site; the first burned to the ground in 1940) was demolished in 1988. With it, most of what remained of Truman Capote's childhood surroundings was destroyed.

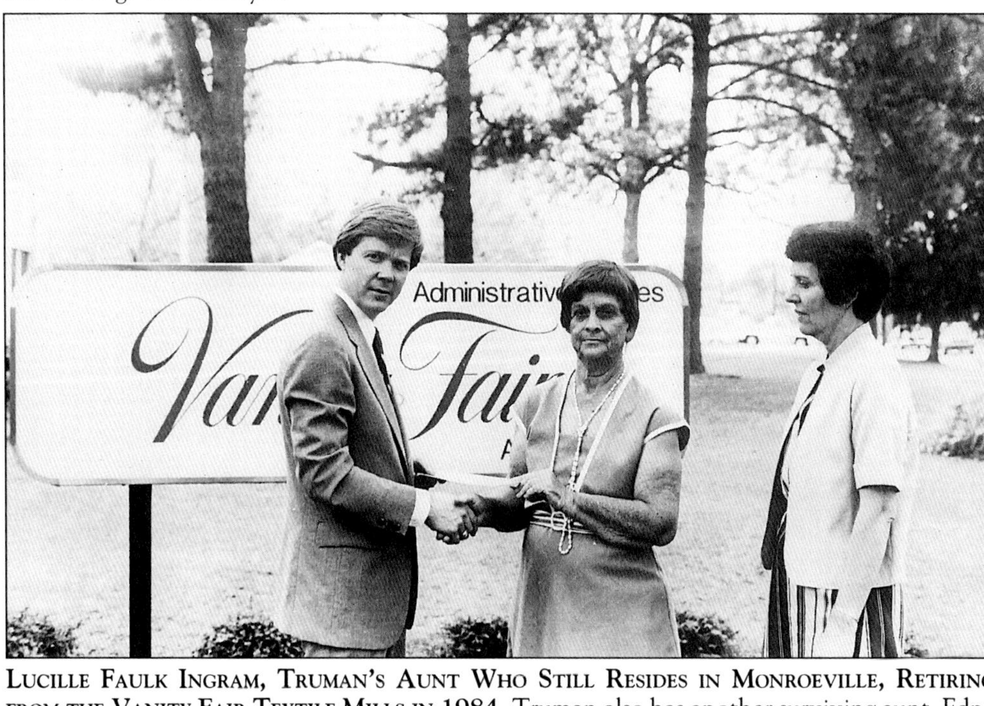

LUCILLE FAULK INGRAM, TRUMAN'S AUNT WHO STILL RESIDES IN MONROEVILLE, RETIRING FROM THE VANITY FAIR TEXTILE MILLS IN 1984. Truman also has another surviving aunt, Edna Marie Faulk Rudisill.

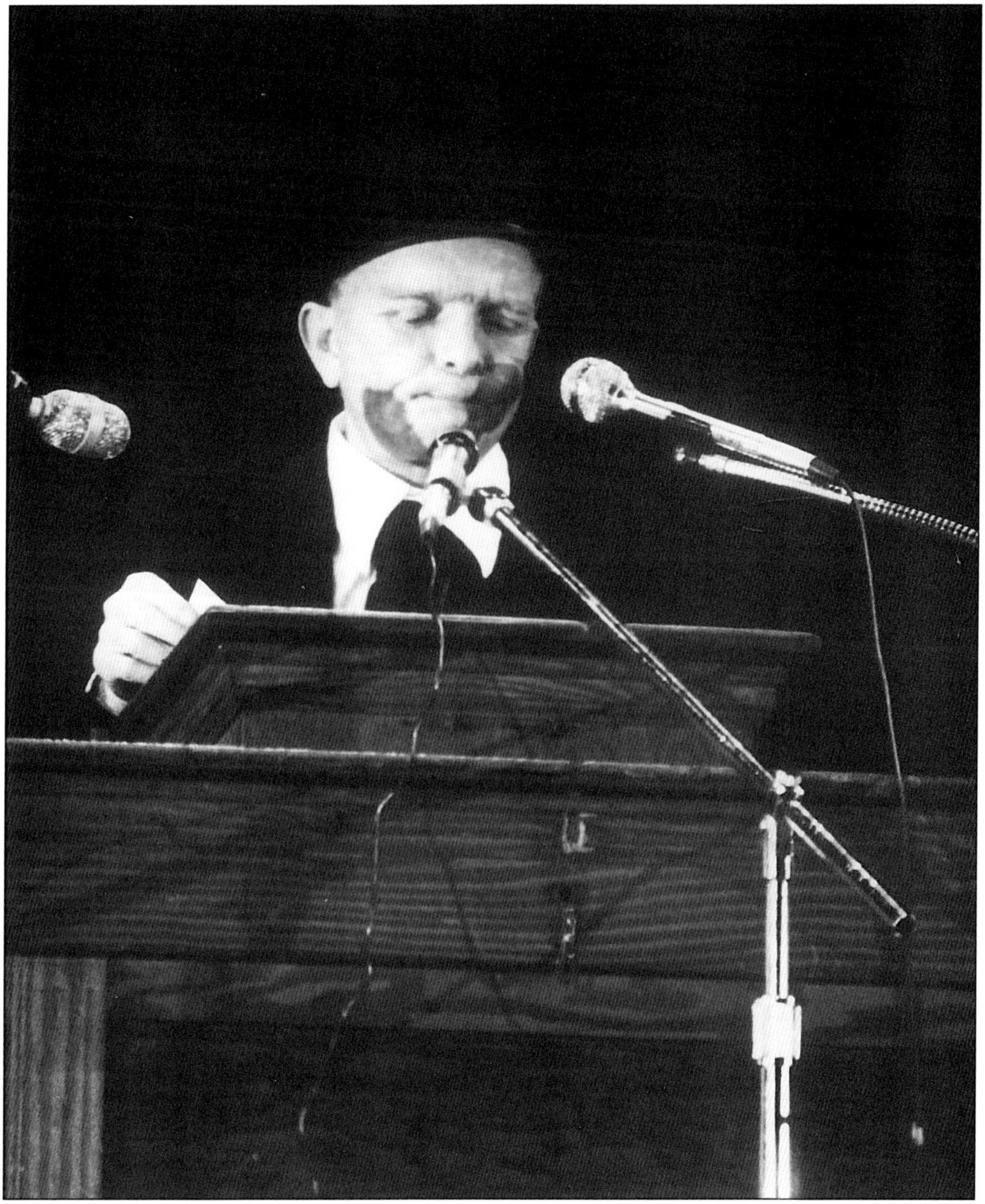

Truman Receiving an Honorary Degree from Auburn University in 1979. After the publication of *In Cold Blood* (in which he received help with research in Kansas from Nelle Harper Lee), Truman enjoyed the rewards of success. The Pulitzer Prize was not among them, however, and it was the only major award which he did not win for his writing. (He had previously won two O. Henry Awards for his short story writing, and in 1959 was awarded a certificate from the American Institute of Arts and Letters.) During the next 18 years, Truman Capote did not publish a full-length novel. He continued to work on *Answered Prayers*, which was published posthumously. This last novel offered a negative group portrait of the society of his time. With the excerpt publication of this book in *Esquire* Magazine, Truman lost many high society friendships that he never regained. Several memoirs about his childhood in Monroeville were published, including *A Christmas Memory*, *The Thanksgiving Visitor*, and *One Christmas*.

He appeared in Neil Simon's play, *Murder By Death*, in 1976. Before his death, his aunt Edna Marie "Tiny" Faulk Rudisill published a book in 1983 recounting her version of his life in Monroeville. Many of Truman's family and friends felt that it painted an inaccurate picture of Truman and his mother. Truman was reportedly devastated. En route to Monroeville in 1983, he overdosed on the drug phenobarbital—a medication used in the control of epileptic seizures—and was taken from his suite at Montgomery's Madison Hotel to the Baptist Medical Center. While it is still unclear as to whether the overdose was accidental, Truman nonetheless remained in the hospital for only three days. At the same time as Truman's illness, Mary Ida Carter was planning to visit her brother-in-law, Marvin Carter, recovering from surgery in the same hospital. Rather than go to Montgomery immediately, however, she decided to wait and visit both when Marvin was able to receive visitors. Finally deciding to go, she arrived at daylight. She called the hospital just on a whim to see if everything was all right, but Truman had left that morning. After several more hospitalizations during the following year, he flew to California to visit his longtime friend Joanne Carson. On the evening of August 25, 1984, he succumbed to the drugs and alcohol which had been a part of his life for so long.

A special thanks to Matt Rhodes for his excellent research on Capoté and for his article in the Museum's magazine *Legacy*, spring/summer 1997 edition.

Seven

HARPER LEE

"*To Kill a Mockingbird* had a lot to do with that [racial climate] in the same way that *Uncle Tom's Cabin* woke people up to injustice 100 years earlier."
—Mark Childress, novelist and native of Monroeville

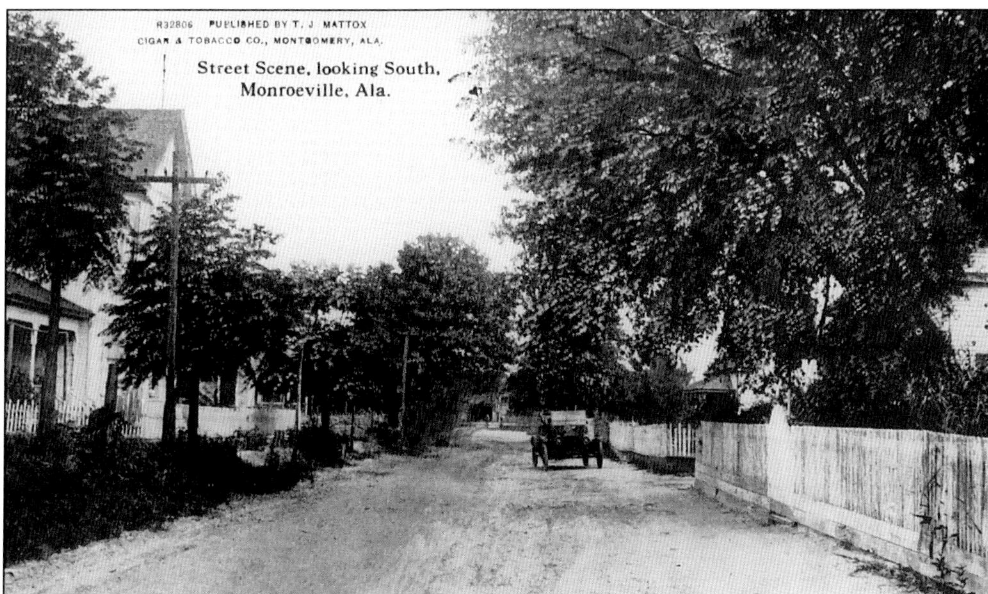

STREET SCENE LOOKING SOUTH, MONROEVILLE. With the publication of Nelle Harper Lee's *To Kill a Mockingbird* in 1960, and the Pulitzer Prize awarded to her the following year, Monroeville would never be the same town again. When she published *Mockingbird*, the civil rights movement was under way, with the white establishment and the South's second-class black citizens hitting head on. While the prosecution in her novel is fictional, similar cases had occurred in Alabama. In 1962, a movie based on the novel received the Academy Award. To date, over 30 million copies of her book have been sold, with translations into over 40 languages.

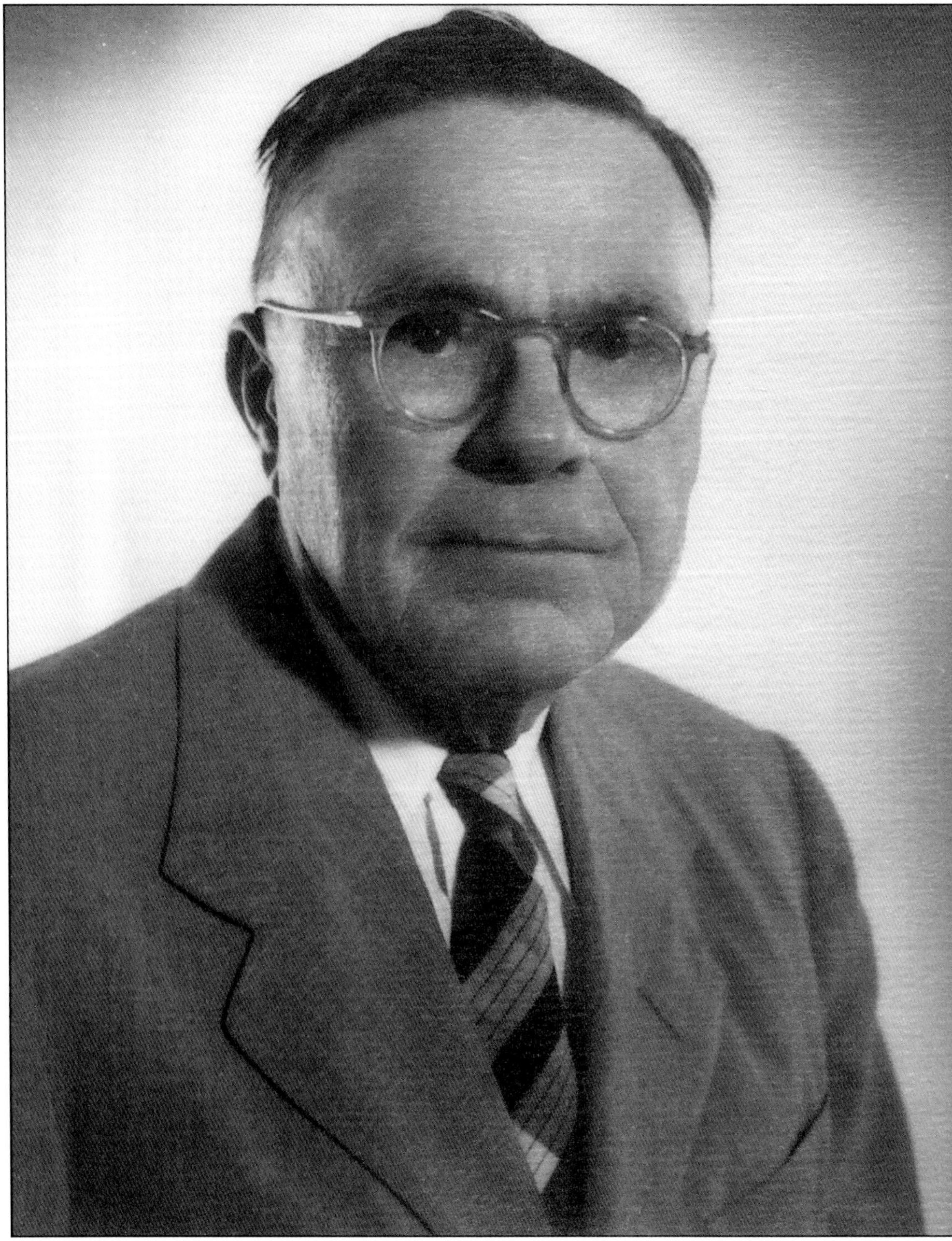

Harper Lee's Father, A.C. Lee, the Dominant Figure in her Childhood. She adored him. A well liked man by many, he was active in the Monroe County Bank and the Methodist Church, and he served as editor of *The Monroe Journal* from 1929 to 1947. He was a partner in the Monroeville law firm of Barnett, Bugg, and Lee. Mr. Lee also served in the Alabama Legislature from 1926 to 1938. Interviewed in 1960, he said that the trial in the novel was purely imaginary. He was a title lawyer and did not normally handle such cases, although he was appointed once by Monroe County Court to defend two black men who killed a merchant living in Lower Peach Tree in Monroe County.

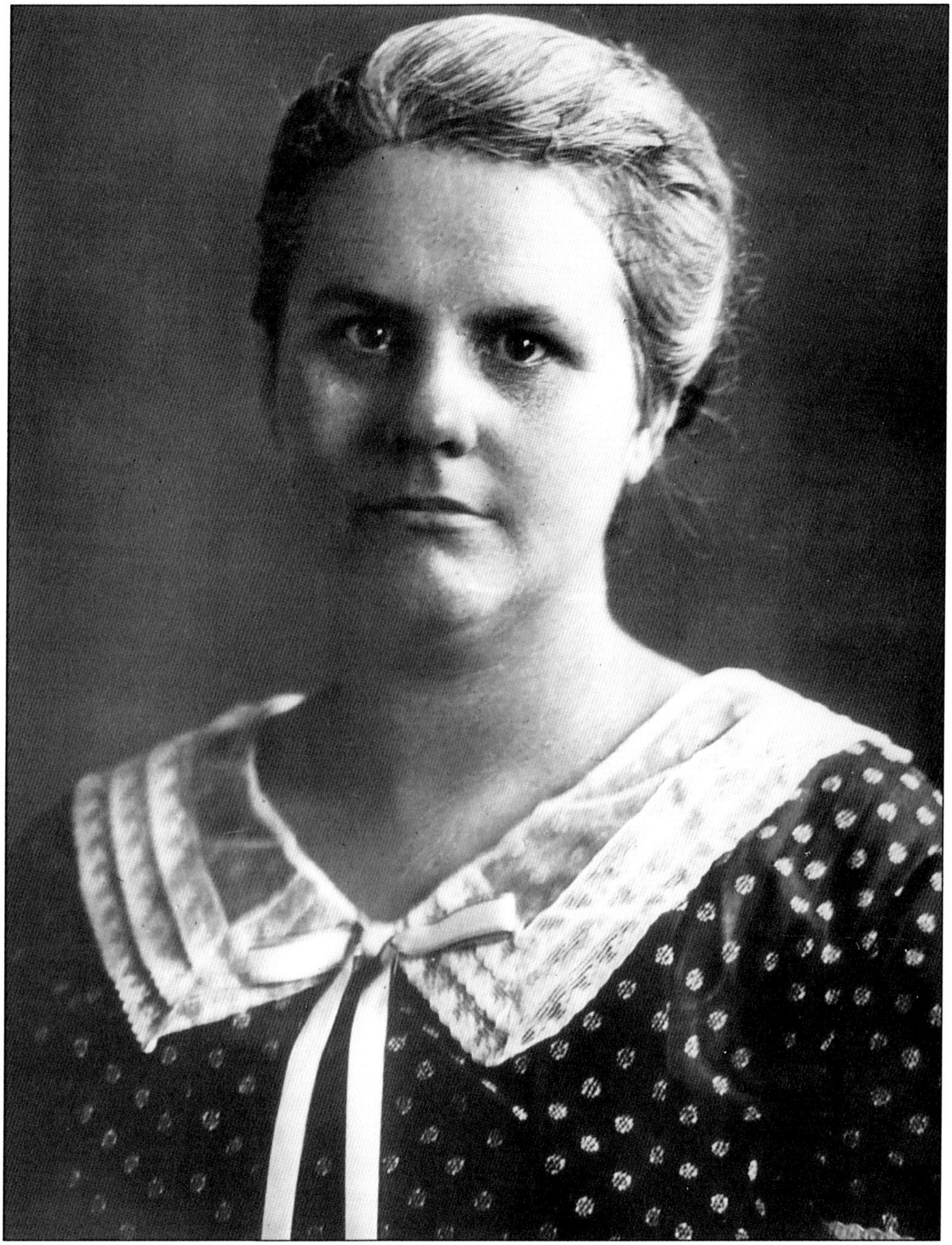

FRANCES FINCH LEE, HARPER'S MOTHER. Mrs. Lee, an accomplished pianist, came from a family which had been early settlers of Monroe County. The Lee family lived two blocks away from the courthouse in a one-story house that no longer stands; today the site is occupied by Mel's Dairy Dream. Nelle was raised with two sisters, Louise and Alice, and a brother, Edwin, now deceased.

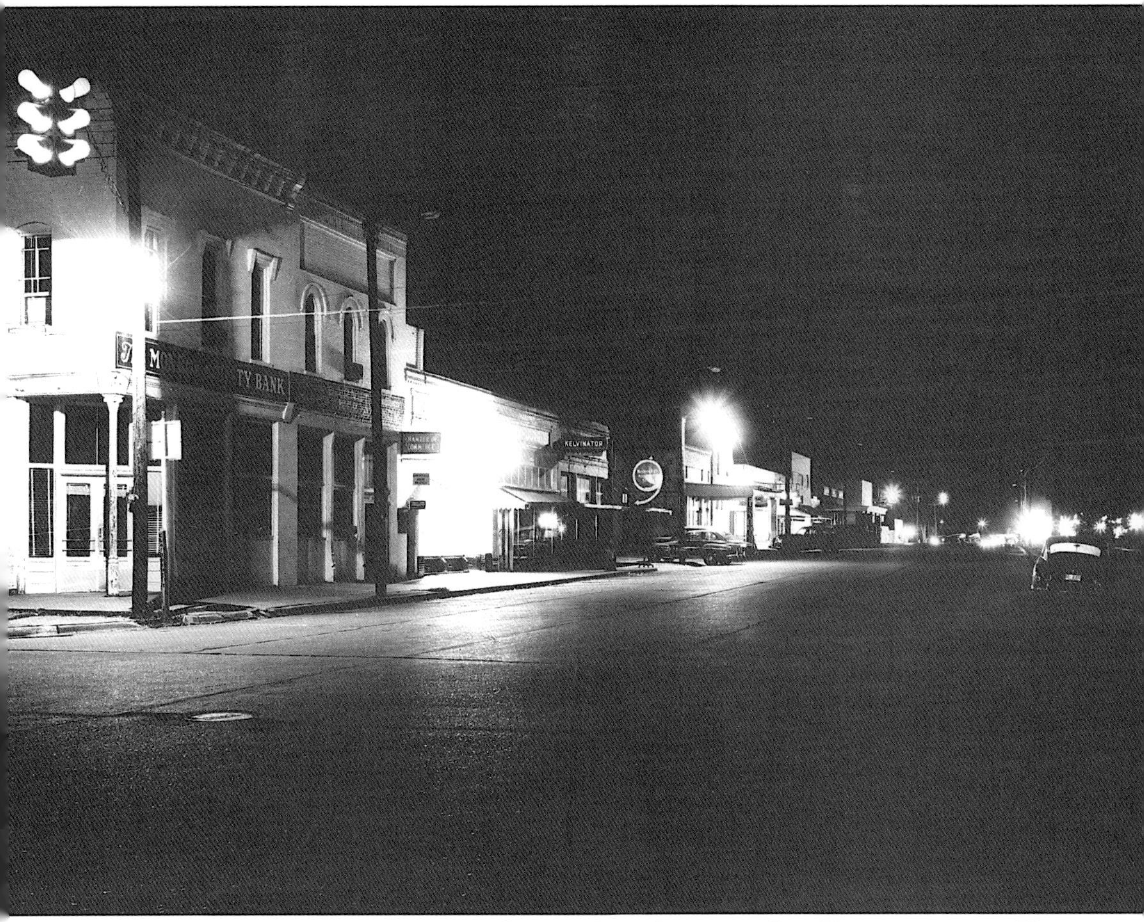

The Building on the Corner—A.C. Lee's Law Office at One Time, and where Harper Lee Supposedly Penned Part of the Novel, *To Kill a Mockingbird*.

"Maycomb" became a town that readers from all over the South related to. Maycomb County could be any small town in the South, but Miss Lee's overwhelming ability to write so realistically about the subject matter surely comes from first-hand interaction. The courage to write such a story in the turbulent late 1950s in America is a Lee characteristic. According to Wayne Flynt, University Distinguished professor of History at Auburn University, the novel ranked fifth in public schools (69 percent assign it) in a 1989 survey of the ten most frequently assigned titles in American high schools. It ranked fourth in Catholic schools and seventh in private schools. Only Shakespeare, Mark Twain, Nathaniel Hawthorne, and F. Scott Fitzgerald ranked higher. When he polled 44 Alabama history students in June, 36 had read *To Kill a Mockingbird*, probably their "single most unifying literary experience." Flynt said one perceptive student observed that although Shakespeare likely is the most universally assigned author in American high schools, Harper Lee is the most universally read. *To Kill a Mockingbird* has been called the great American novel. Each year thousands of people travel to the old courthouse on the square to see the courtroom made famous by the movie. They come from Russia, Singapore, England, Australia, Finland, and Germany. Some bring their copies of *To Kill a Mockingbird*.

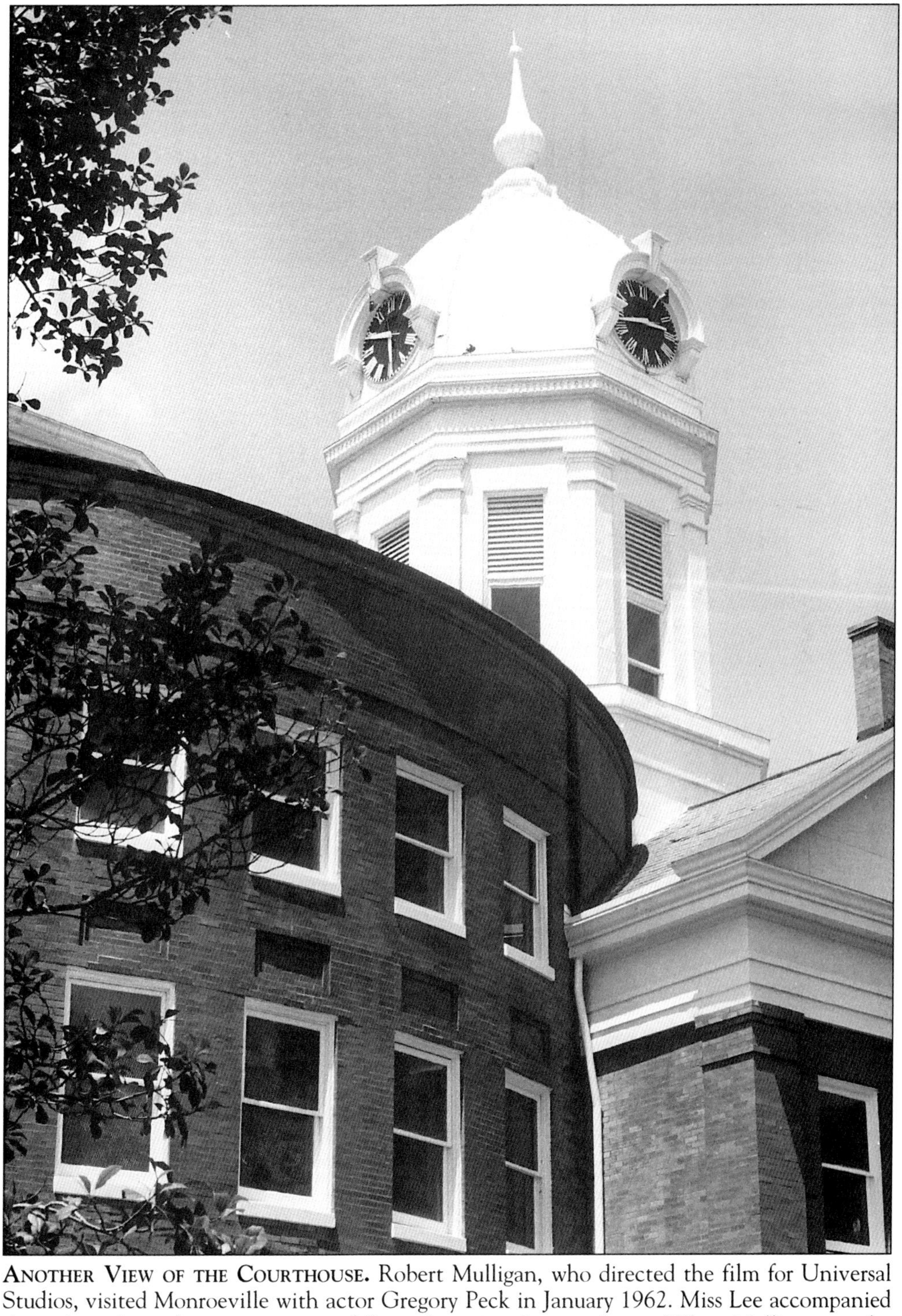

ANOTHER VIEW OF THE COURTHOUSE. Robert Mulligan, who directed the film for Universal Studios, visited Monroeville with actor Gregory Peck in January 1962. Miss Lee accompanied them throughout the town, meeting folks and visiting the courthouse. When Mulligan saw the old courtroom, he remarked, "The balcony is particularly beautiful, the prettiest I have ever seen. It is a marvelous old courthouse, and we are going to get as close to it as we can."

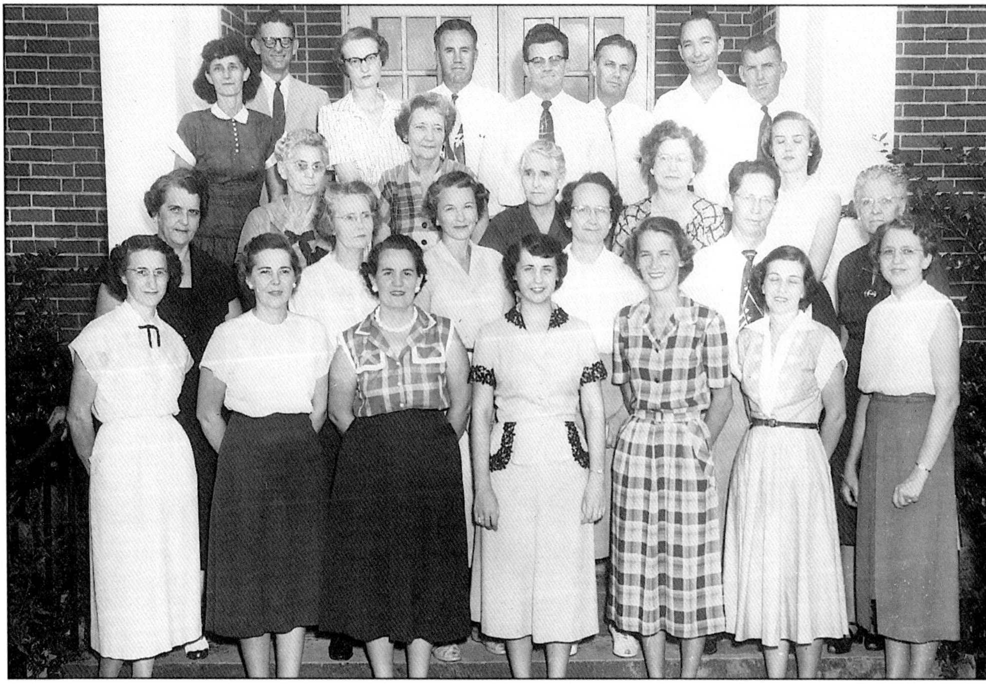

Lee's English Teacher, Gladys Watson Burkett, third from left on the top row. Mrs. Burkett lived across the street from the old Lee house. Ida Shomo (shown third row, first on left) was a beloved history teacher for many years in Monroe County.

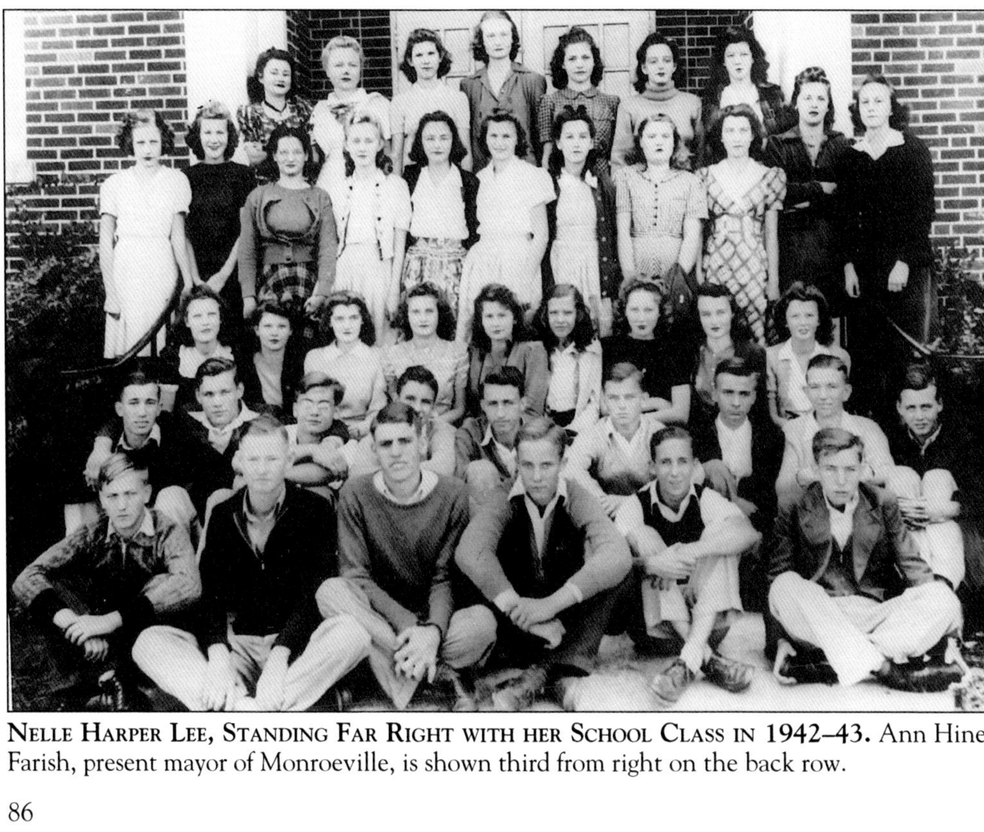

Nelle Harper Lee, standing far right with her School Class in 1942–43. Ann Hines Farish, present mayor of Monroeville, is shown third from right on the back row.

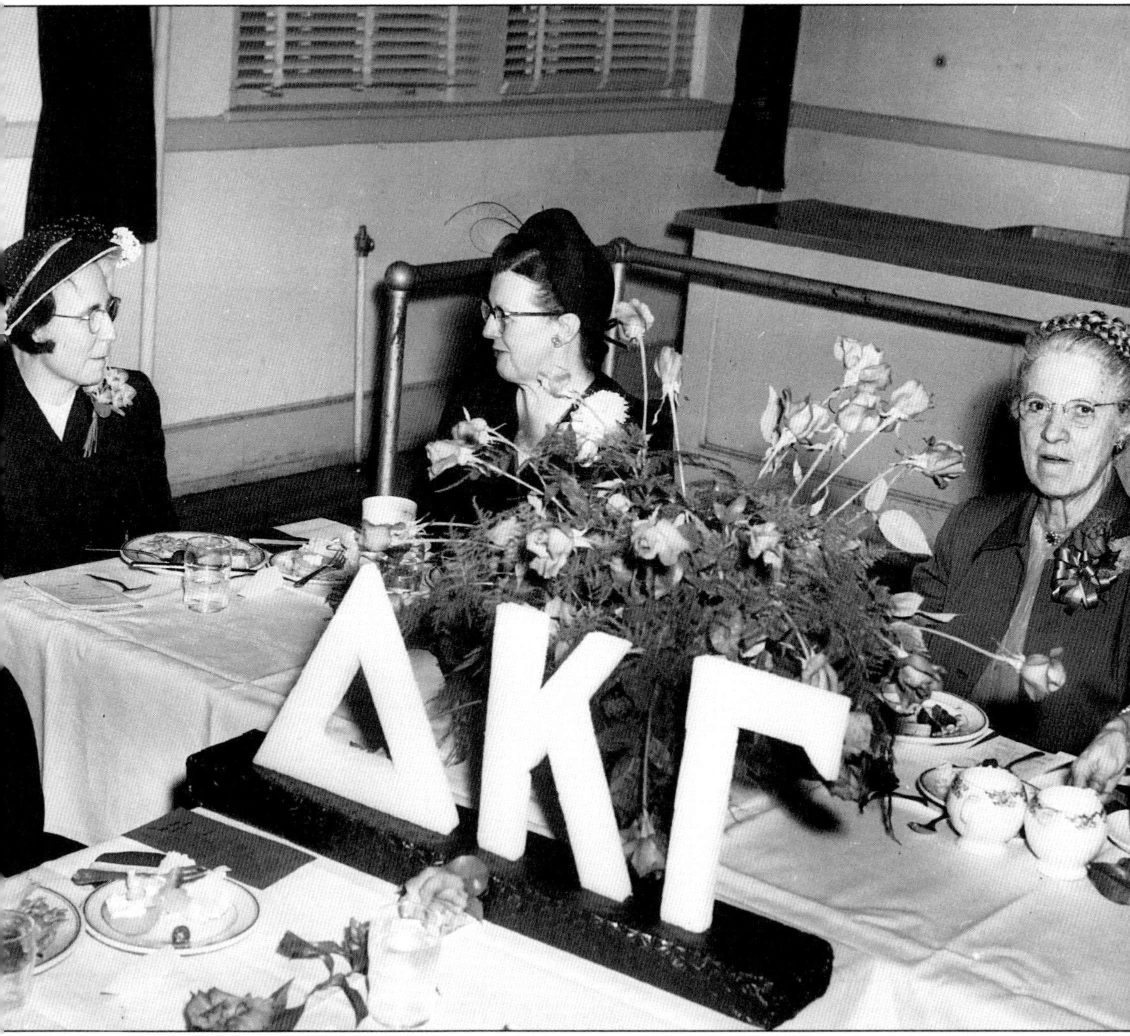

Alice Finch Lee, Sister of Harper Lee, on the Left at a Social Function in Monroeville in the 1940s. Miss Lee is a practicing attorney in Monroeville.

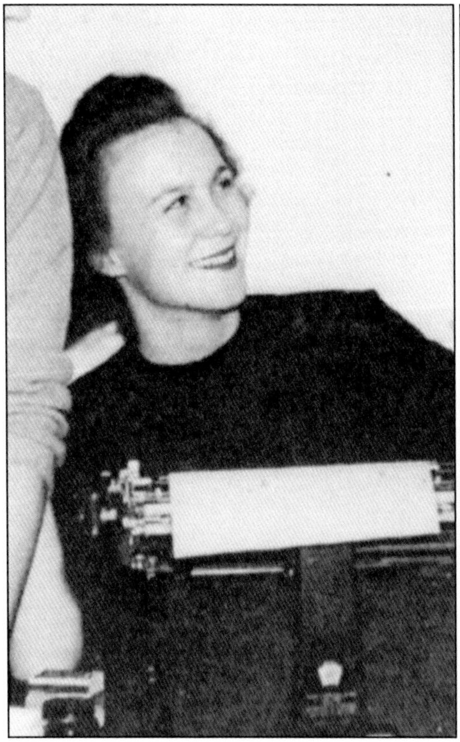

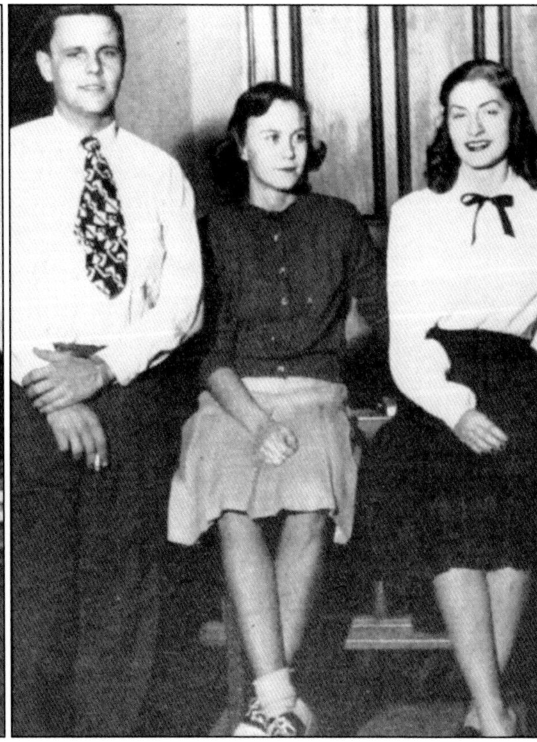

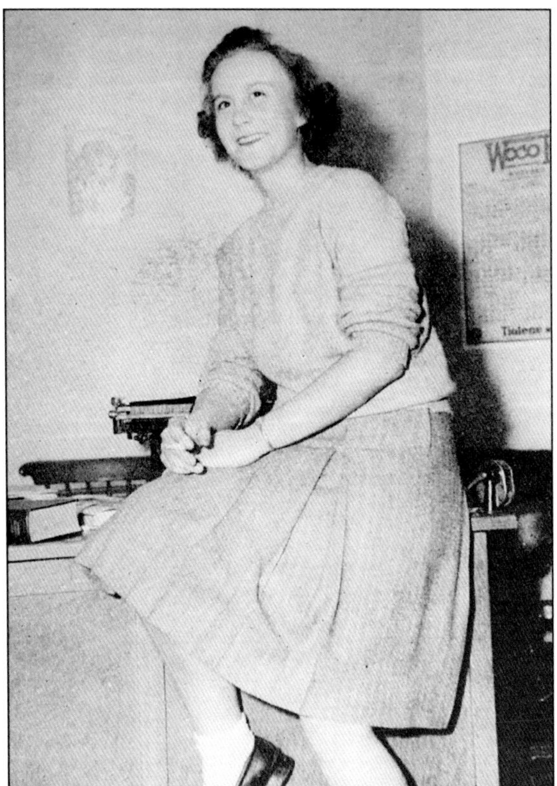

PHOTOGRAPHS TAKEN FROM THE UNIVERSITY OF ALABAMA'S YEARBOOK, *THE COROLLA*, 1947.

As a child, Nelle was a great reader, much like her neighbor for several years and lifelong friend, Truman Capote. She attended Huntingdon College in Montgomery and then the University of Alabama in Tuscaloosa, where she was a law student. She was the editor of a humor magazine, *Rammer-Jammer*.

According to an interview in the school newspaper, she said, "I'll probably write a book someday." She never received a law degree, but was awarded an honorary Doctor of Letters degree on May 11, 1991. In 1993 she was given an honorary degree by the University of Alabama. This was a rare public appearance for Miss Lee, who has not given an interview since the 1960s.

Miss Lee went to New York in the mid-1950s and supported herself as an airline reservation clerk. Her good friend Capote and other fellow

Alabamians would meet and socialize in the "Big Apple." Truman had already published his first novel and had written several stories in *Mademoiselle* and *Harper's Bazaar* magazines.

A wealthy New York couple gave her a special Christmas gift one year, an envelope with a note saying, "You have one year off from your job to write whatever you please. Merry Christmas." Later, Miss Lee would write that the gift was an expression of her friends' faith in her, "not given me by an act of generosity, but by an act of love . . . " *To Kill a Mockingbird* became Miss Lee's expression of love for a family and a community.

"Miss Nelle" lives in New York part of the year and returns to Monroeville to spend several months visiting relatives and friends. She is a neighbor and is respected as such. "Recluse" has been a word that the media likes to use to describe Miss Lee, but nothing could be further from the truth. She simply does not care for publicity or being viewed as an object. She is a person who enjoys golf, reading, traveling, being with good friends, and listening to local "talk." Her neighbors respect her and her wishes for privacy.

Above all, Miss Lee is a Southerner in the truest form. She once told an interviewer her two favorite persons in history were Robert E. Lee and Thomas Jefferson. Both were individuals of courage and honor, the two main characteristics of her father and Atticus Finch.

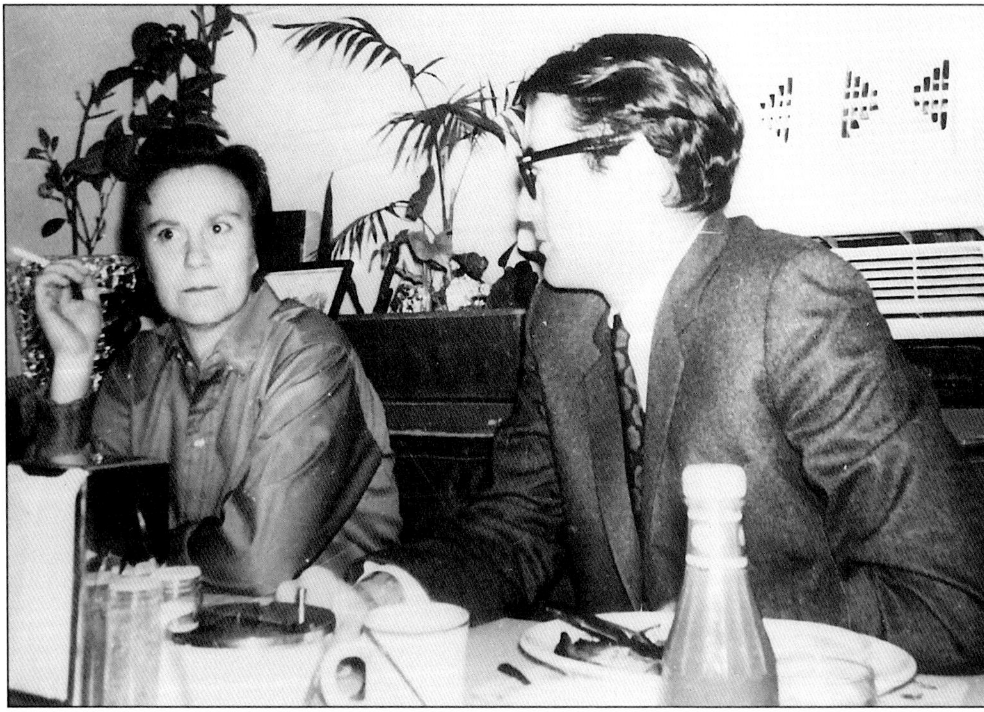

Harper Lee and Gregory Peck in 1962 at the Wee Diner on Pineville Road, Just off the Square. Peck and directors from Hollywood made a visit to Monroeville to view the old courthouse and the town to gather ideas for the movie sets of *To Kill a Mockingbird*.

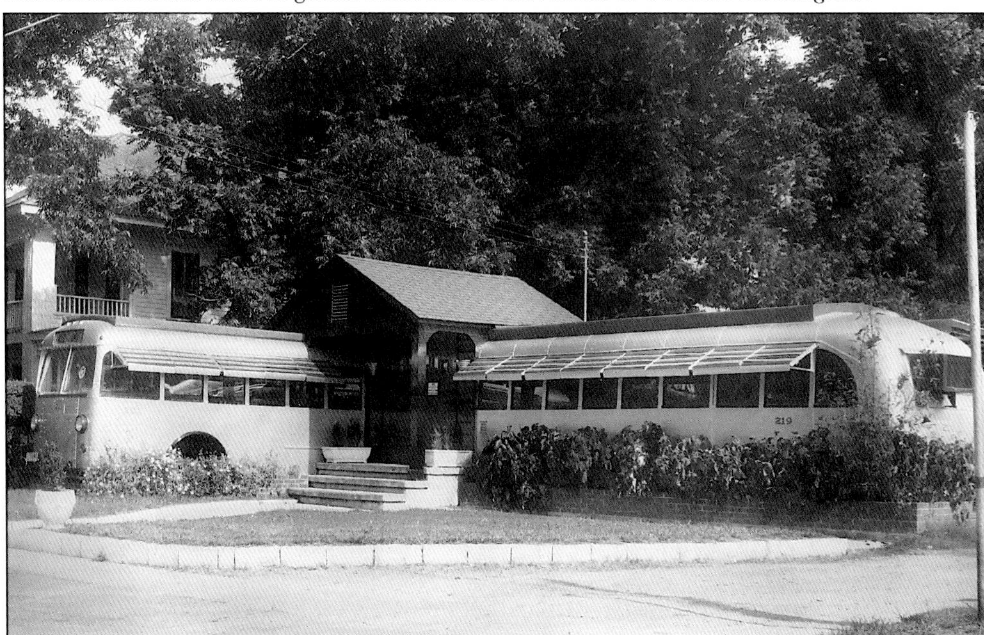

The Wee Diner. The diner, owned by Mr. Frank Meigs, was a favorite eating spot for "good steaks and salads." Ms. Sally Montgomery, daughter of Mr. Meigs, plays the part of Miss Maudie in the local production of the play each spring.

Harper Lee with Actress Mary Badham (Who Played Scout in the movie version), on the Set of *To Kill a Mockingbird*.

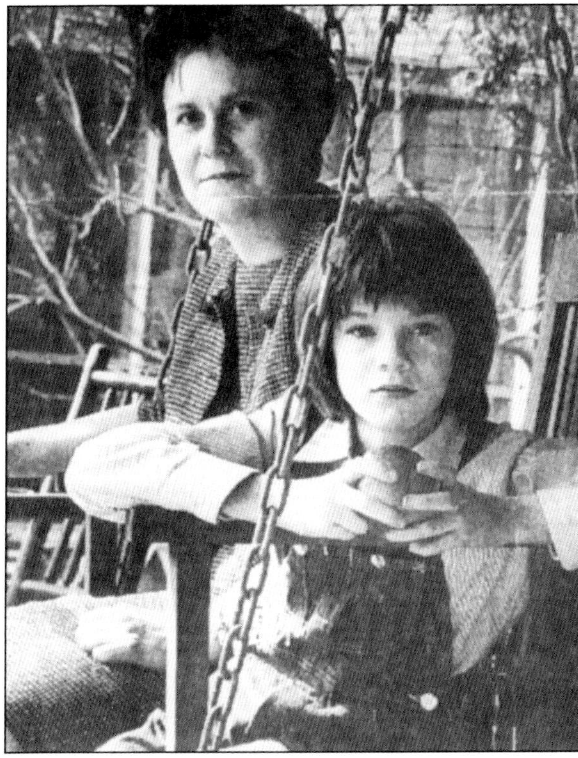

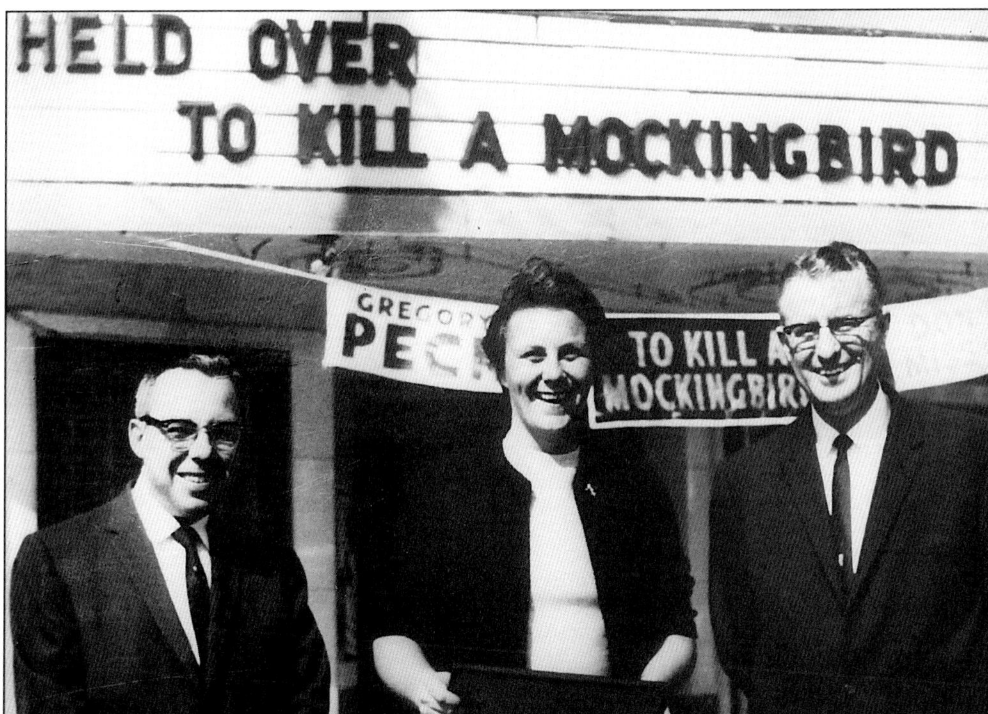

William Bowden (left), Harper Lee, and John Barnett Jr. (right) in front of the Monroe Movie Theatre.

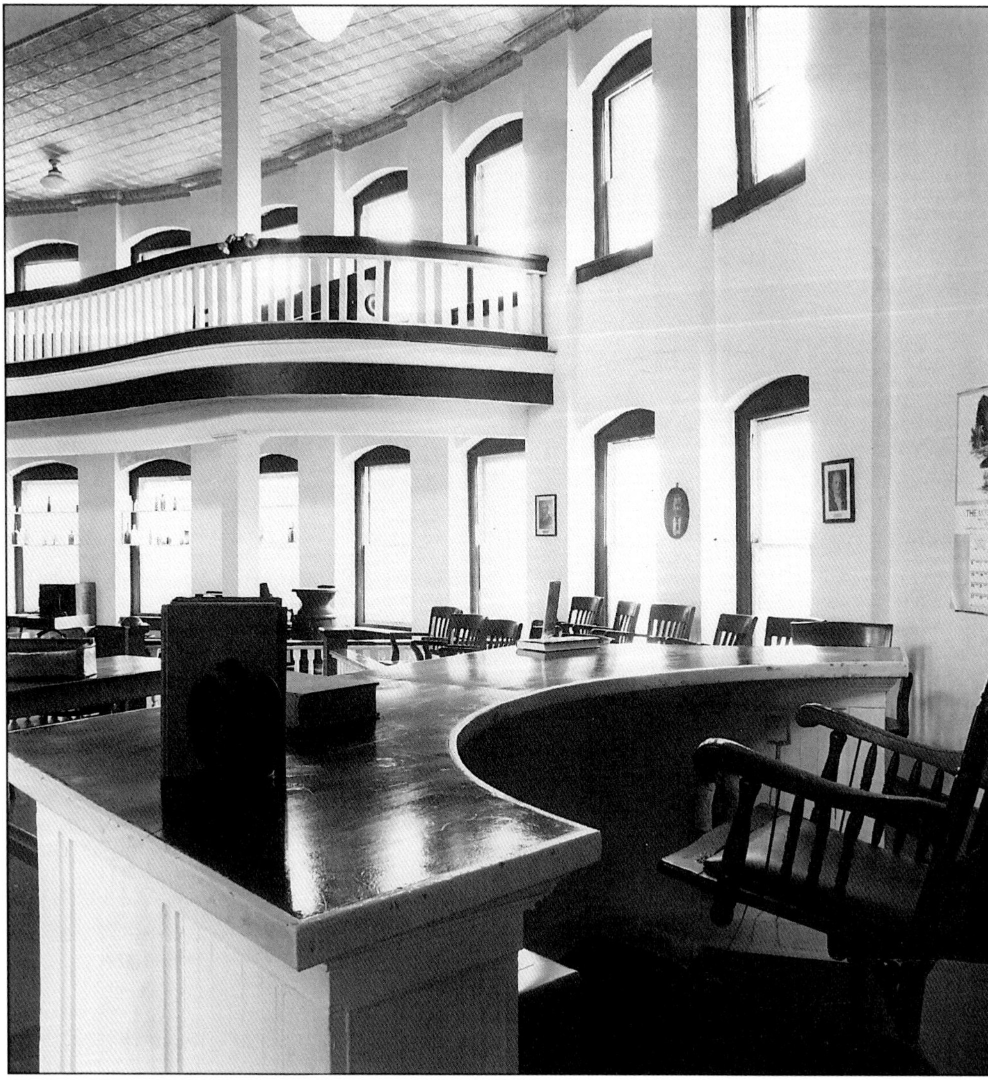

The Old Monroe County Courthouse Courtroom. The courtroom is the epitome of the old southern courtroom—judge's bench and the "colored" balcony, flanked by windows on each side which cool the room. Two large, potbellied stoves still sit on the black-gum floors. The lawyers' table, an old, much-worn piece, is piled with 1930s law books. A person can sit on one of the benches and gaze up at the tin ceiling patterned with dogwood flowers.

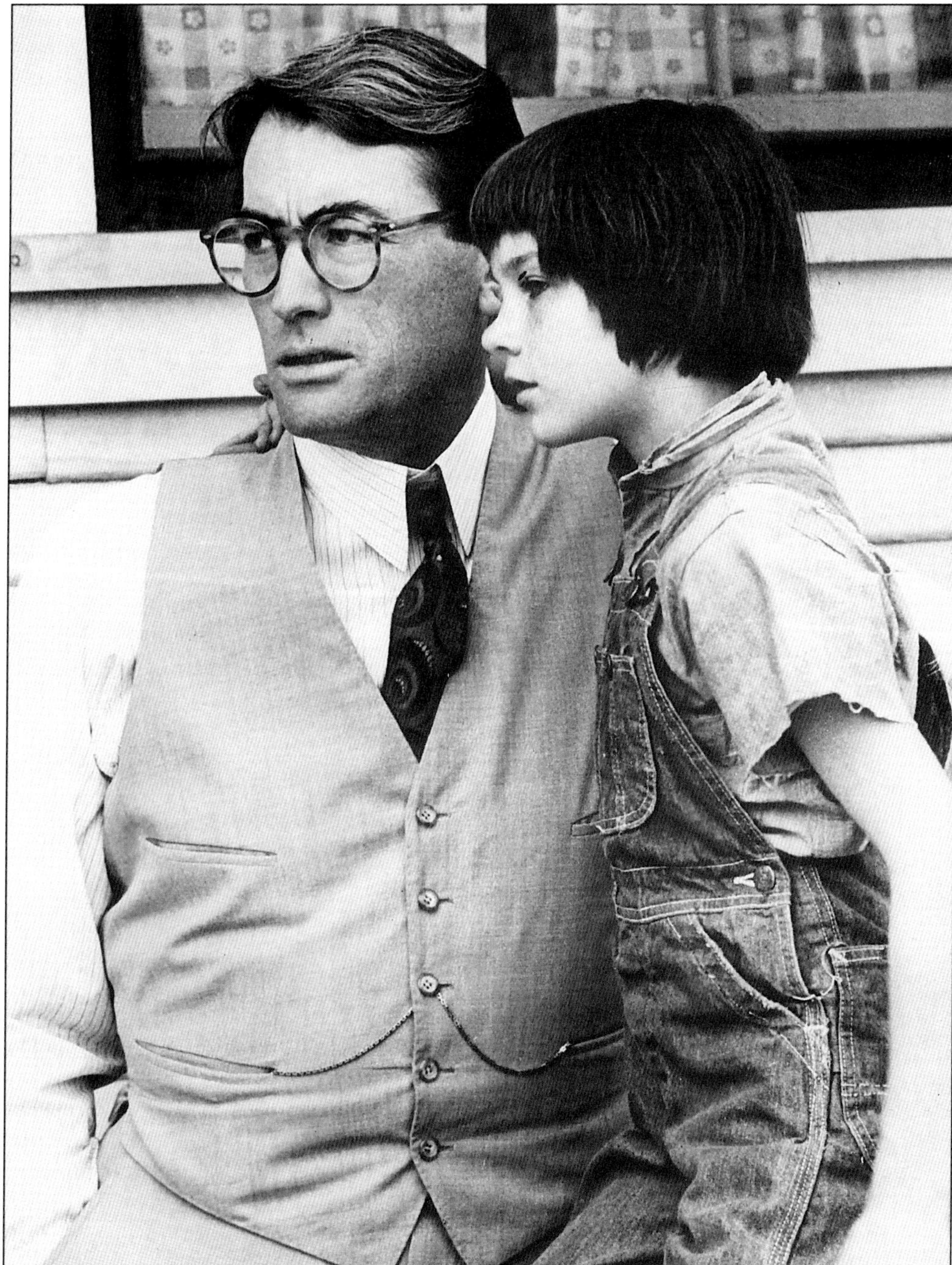

NBC-TV PHOTO OF GREGORY PECK AND MARY BADHAM. The movie was telecast on the "NBC Saturday Night at the Movies" on September 13, 1968, in black and white. In 1997 on Christmas Day, this movie once again was telecast on national networks.

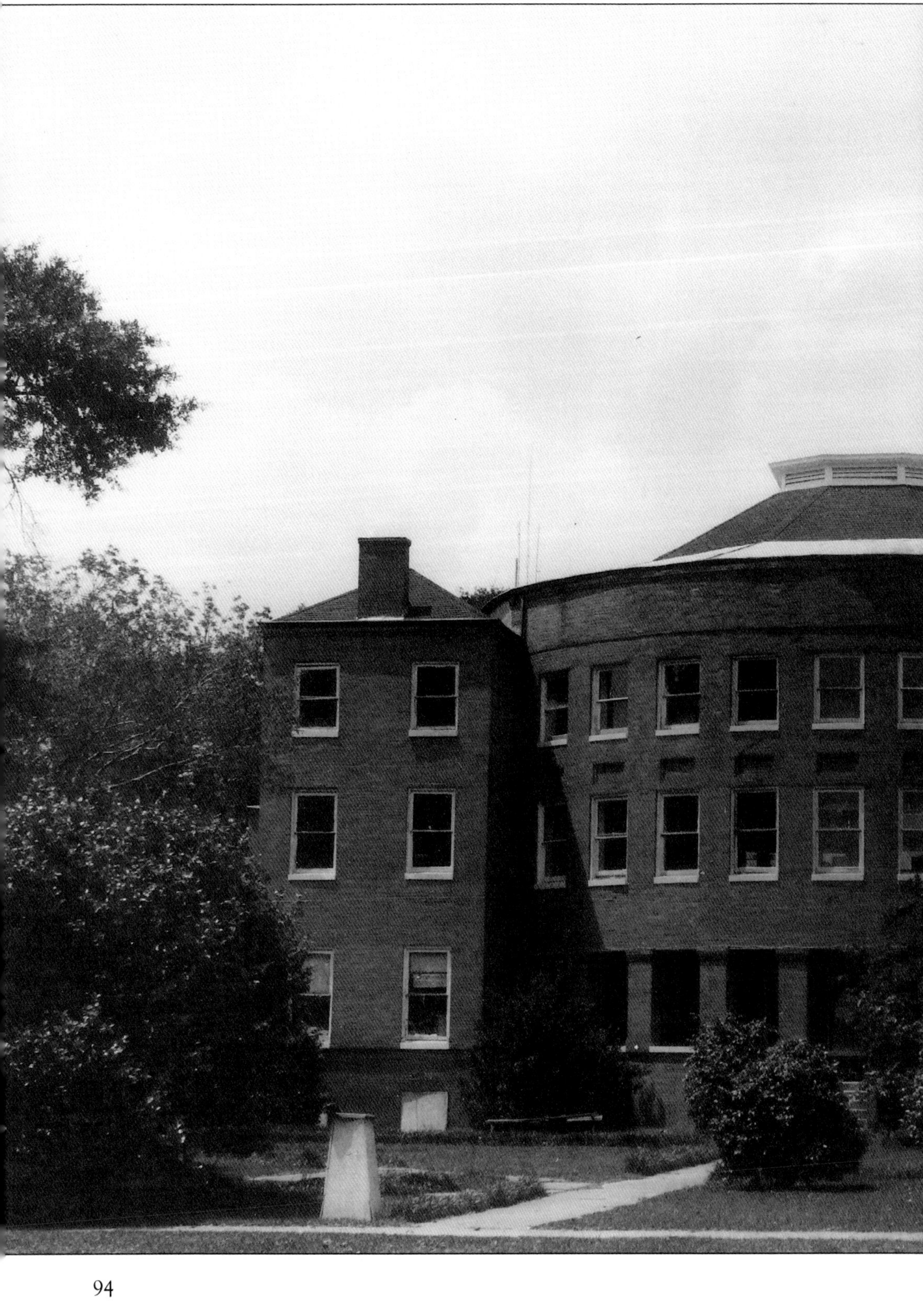

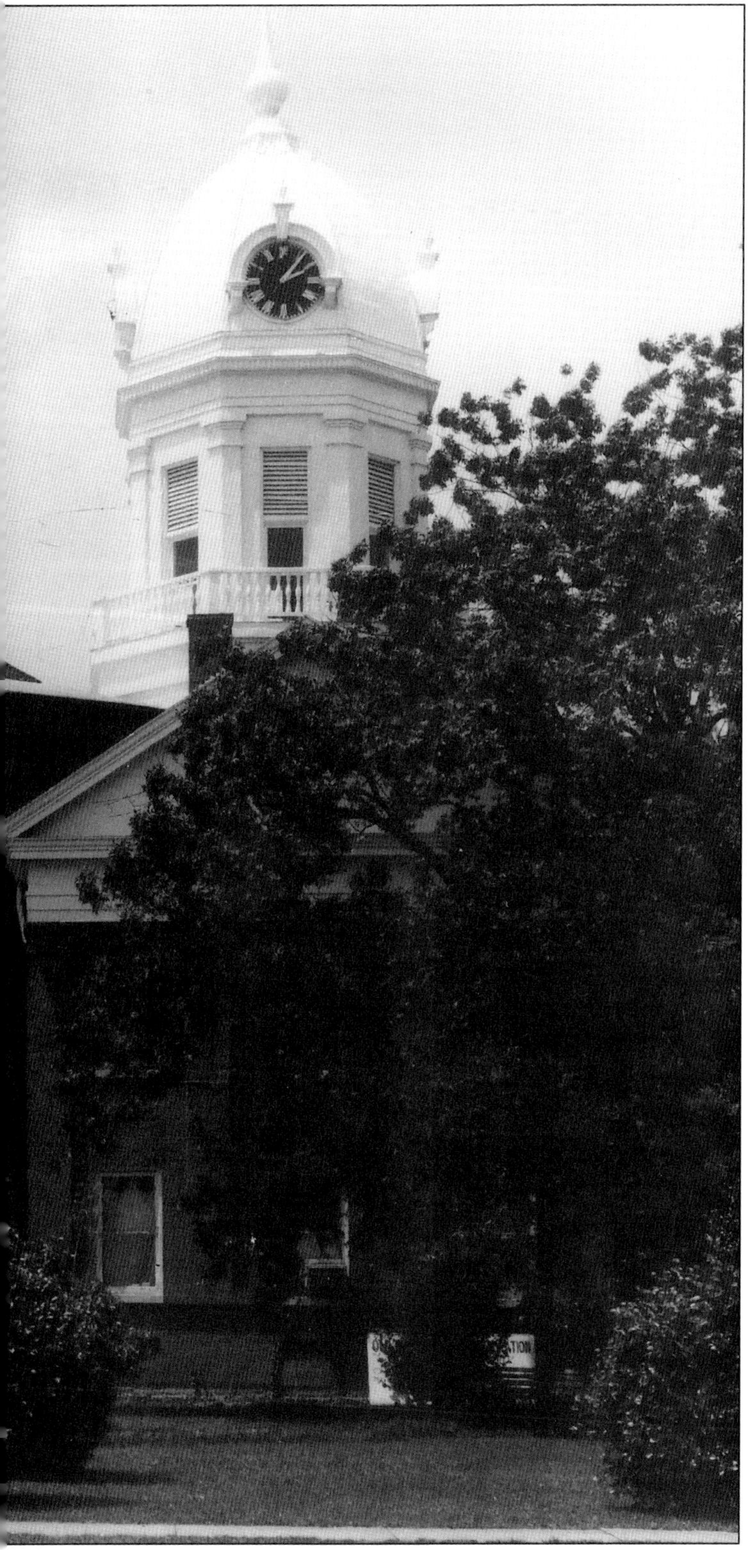

The Production of *To Kill a Mockingbird*. Each year in May, the Monroe County Heritage Museums produces the play *To Kill A Mockingbird*. Museums Director Kathy McCoy directs the play with an all-local, amateur cast. The play has two acts. The first is performed on the back lawn of the courthouse, where a set has been created for Atticus's, Boo Radley's, and Miss Maudie's and Miss Dubose's houses. The second act is performed in the courtroom upstairs of the old courthouse, which is now a museum. This courtroom is the one Harper Lee used as a model for her book. The production was presented in 1996 in Jerusalem, Israel, at the international Israel Festival; presented in 1998 at the Alabama Supreme Court Justice Building in Montgomery; and presented in Kingston-upon-Hull, England, in September 1998.

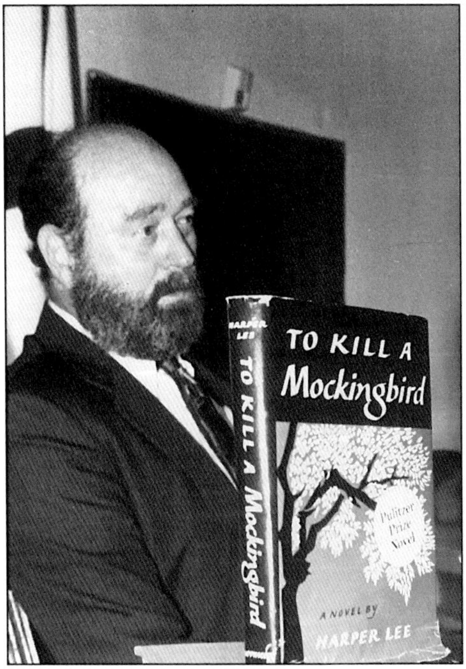

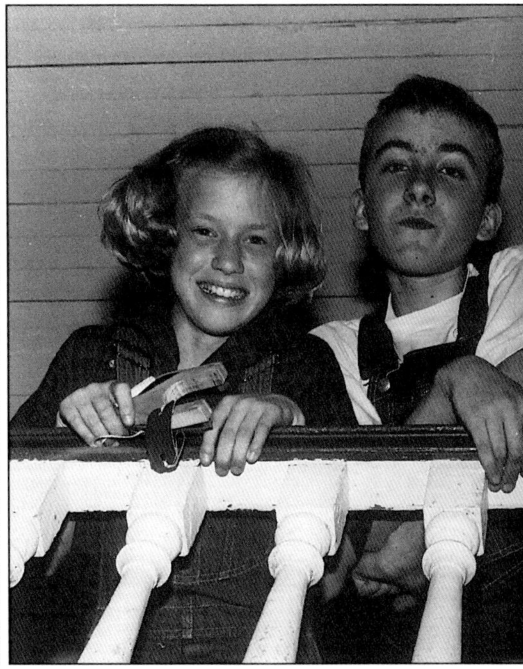

RAY SASSER, JUDGE TAYLOR IN THE LOCAL PRODUCTION. Sasser (above left) is a professor of psychology at Alabama Southern Community College. Stewart Coxwell and Matthew Eubanks (above right) portrayed Scout and Jem in 1993. (Allison Brown was the first Scout, followed by Courtney Barnett and Stewart Coxwell.)

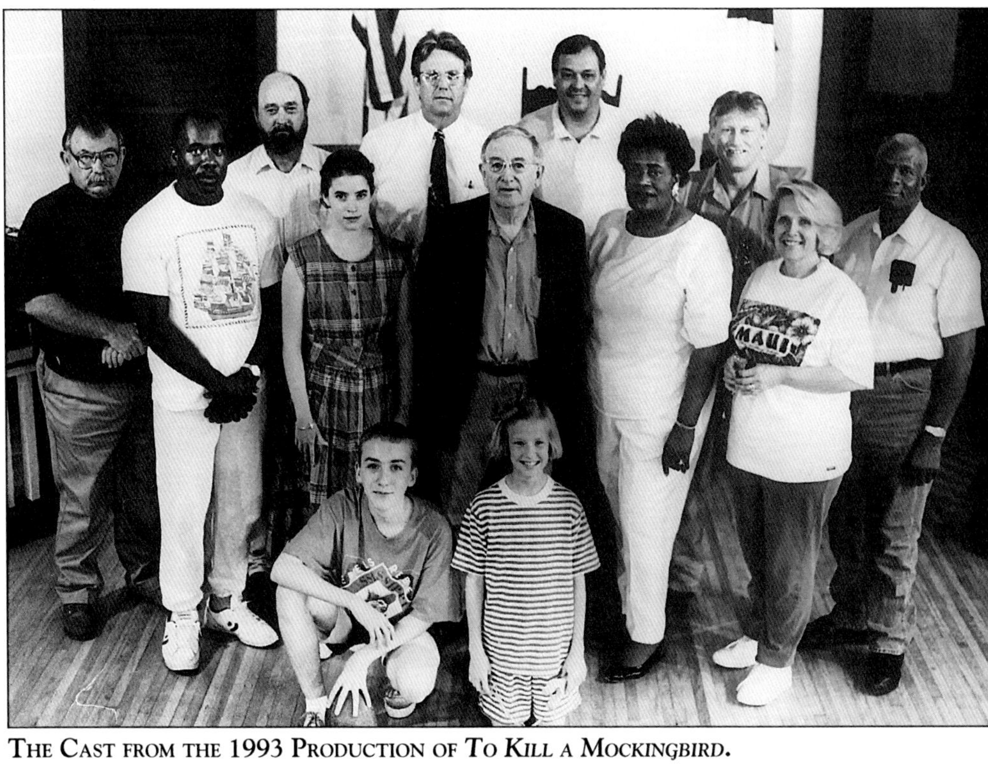

THE CAST FROM THE 1993 PRODUCTION OF *TO KILL A MOCKINGBIRD*.

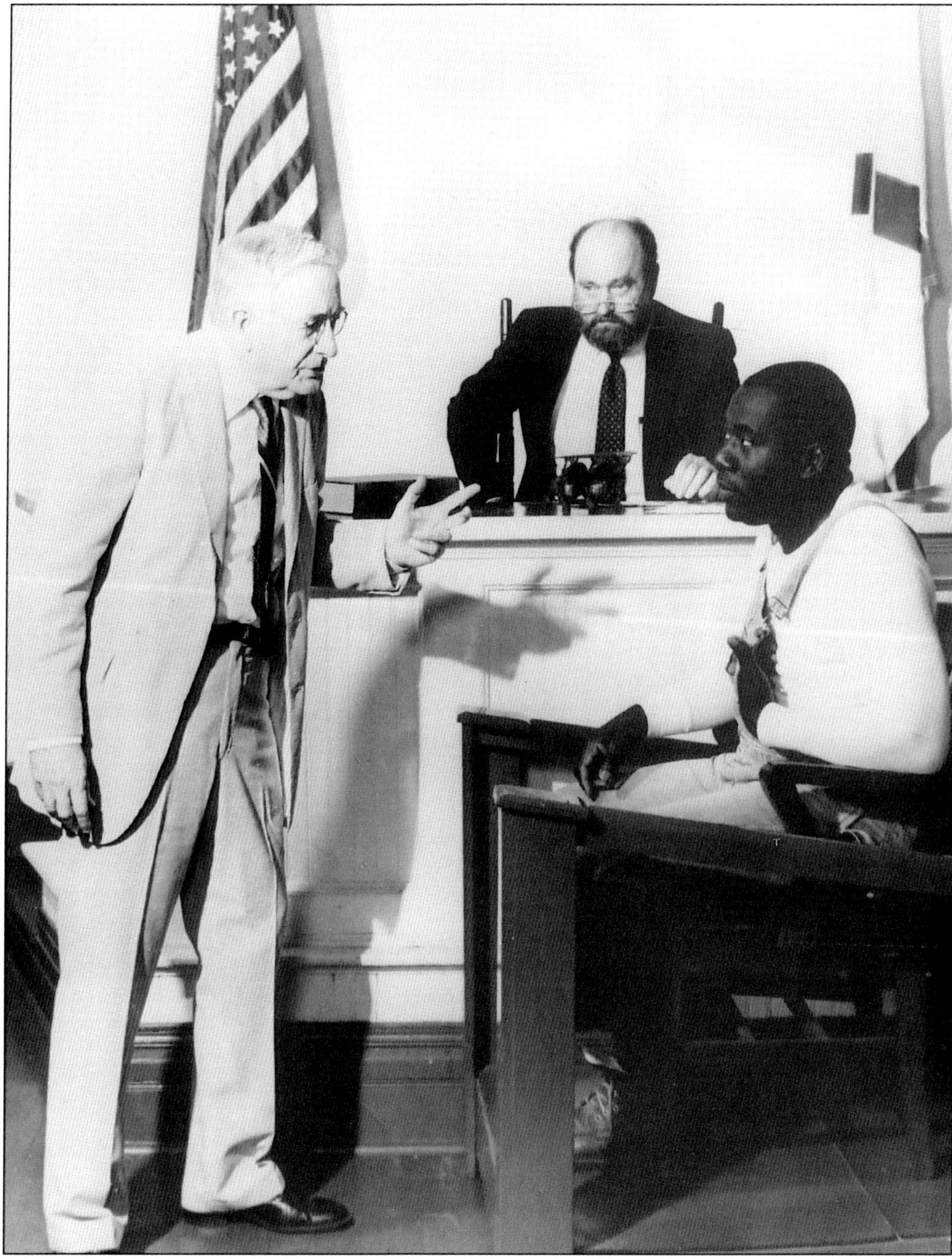

RAY SASSER AS JUDGE TAYLOR, CHARLIE MCCORVEY AS TOM ROBINSON, AND T.M. (MORT) MCMILLAN JR., AS ATTICUS FINCH. McMillan was Atticus in the first production in 1991, and portrayed the part for six years. McCorvey, who has portrayed Tom Robinson since 1991, is a county commissioner, a teacher, and a farmer.

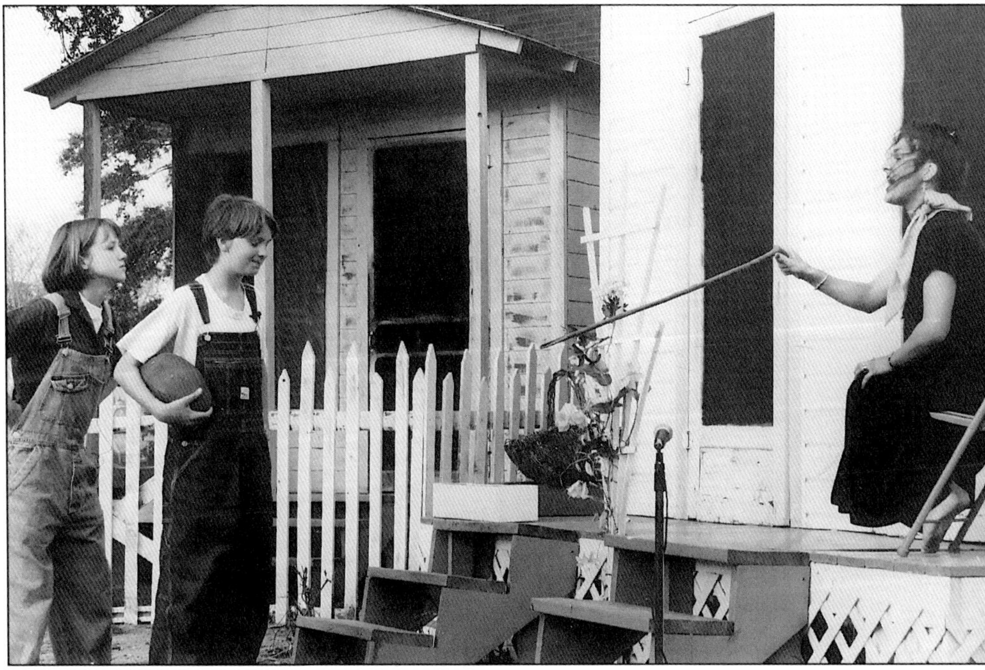

A Confrontation with Miss Dubose. Jared Handley as Jem, and Stewart Coxwell as Scout, have a confrontation with Miss Dubose, played by local attorney Sherrie McKenzie.

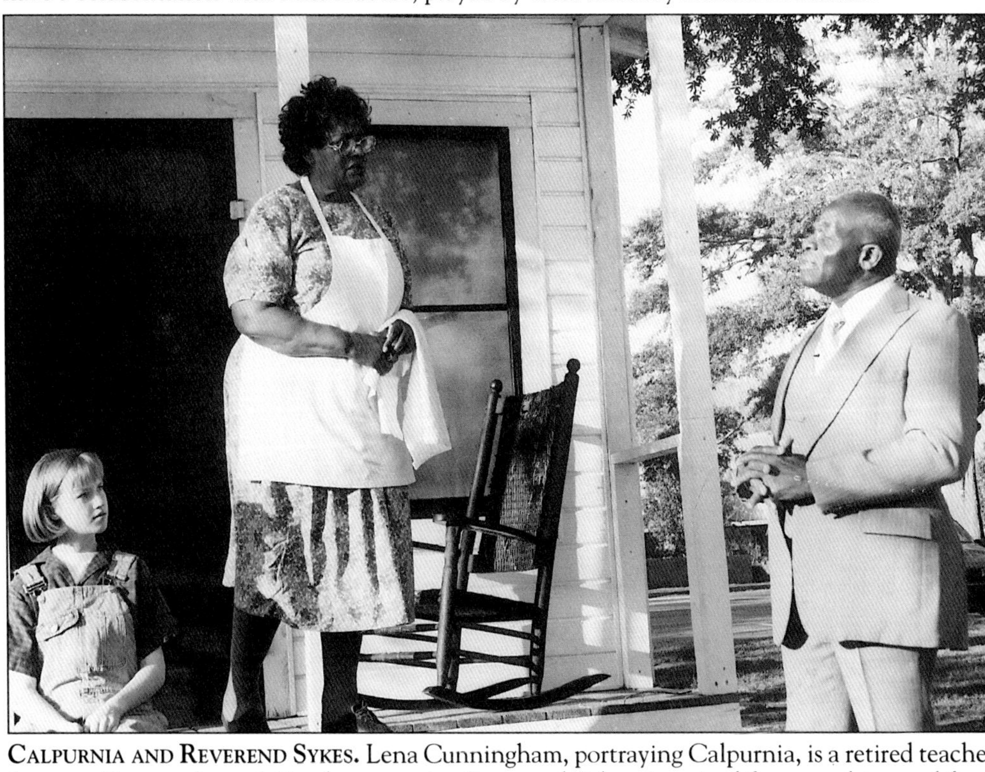

Calpurnia and Reverend Sykes. Lena Cunningham, portraying Calpurnia, is a retired teacher for over 40 years. Lavord Crook, portraying Reverend Sykes, is retired from teaching and from the Alabama Department of Education.

Jimmy Blackman as Atticus and Andrea Godwin as Scout in the Production in the Old Courtroom, 1997. Blackman is a local preacher.

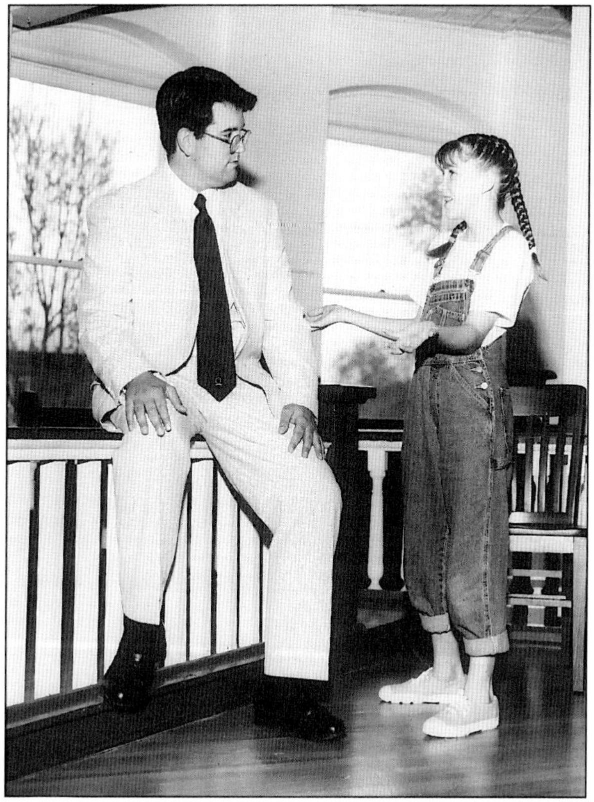

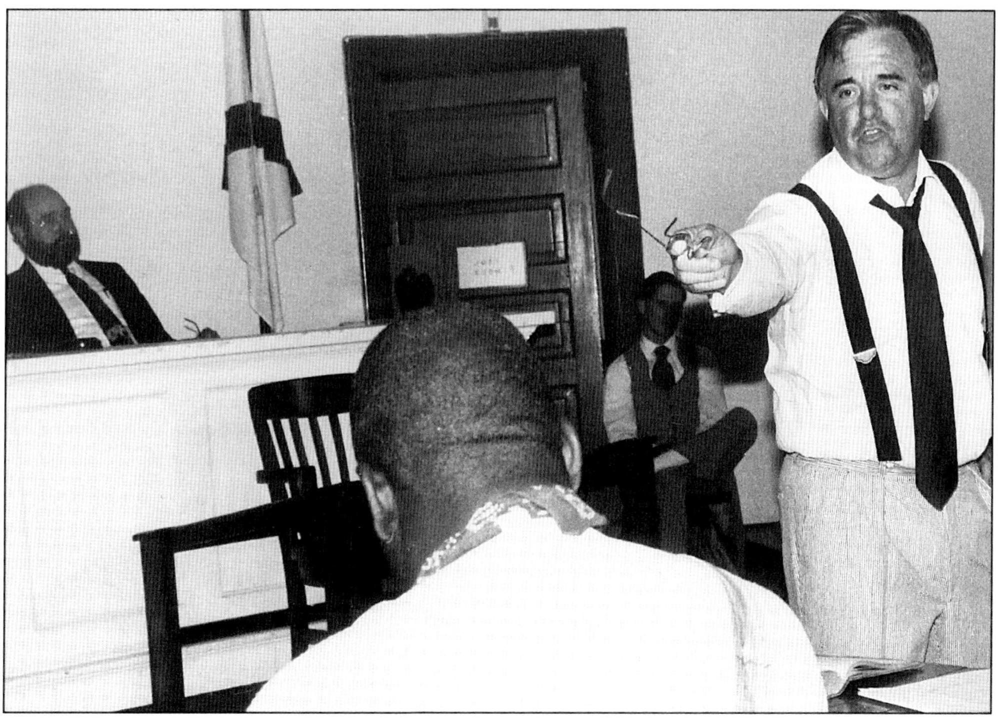

Everette Price. This attorney has portrayed Atticus since 1995.

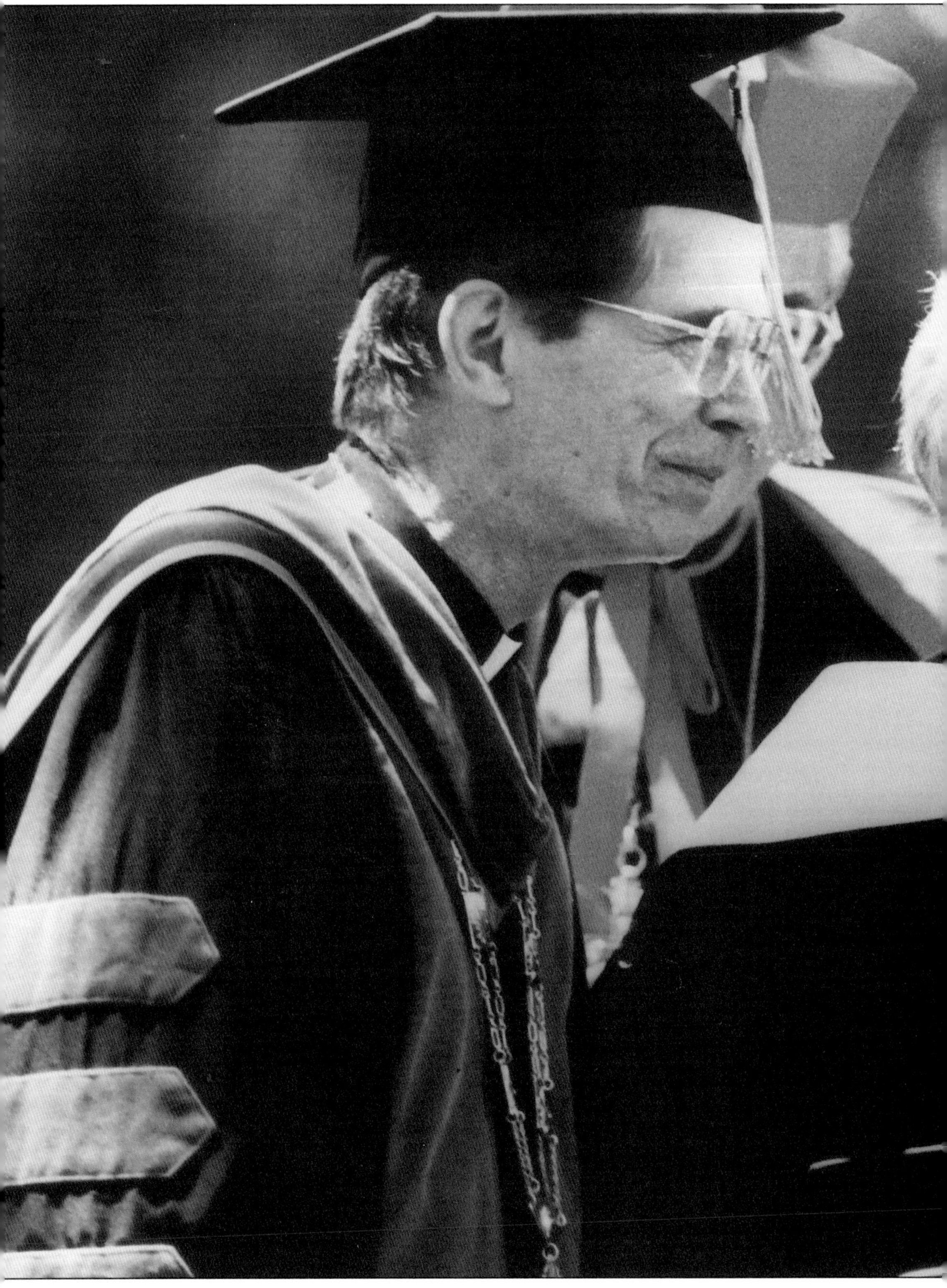

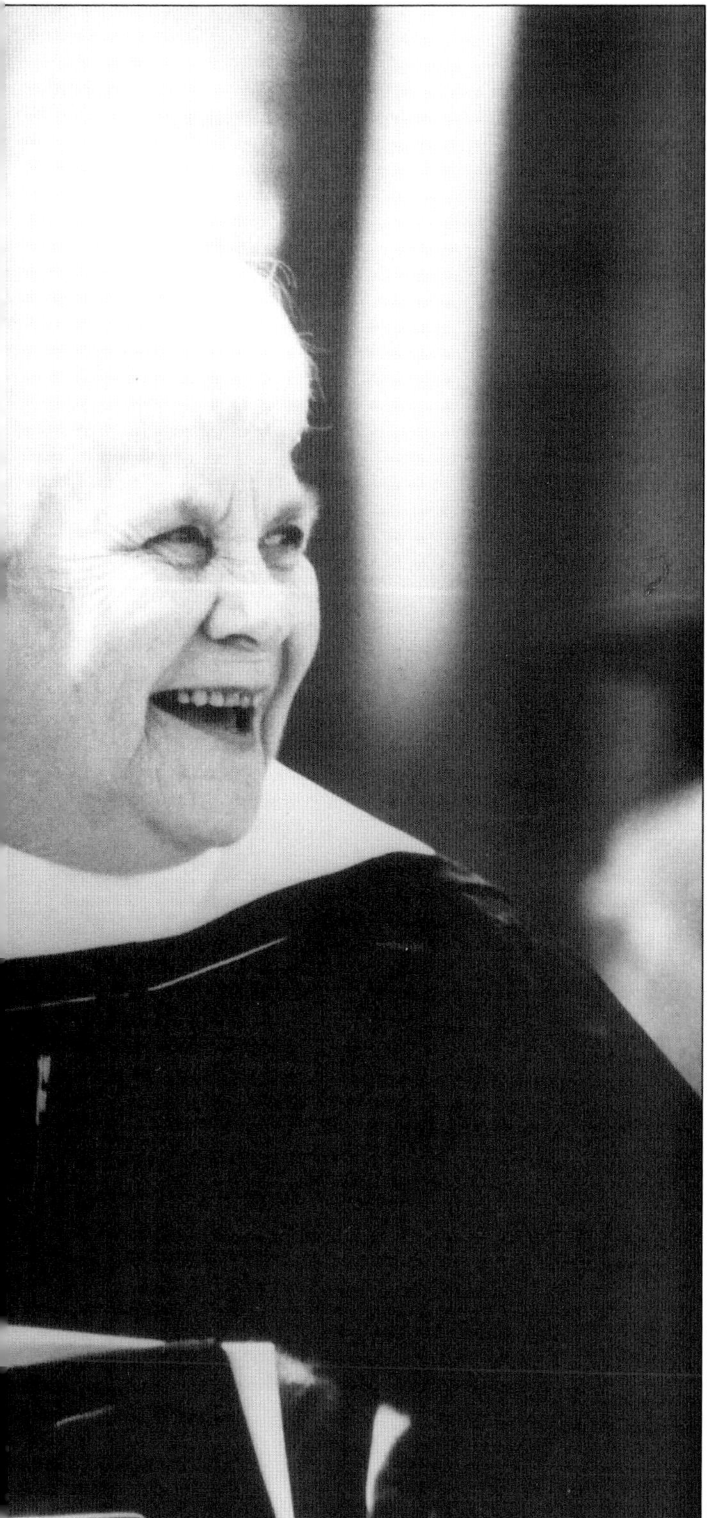

HARPER LEE RECEIVING HONORARY DEGREE FROM SPRINGHILL COLLEGE IN MOBILE, ALABAMA, IN 1997.

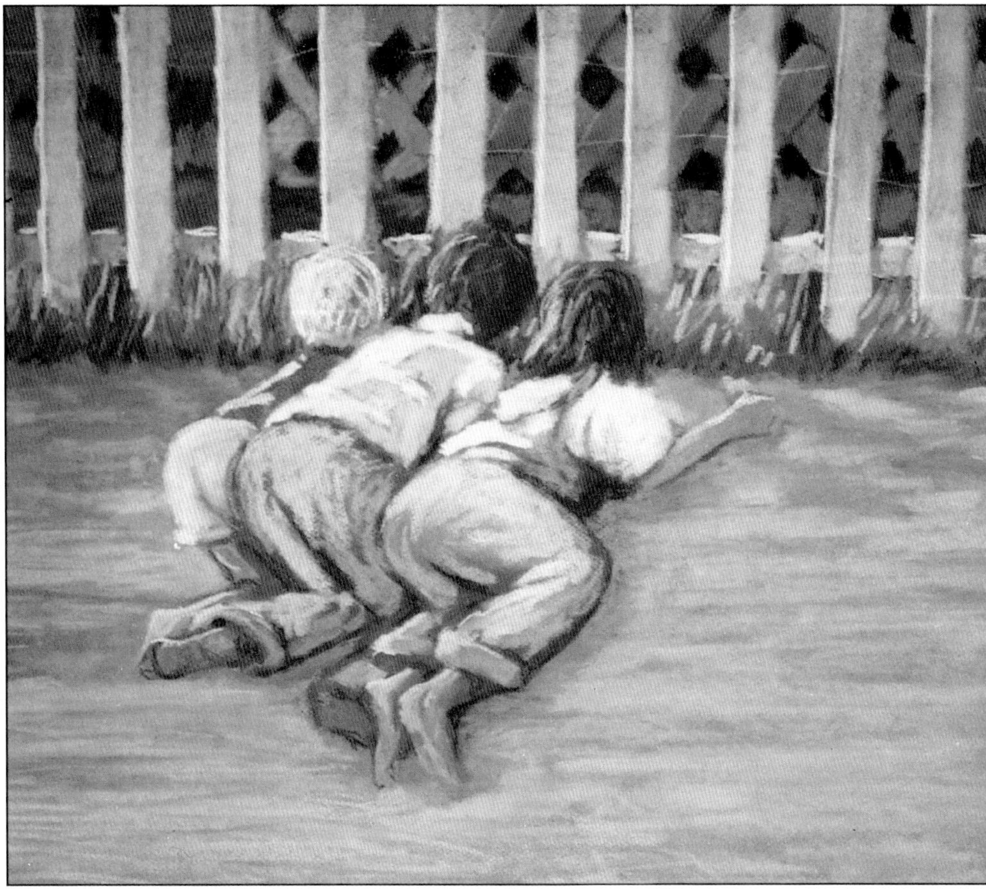

The Downtown Mural (detail). Artist William (Bill) Harrison was commissioned by the city of Monroeville to execute a mural just off the courthouse square in conjunction with students from local Alabama Southern Community College. The mural depicts three children—Scout, Jem, and Dill—looking through a fence, with the Old Monroe County Courthouse in the background. Visitors to Monroeville are captivated by the mural as they arrive on the square.

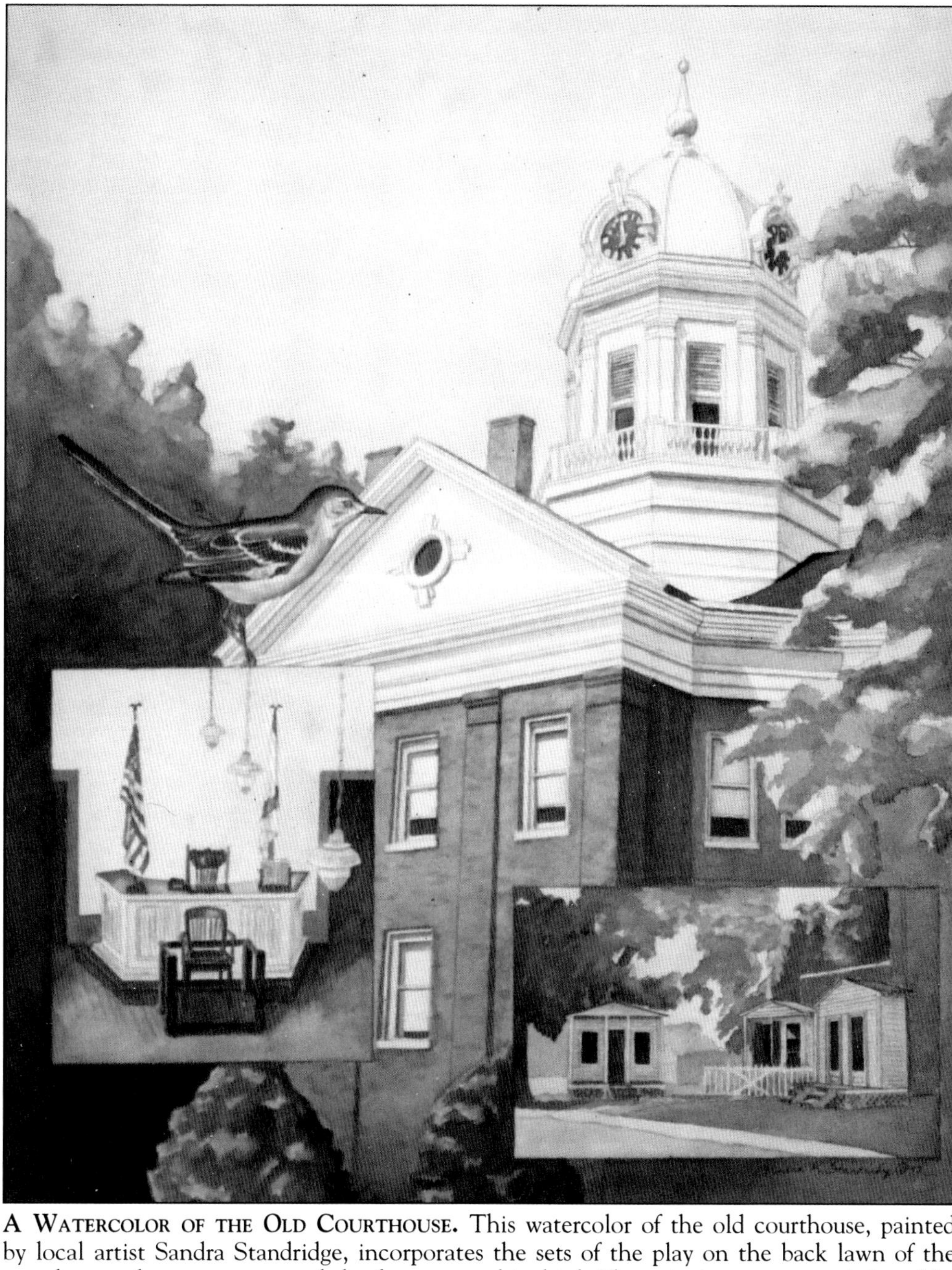

A WATERCOLOR OF THE OLD COURTHOUSE. This watercolor of the old courthouse, painted by local artist Sandra Standridge, incorporates the sets of the play on the back lawn of the courthouse, the courtroom, and the famous mockingbird. The painting was commissioned by Everette Price, actor in the play, who then donated the watercolor to the Monroe County Heritage Museums. Prints are available at the Museums.

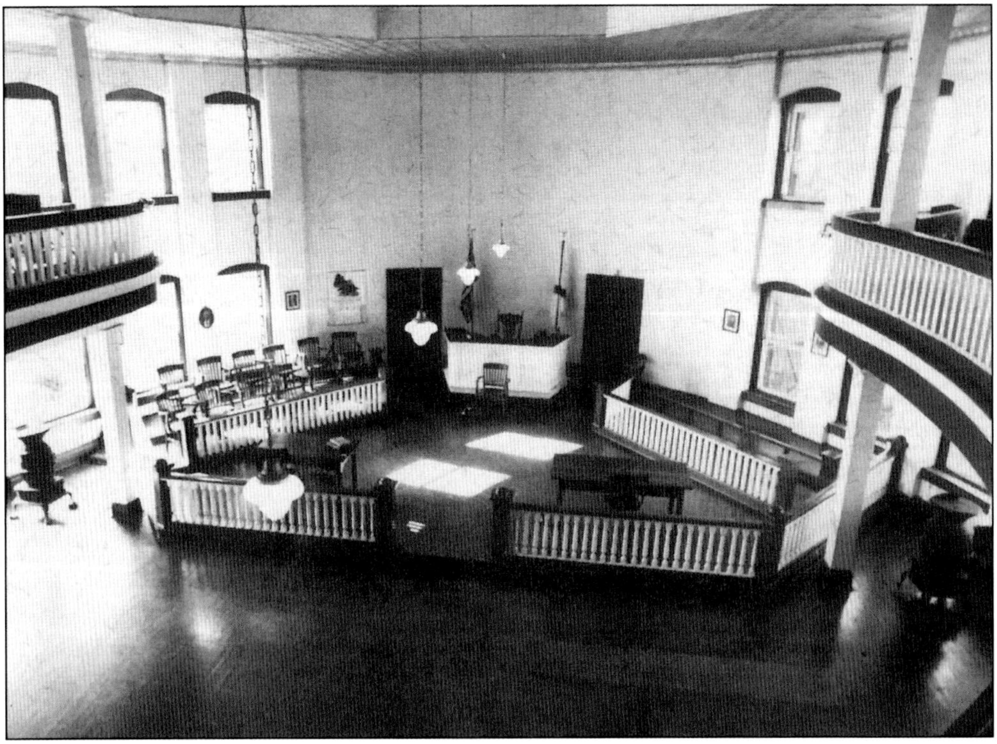

The Old Monroe County Courtroom. As a breeze lightly brushes across the courtroom, one can almost hear Atticus's voice ringing out, "In the name of God, do your duty." (Photograph by Aaron White.)

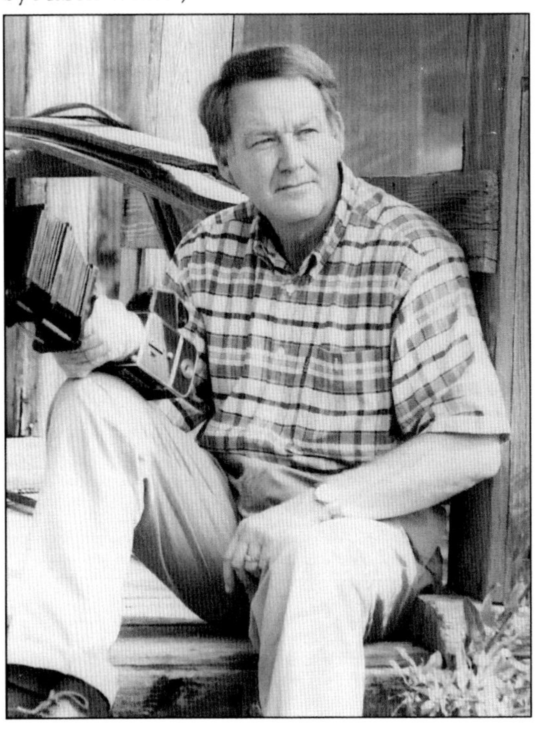

Aaron White, Photographer. Aaron is a professional photographer in Monroeville. He has photographed the people and places of Monroe County for over 28 years, and has graciously shared with the Museums many of the photographs in this book. In 1993 Aaron's photo of the old courtroom in the courthouse was chosen for the cover of Shelby Foote's republished book *Follow Me Down*.

The Monroe County Heritage Museums, housed in the Old Monroe County Courthouse, was established as a volunteer organization in the 1960s by the Monroe County Historical Society. The courtroom was made famous through the country and the world by the Pulitzer prize-winning novel, *To Kill a Mockingbird* by Monroeville resident Nelle Harper Lee.

In 1991, the Old Courthouse Restoration Committee and the Monroe County Commission established a nonprofit museum board and hired a museum director. Restoration on the courthouse was begun and continues today. The Museums has expanded in the old courthouse to include several rooms on the first floor with rotating exhibits illustrating the colorful past of Monroe County.

The Museums seeks to foster understanding of the heritage of southwest Alabama. To fulfill this purpose, the Museums acquires, preserves, exhibits, and interprets documents, maps, publications, artifacts, and any items of historical significance pertaining to southwest Alabama, with emphasis on the area known as Monroe County, Alabama.

The Museums' mission is to bring people and history together. This mission is founded on two beliefs: That understanding of our regional history enriches people's lives, and that our heritage is most thoroughly perceived, best understood, and most enjoyed through individual first-hand experience observing well-presented displays designed to tell the story of our past. To provide a permanent cultural resource for the enrichment of its community, the Museums acquires items of importance to our regional heritage. To recognize the importance of our regional heritage and to enhance understanding of history, the Museums presents special exhibitions and programs.

Each year the Monroe County Heritage Museums presents the Mockingbird Players in a two-act version of the play *To Kill a Mockingbird*, written by Christopher Sergel. People from all over the country migrate to Monroeville to watch as the all-local cast performs the play in the infamous setting. Playgoers are spellbound as the story unfolds, the experience heightened by the gospel singing of the Monroe County Interdenominational Choir at poignant times during the play.

The Museums is more than just the play, however. It is involved in many activities, including the managing of Rikard's Mill, a 150-year-old gristmill in north Monroe County, and Bethany Church in Burnt Corn, Alabama. Rotating collections of artifacts and relics from important periods in Monroe County and Alabama history are housed, along with regularly scheduled art exhibits and traveling exhibits. Numerous activities are scheduled throughout the year to promote the celebration of the history of Monroe County and Alabama.

The Old Courthouse Museum houses one of the largest collections of memorabilia and information related to Harper Lee and *To Kill A Mockingbird*. These collections also include memorabilia and information about critically acclaimed author Truman Capote. A permanent exhibit on both authors is displayed in the museum.

In 1997, the Alabama State Legislature declared Monroeville and Monroe County "Literary Capital of Alabama," since many authors have emerged from her populous. In addition to Lee and Capote, authors such as Mark Childress and internationally-known journalist Cynthia Tucker drew inspiration from this town.

The first annual Alabama Writers Symposium was held in 1998 in Monroeville, sponsored by Alabama Southern Community College and many other local organizations, including the Museums. The symposium gave the first Harper Lee Award for Alabama's Distinguished Writer 1998 to Albert Murray, noted Alabama author of such books as *The Spyglass Tree*, and *Down South To A Very Old Place*. The Eugene-Currant-Garcia Award for Alabama's Distinguished Literary Scholar 1998 was presented to Claudia Durst-Johnson, author of *Understanding "To Kill a Mockingbird."*

"TO KILL A MOCKINGBIRD *was written through a child's eyes, and therein lies its appeal. We share concerns that could only bear significance to the young Scout. The unnoticed suddenly becomes the extraordinary as we enter the children's world, unfolding the plot from their perspective.*

To Kill A Mockingbird *is Jem looking for a more physical representation from his aging father and being upset when he won't play football for* 'the Methodists.' *It's having to read to* Miss Dubose *as punishment only to find she's not so bad after all. Or Calpurnia fearing for the children's religious welfare, taking them to her own service much to the annoyance of Atticus's prim sister. Most of all, it's Boo Radley 'coming out.'*

That a trial encompassing a social issue takes place is, I won't say secondary, but follows a different perspective when viewed by the children. To Kill A Mockingbird *is several formative years in the development of a young southern girl. I will always remember the scene from the movie of Jem leading Scout home from the school play dressed in a paper maché ham silhouetted in the moonlight through the windswept leaves with haunting soundtrack.*

On something of a quest, I have photographed subjects all over Alabama with a desire to recapture Scout's world some fifty years later. I hope the images you see do justice, if even in part, to the book."

—Richard Maloney

Eight

In Search of Atticus Finch

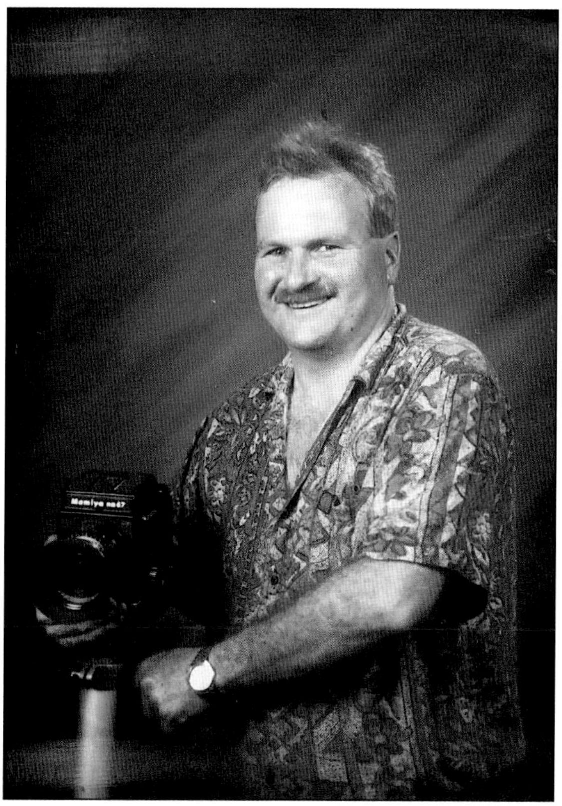

RICHARD MALONEY, PHOTOGRAPHER. Richard Maloney is a photographer from Melbourne, Australia. He has studied fine art at the Royal Melbourne Institute of Technology and completed studies in photography at the Photography Studies Institute in Melbourne. He was the recipient of the Borg Anderson Award for Photojournalism in 1990 in Melbourne. He lives and works in Australia.

Having exhibited in Australia prior to his visit to Monroeville, the Monroe County Heritage Museums housed his first exhibit in America in 1993. He entitled this collection of photographs "In Search of Atticus Finch." The following photographs are excerpts from the collection.

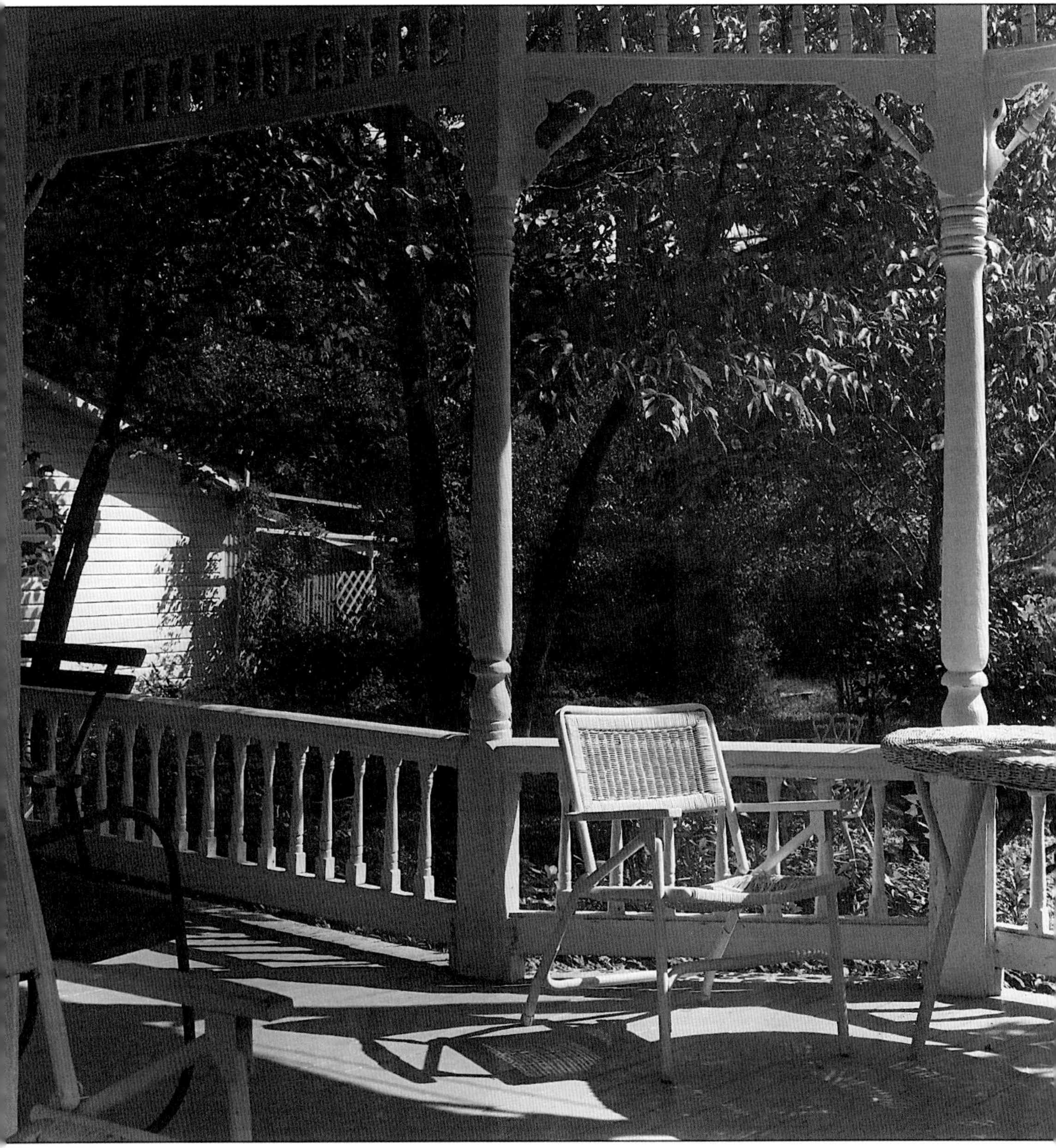

PORCH OF THE STALLWORTH-HARE HOME. This home was built at the turn of the century by Probate Judge Nicholas James Stallworth, who commissioned the building of the 1903 courthouse.

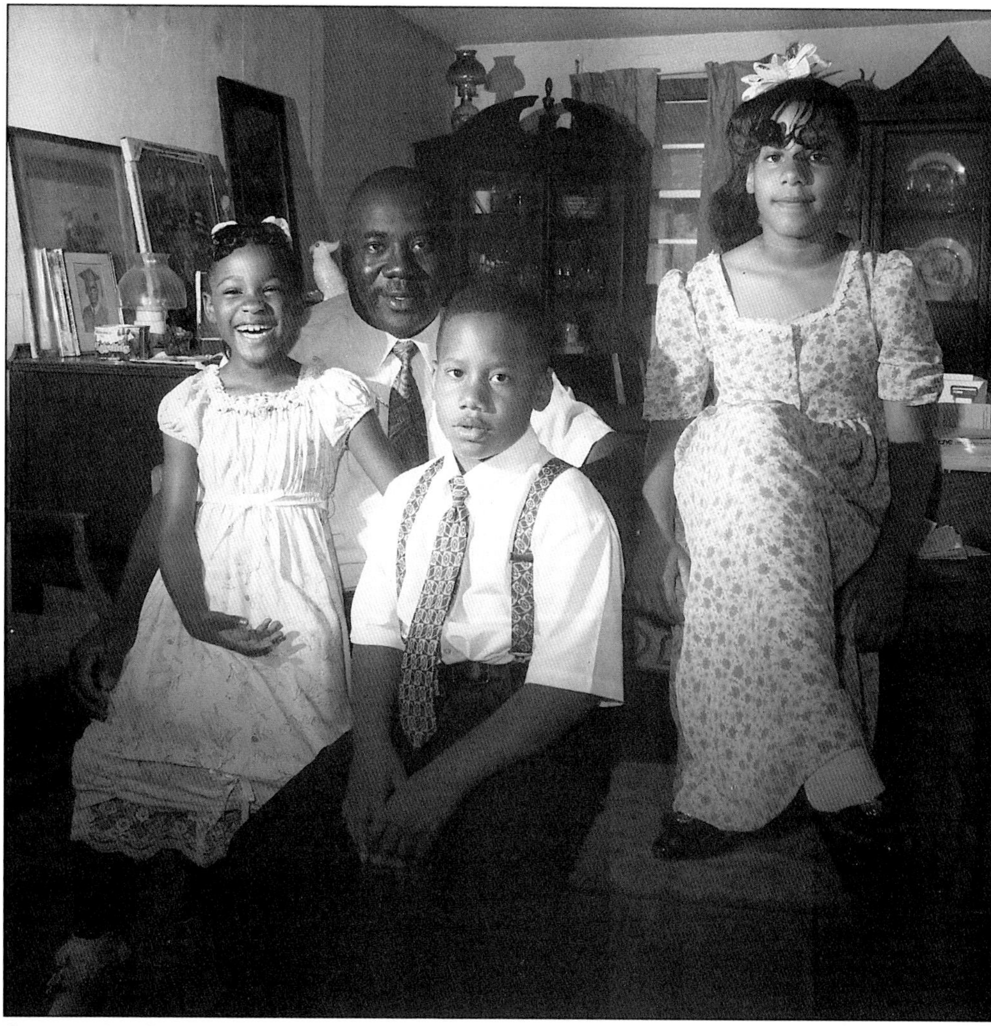

CHARLES MCCORVEY JR. AND HIS THREE CHILDREN AT THEIR HOME. Charlie, a school teacher, farmer, and Monroe County Commissioner, plays the role of Tom Robinson in the Museums' annual production *To Kill A Mockingbird*.

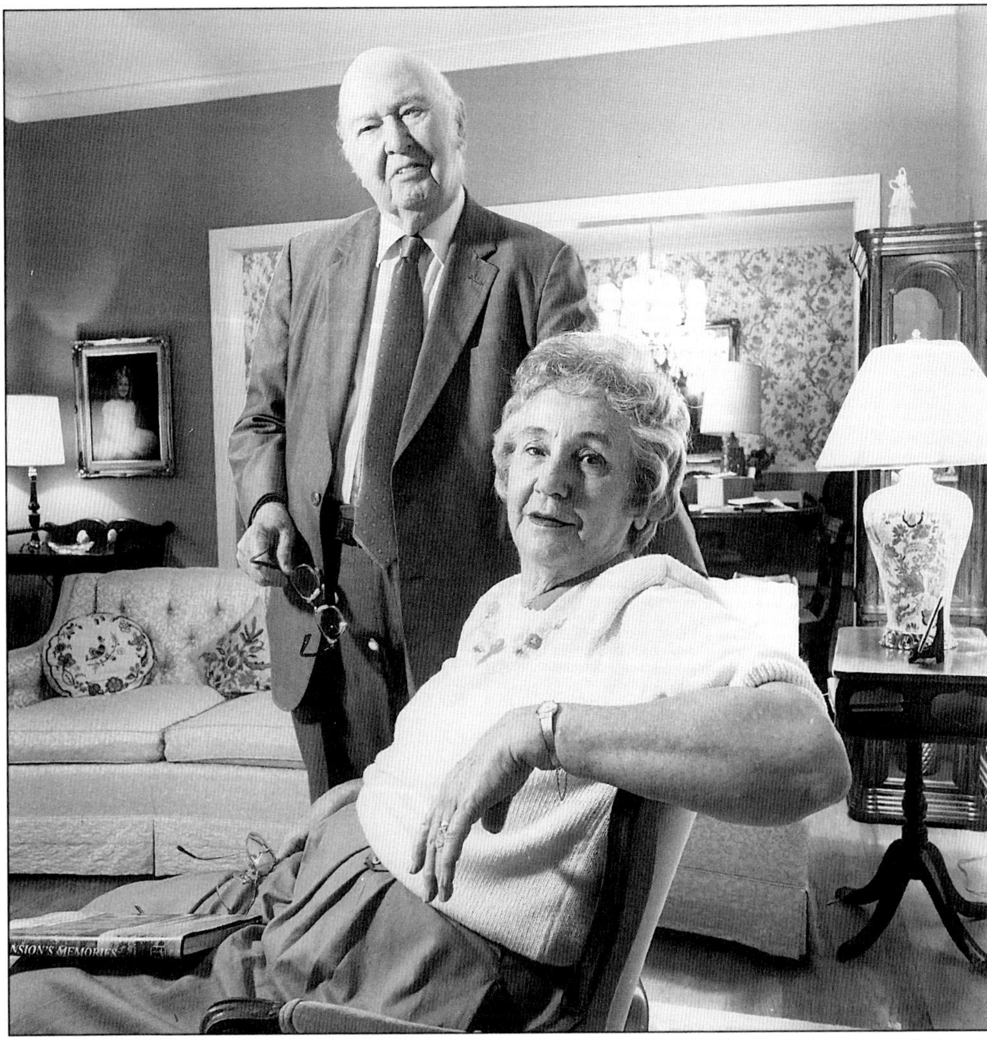

Dr. Woodrow Eddins and Anna Ruth Williams Eddins. Dr. Eddins practiced medicine in Monroe County for over 52 years. He was born the day Woodrow Wilson was elected President in 1912.

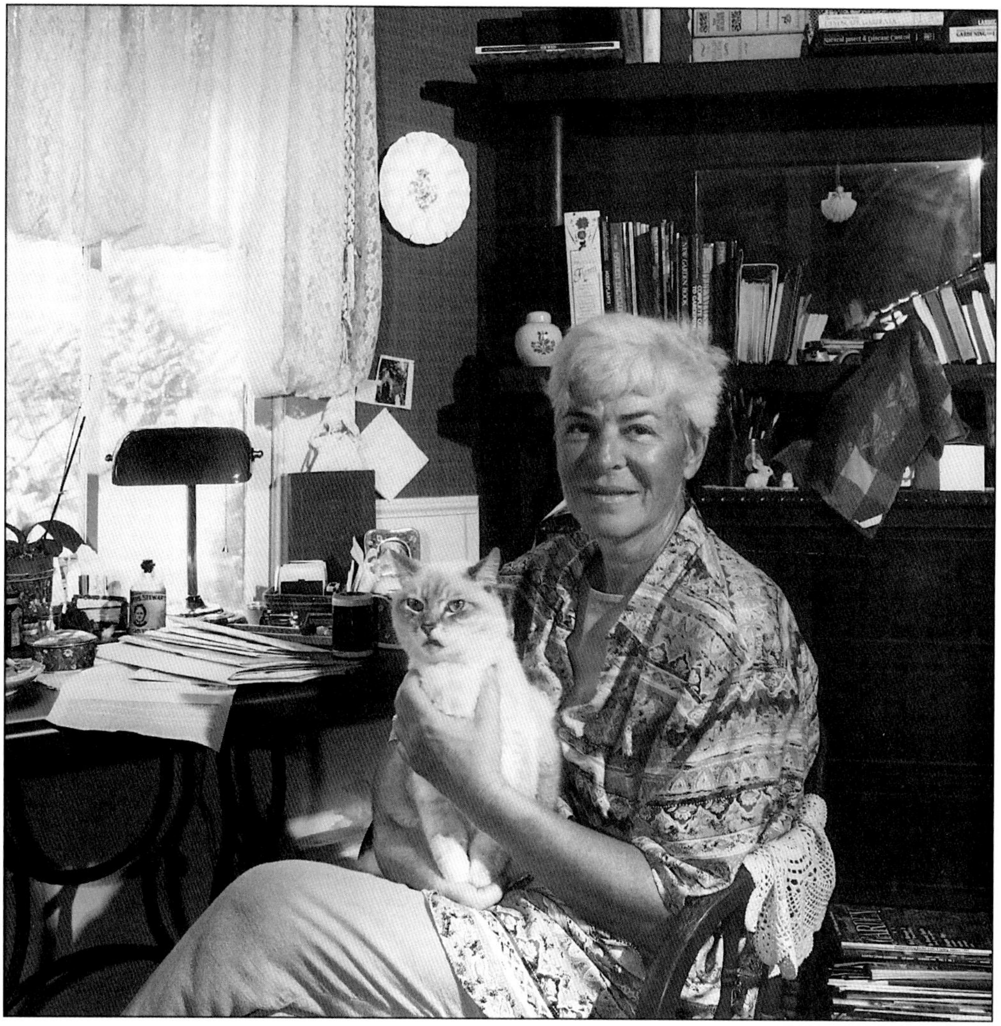

Vearl Cofield. Ms. Cofield owns and operates her own landscaping business in Monroeville. A California transplant, Vearl is known as "Plant Nanny."

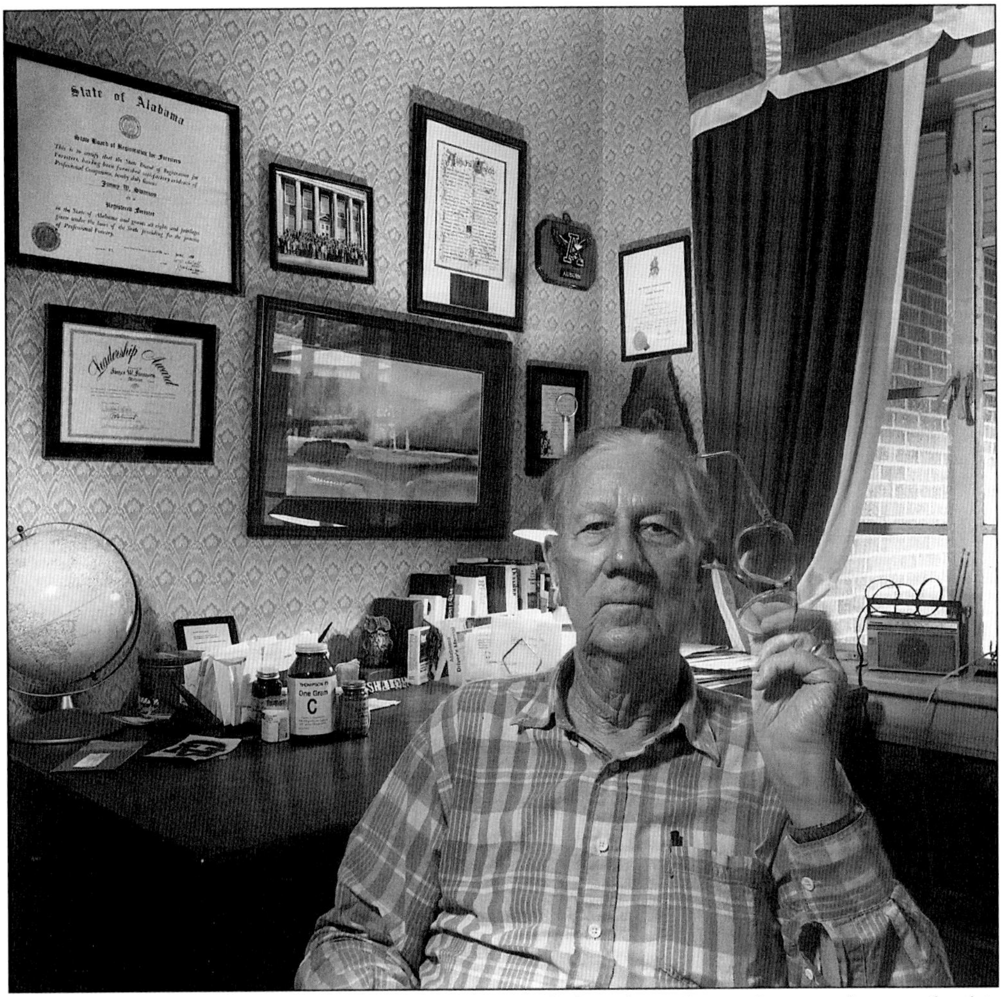

The Late Jimmy Swanson. Mr. Swanson was a beloved resident who was famous for his "one liners."

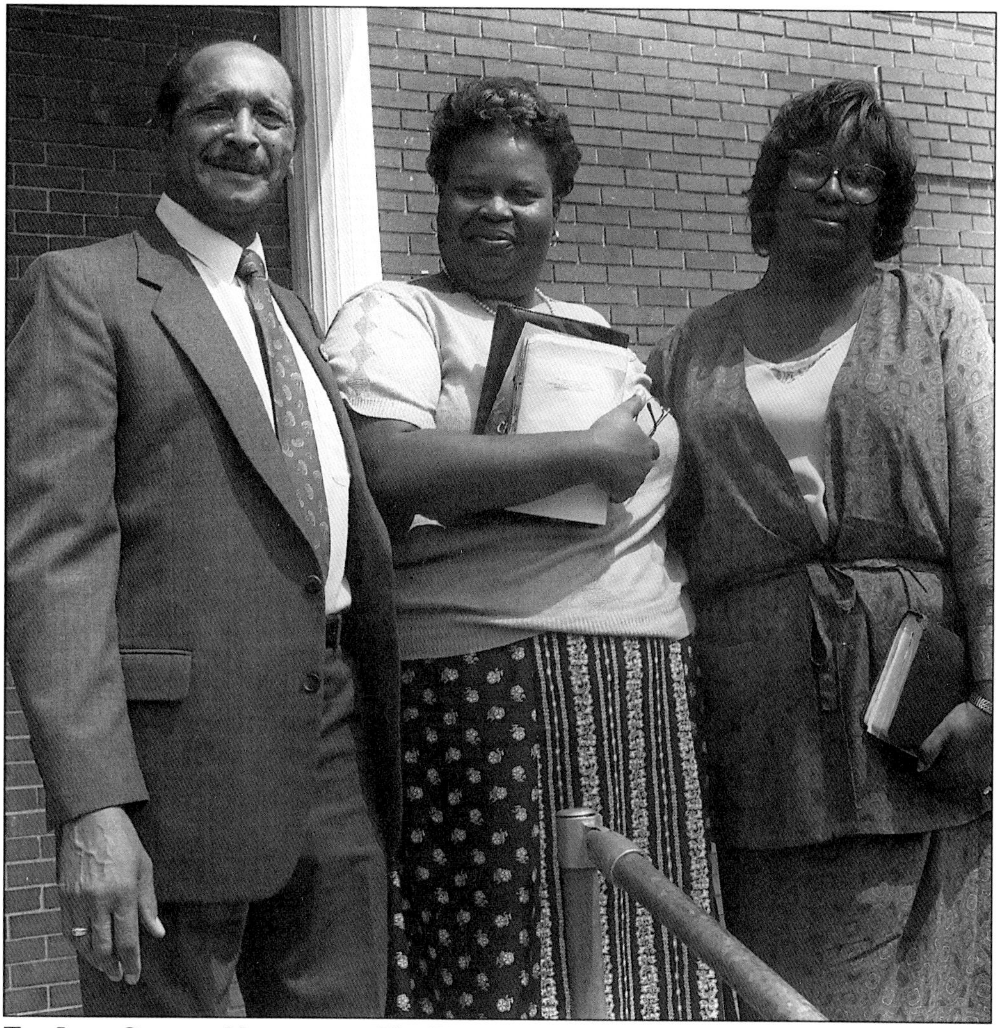

The Late Clement Nettles and His Wife Jackie with a Friend on the Steps of Their Church, Bethel Baptist. Jackie is the director of the Monroe County Interdenominational Mass Choir and teaches music at Wilcox County High School.

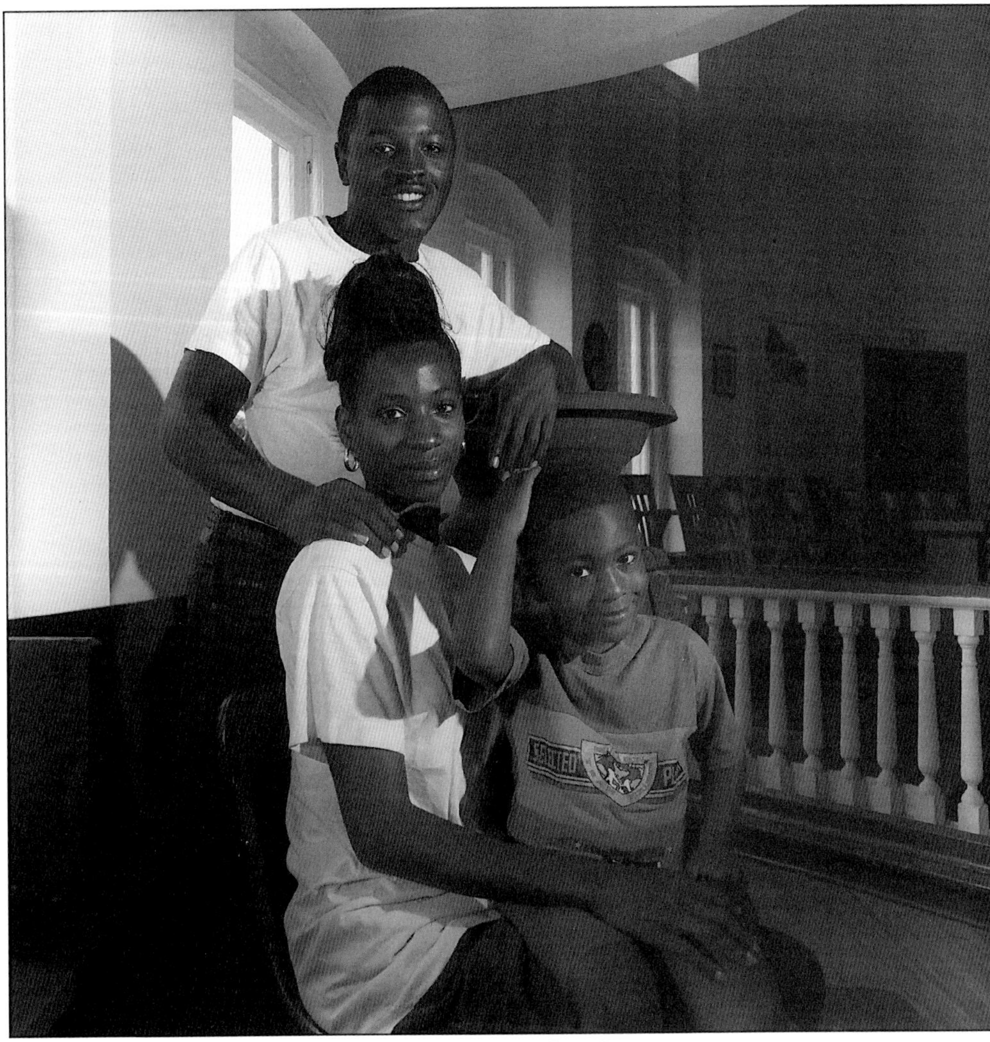

Eric and Vickie Burton and Their Son, in the Old Courtroom.

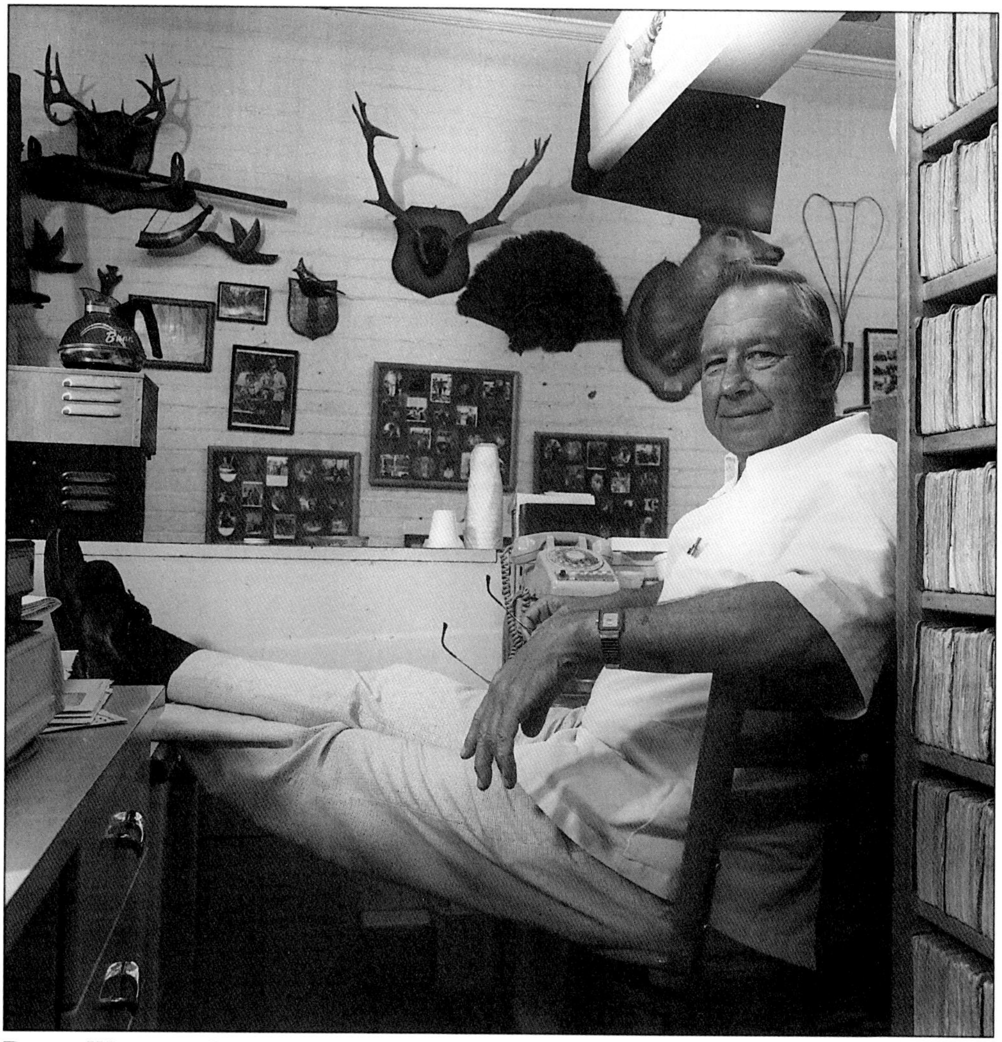

DICKIE WILLIAMS, PHARMACIST, AVID HUNTER AND LOCAL HISTORIAN AT HIS DRUGSTORE LOCATED ON THE COURTHOUSE SQUARE. Dickie's favorite motto is "never sweat the little things."

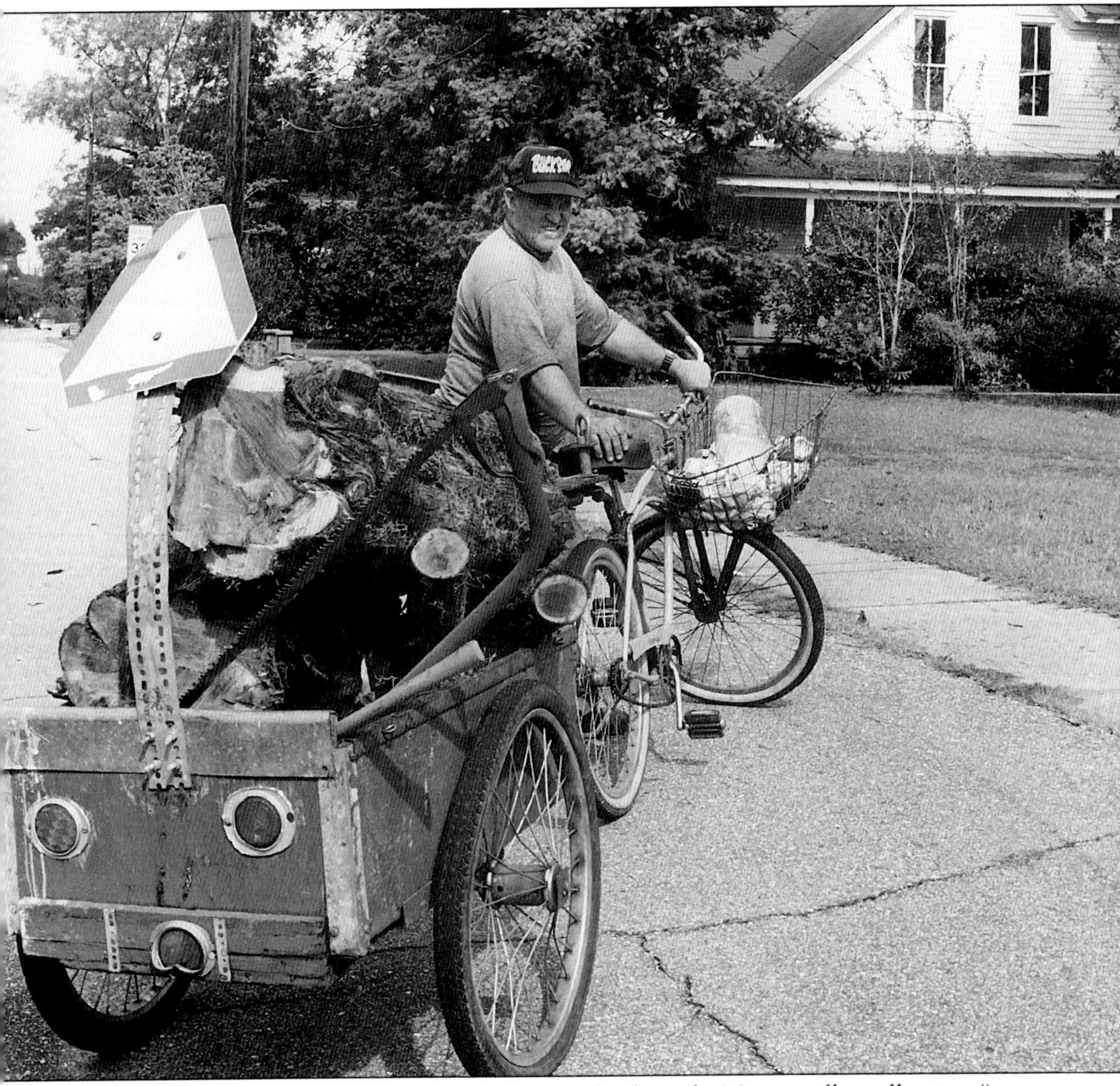

Mr. Ezell. Mr. Ezell makes his daily rounds through Monroeville collecting "treasures from trash."

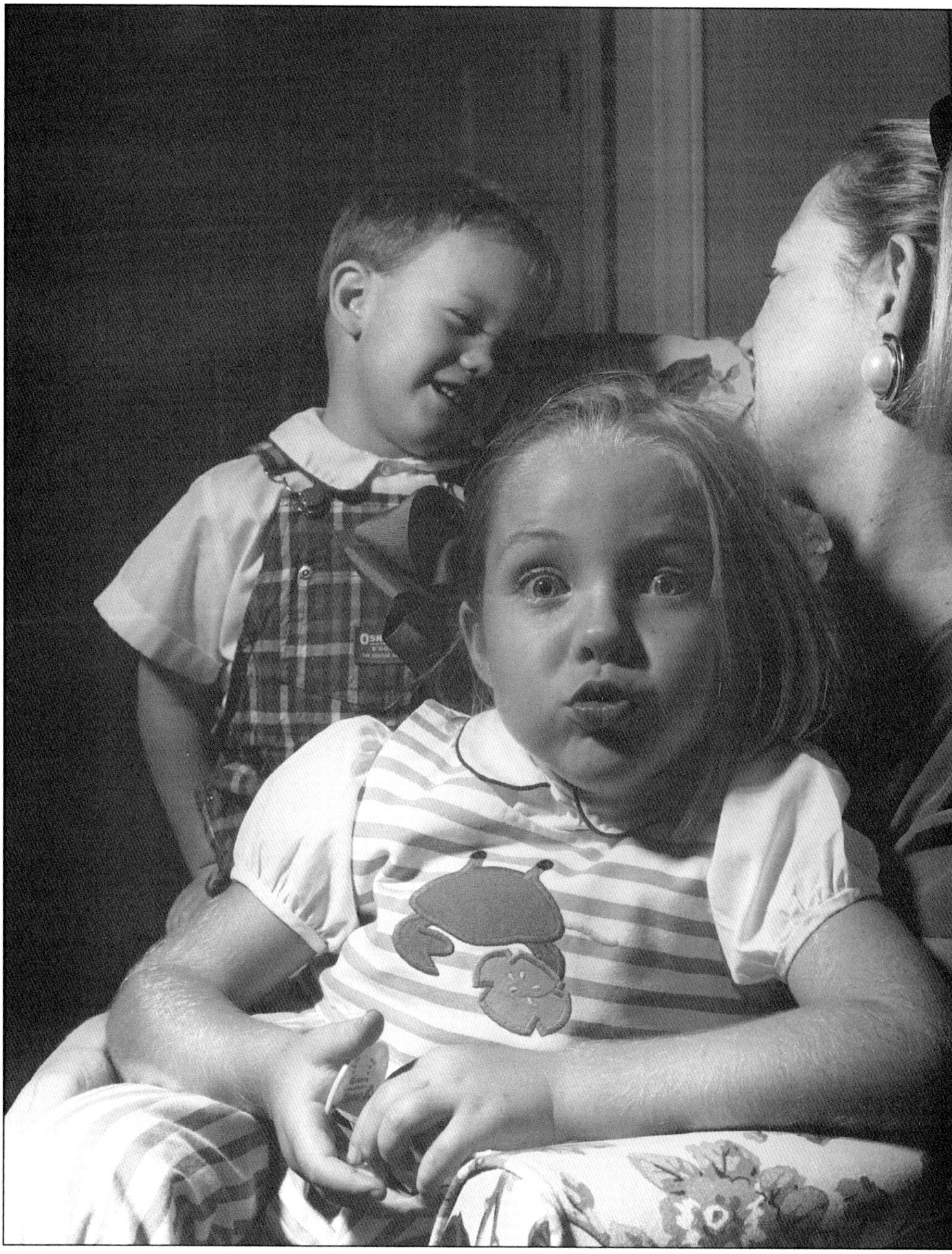

Sandy Cline Smith and her Children Rayford and Haller. Sandy is the director of the Chamber of Commerce, and her husband Rayford is a third generation Monroe Countian.

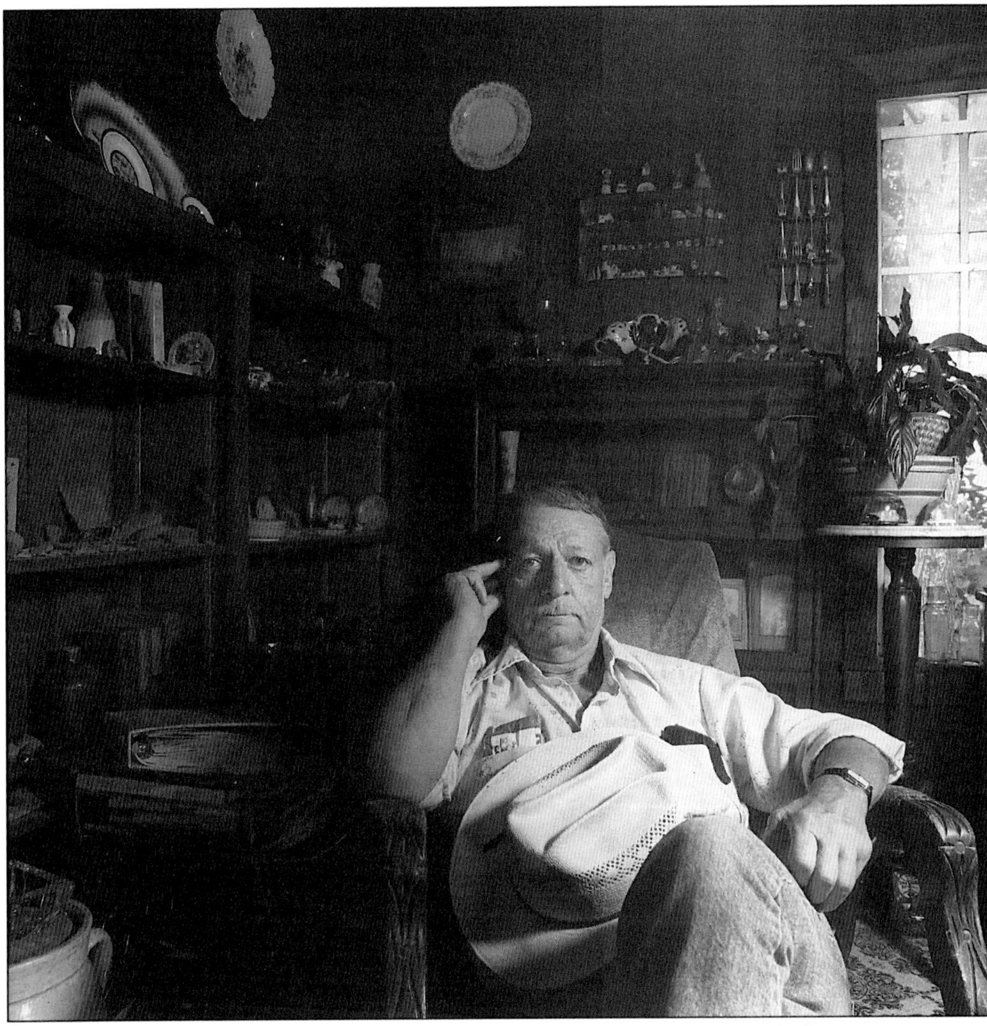

John Byron Carter. Mr. Carter, known as "J.B.," was Truman Capote's first cousin, son of Truman's favorite aunt, Mary Ida Carter. He was an avid historian.

Nine

MONROEVILLE

"The pleasure was all mine."
—Sara Jane Rumens

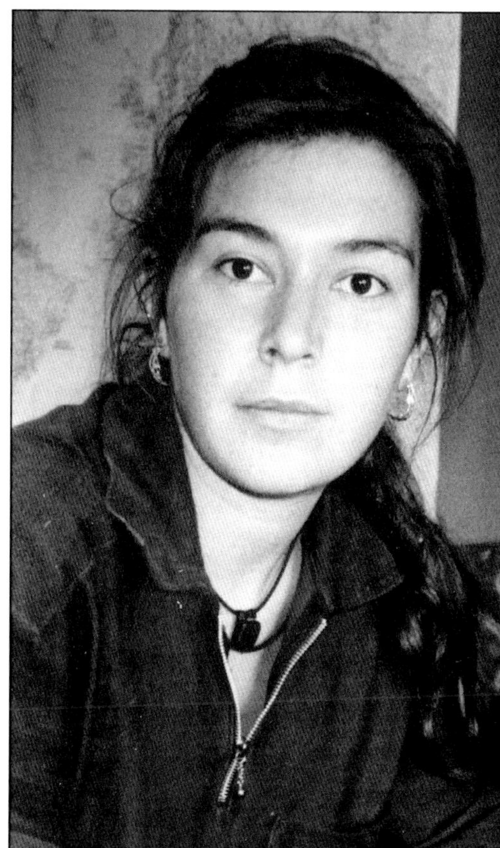

SARA JANE RUMENS. Just in the early stages of her photographic career, Sara Jane Rumens still sees herself in the "getting experience" period. Before taking up photography seriously, she wanted to be involved with travel and tourism. She soon discovered she was more interested in the people she found while traveling than the physical environment they lived in.

Her family home is in the rural county of Suffolk, England. After gaining her bachelor of science degree in geography in Northern Ireland, she studied photojournalism in London, where she aims to base herself. Sara has been taking photographs since she began traveling. Her travels led her to Monroeville, where she lived and worked for a brief time, photographing the people and personalities of the area.

"Being a photographer, I concentrated more upon pictures than words. However, given more time, I would love to return and satisfy curious questions by giving the faces louder voices."

"The pleasure was all mine." (See p. 106 for an example.)—Sara Jane Rumens

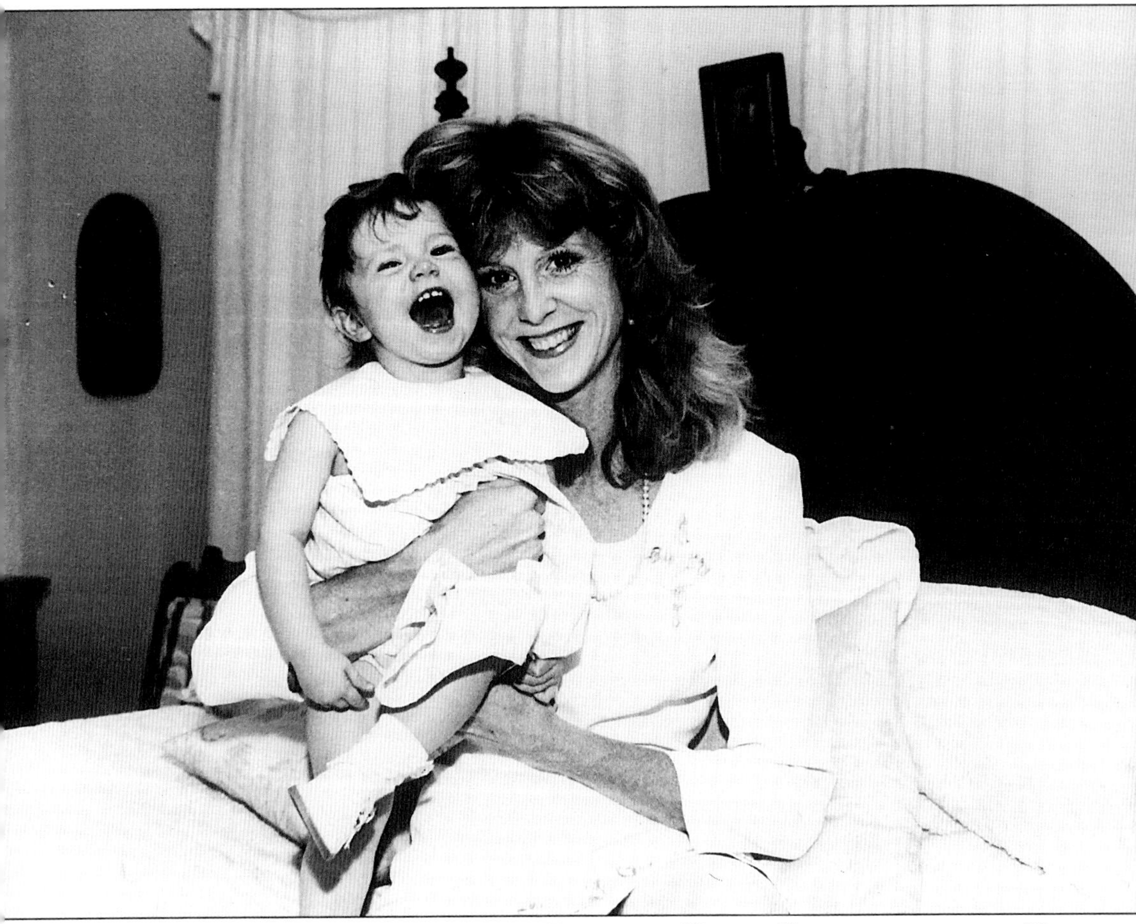

Susan Yarlbrough Brown and her Daughter Hanna Kathryn, at their Home. Grandparents Dr. Sam and Alma Yarlbrough built the house in the 1920s. Susan is an artist and has taught at Alabama Southern Community College for many years.

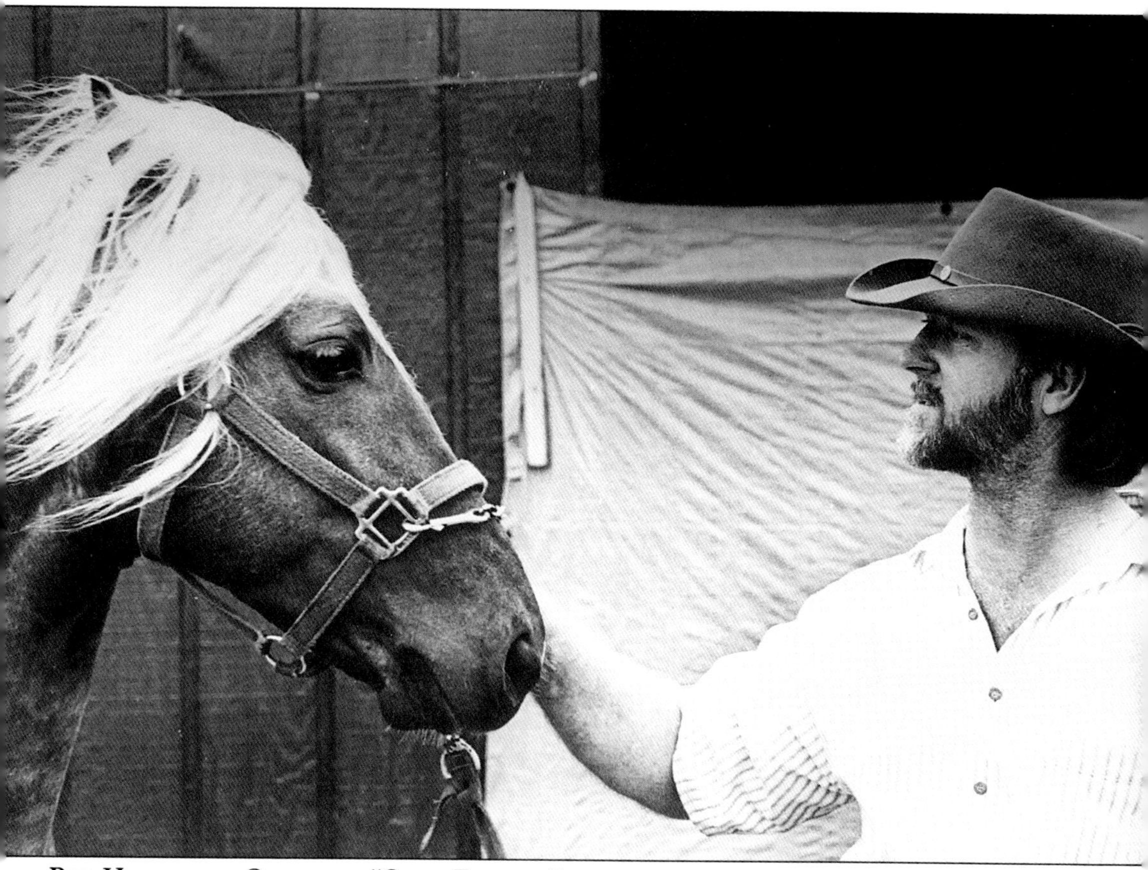

BILL HARPER AND ONE OF HIS "CLOSE FRIENDS."

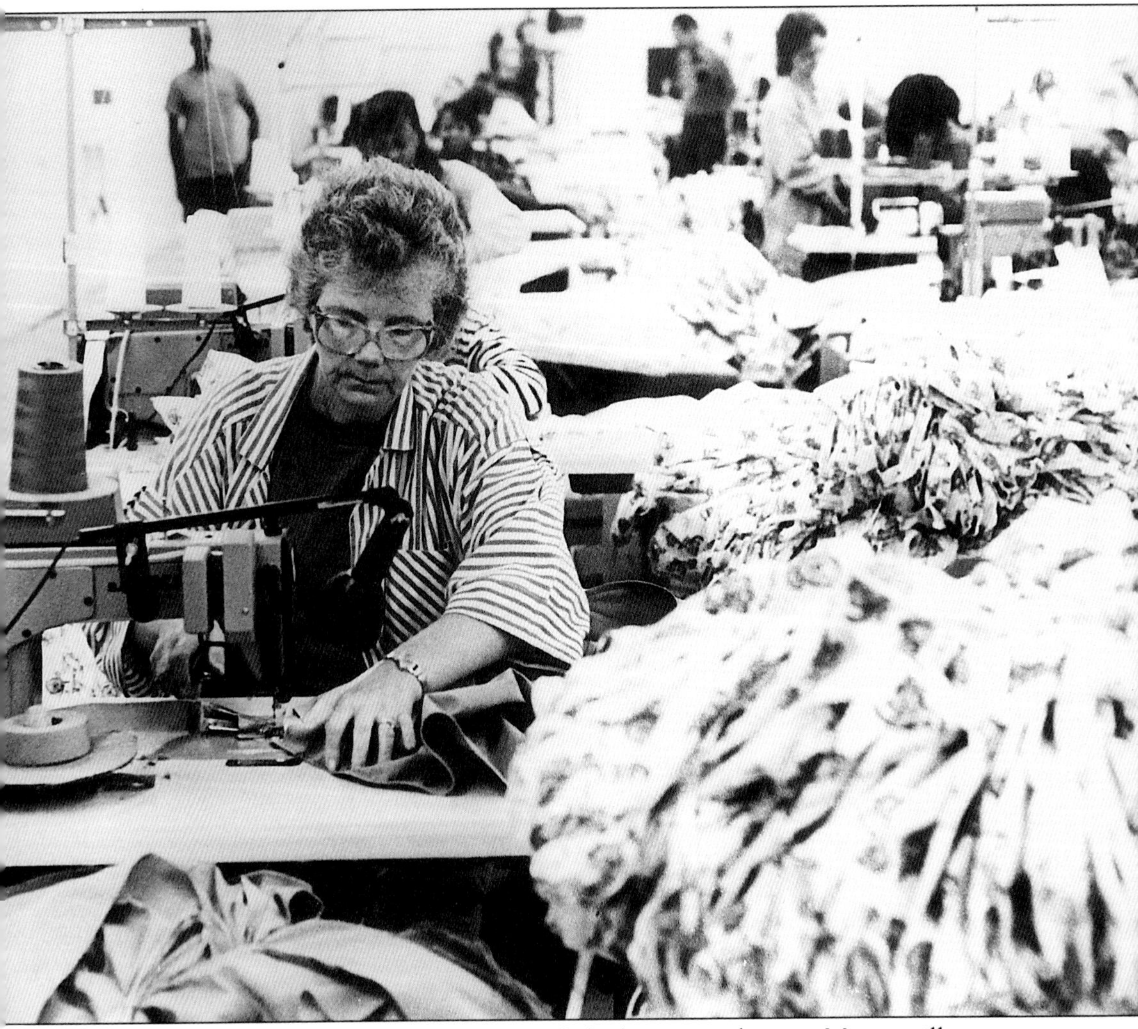

Vanity Fair Mills. Vanity Fair Mills is still the largest employer in Monroeville.

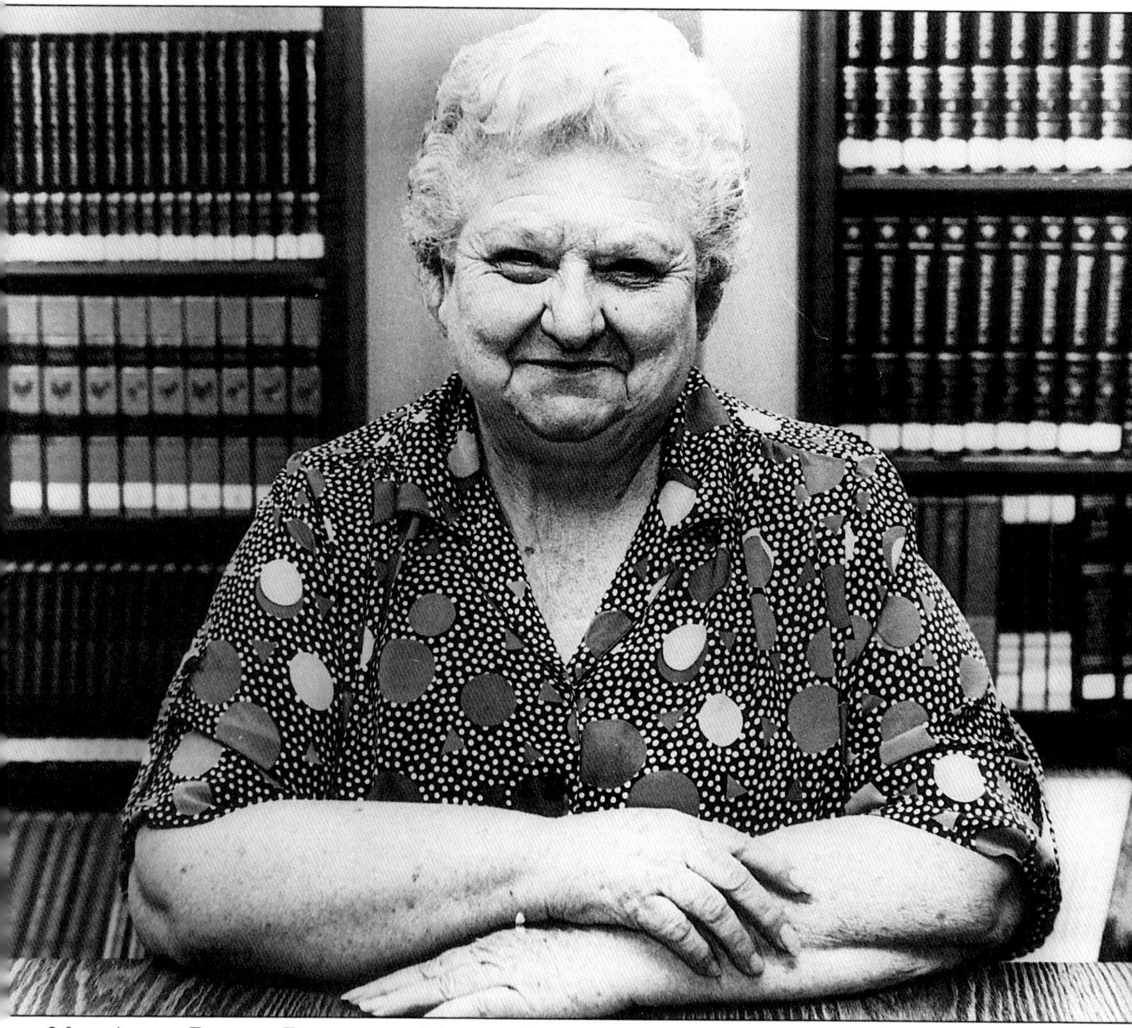

Mrs. Aileen Brooks, Part of the Monroe County Library Staff and Entrusted Keeper of the "Alabama Genealogy Room."

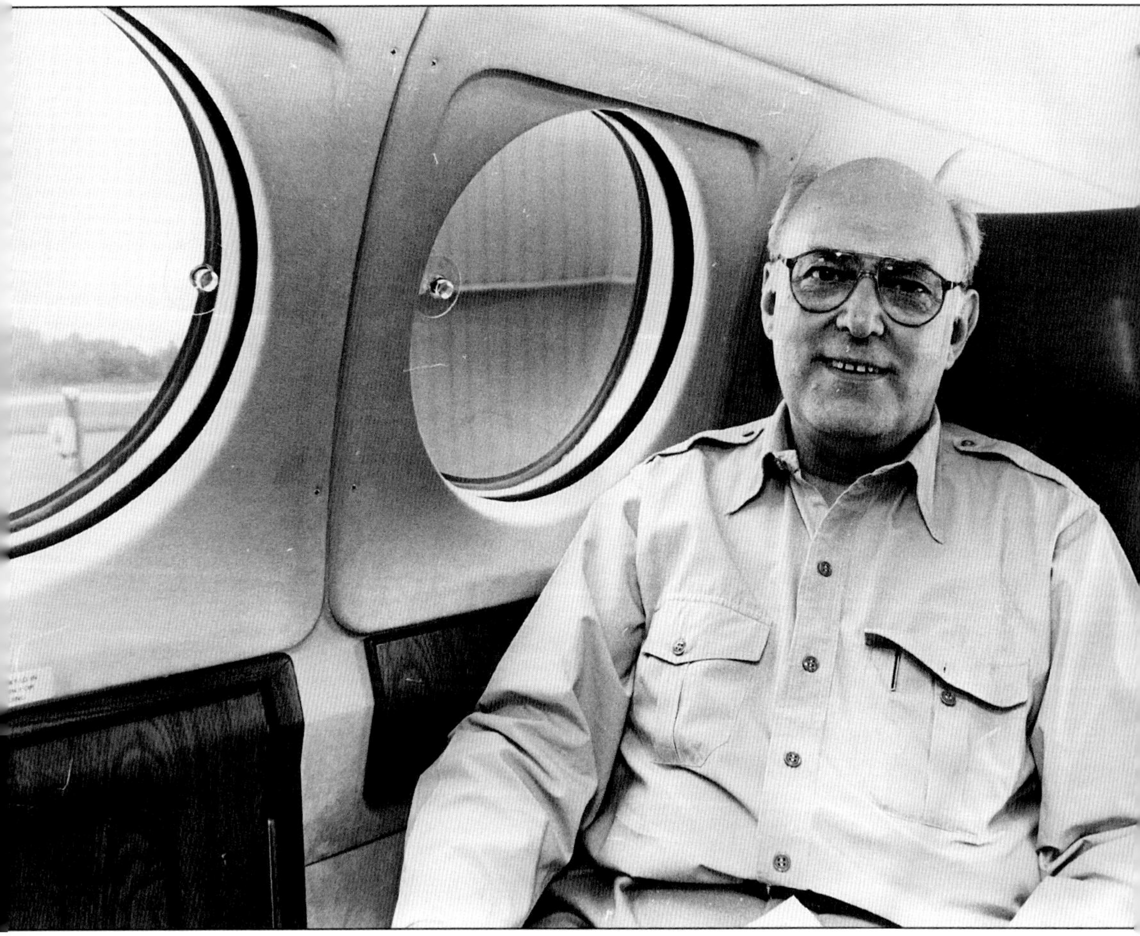

Dr. Luigi Terziotti. Dr. Terziotti is past executive vice-president-general manager of Alabama River Pulp and Alabama Pine Pulp. He is much respected and loved by those with whom he has worked since the mill's construction and beginning operations.

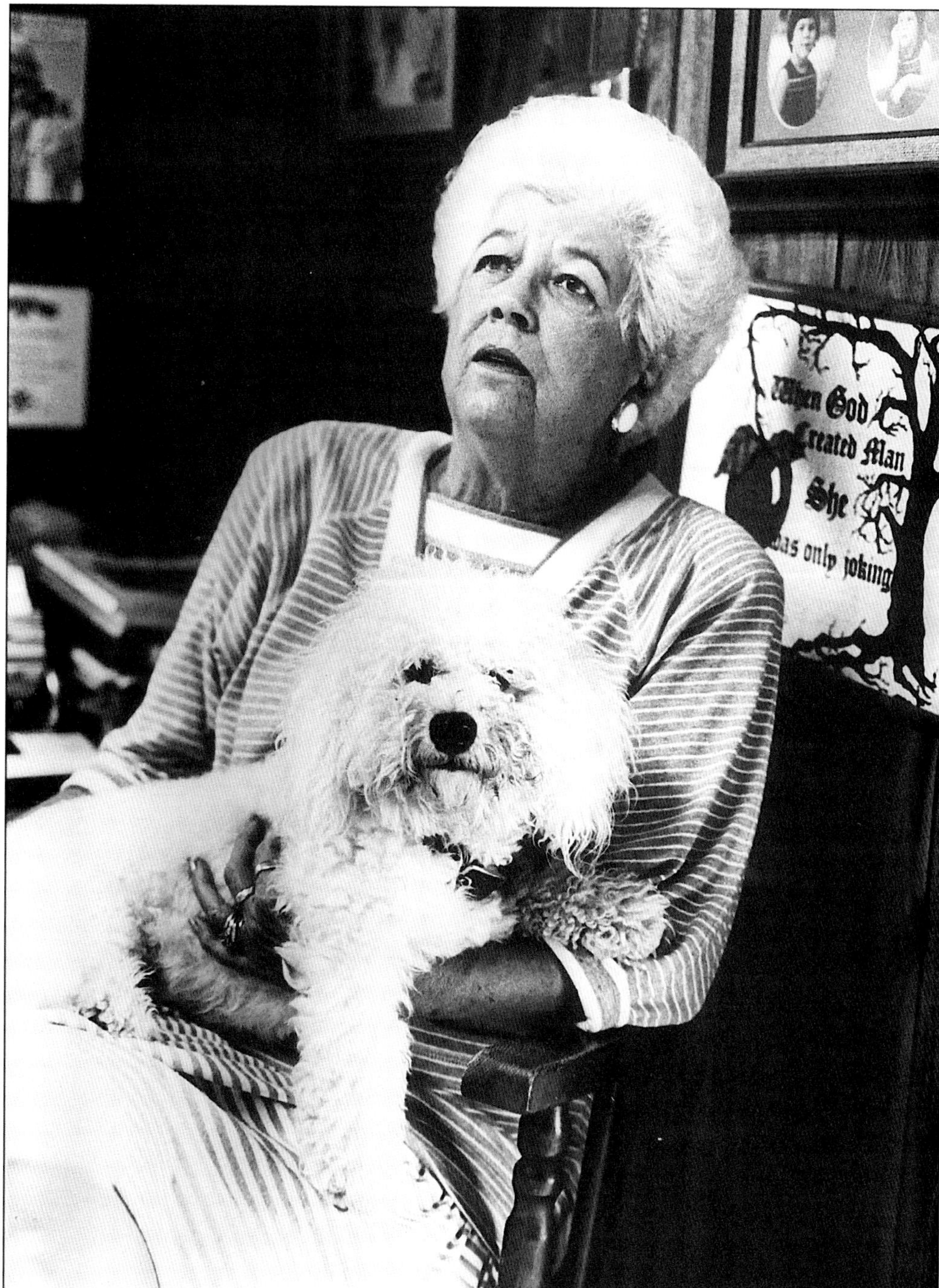

Mayor Anne Hines Farish. Mayor Farish's father, Dr. Jack Hines, was also mayor of Monroeville.

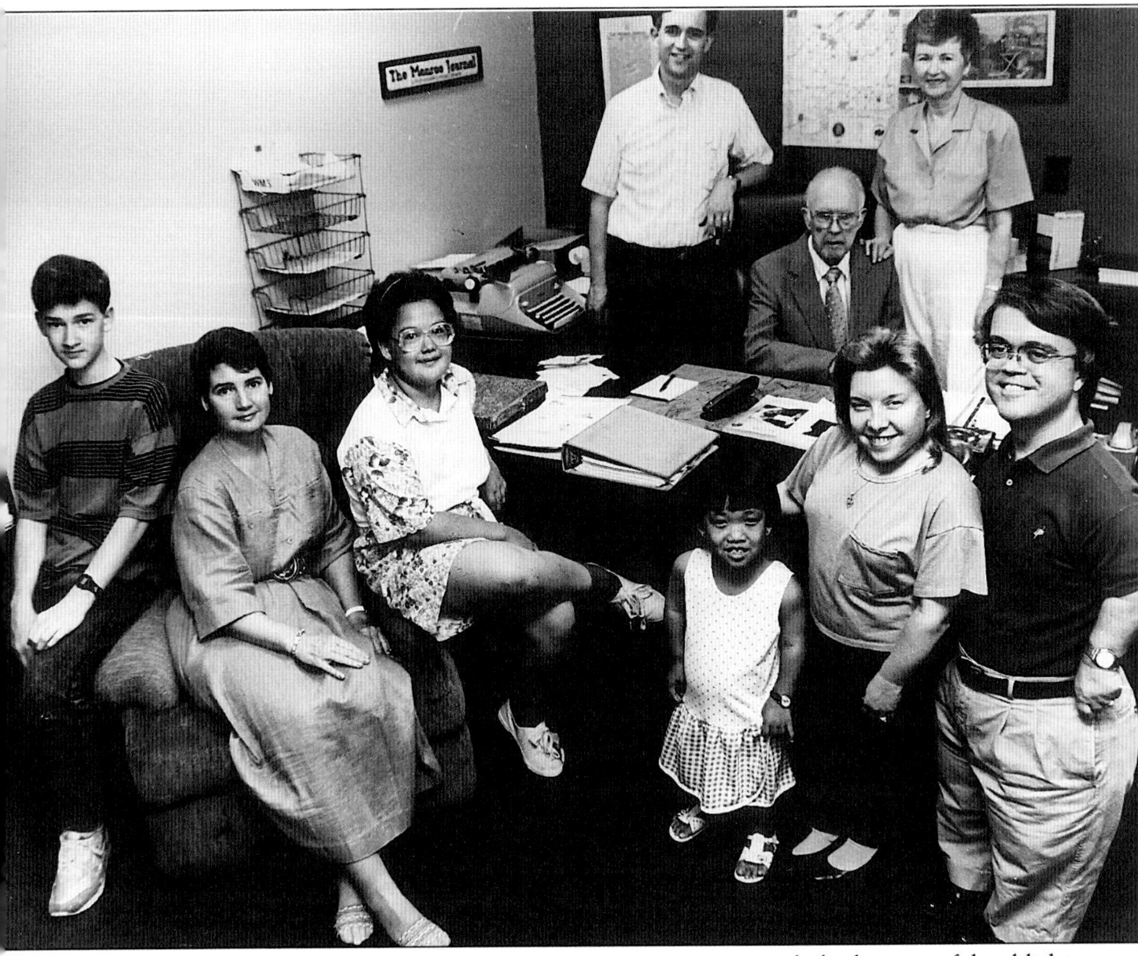

The Late Bill Stewart (seated at back). Mr. Stewart not only built successful publishing and broadcast companies, but also earned the highest respect from all his employees. Rumens remarked, "I only heard the kindest words about 'Mr. Bill.' " His sons ran the family business, with Steve Stewart as publisher of *The Monroe Journal* and David Stewart as manager of WMFC radio station. Today, *The Monroe Journal* is owned by Bo Bolton.

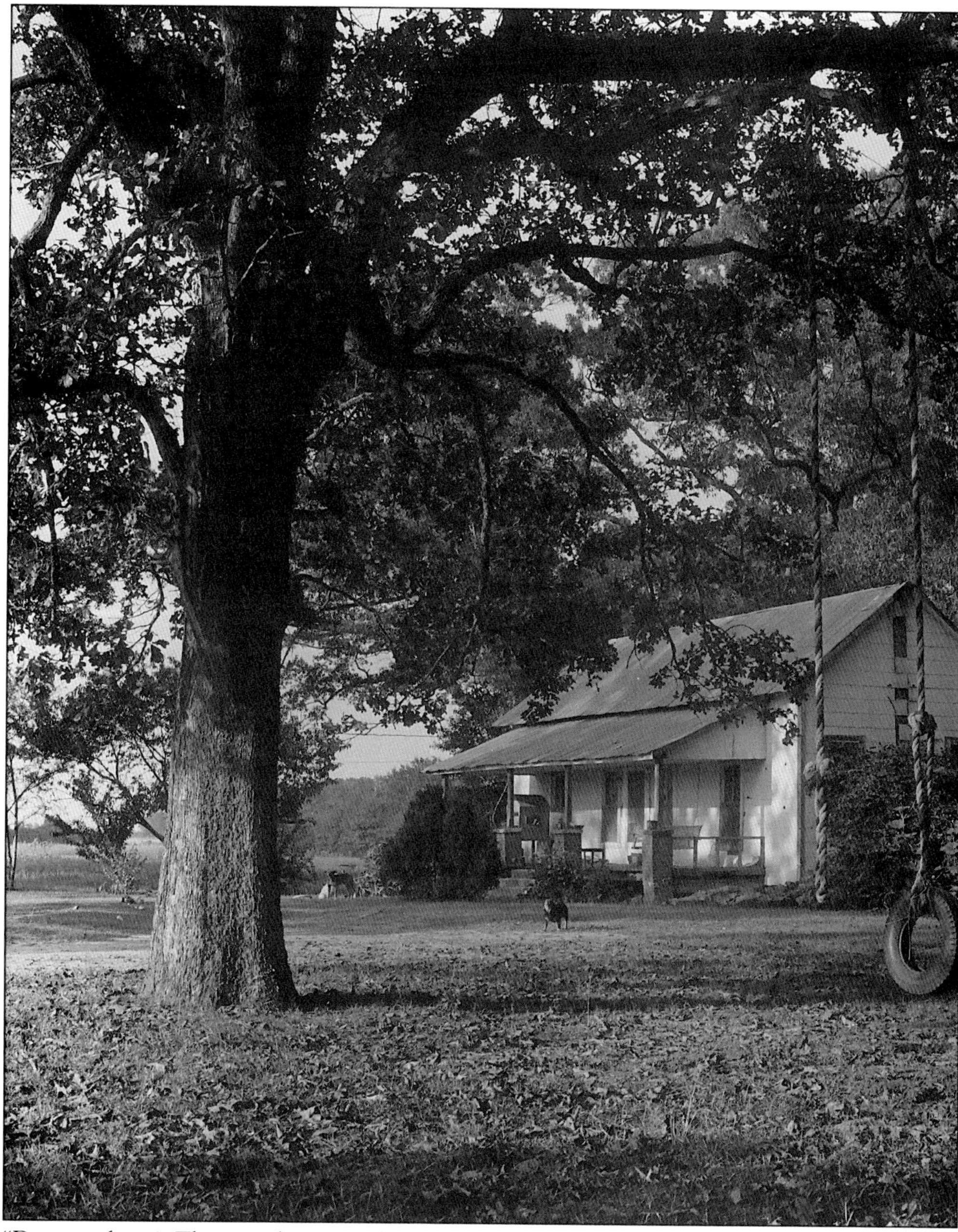

"Do you hear? That is the grass harp, always telling a story—it knows the stories of all the people who ever lived, and when we are dead it will tell ours, too."—Truman Capote, *The Grass Harp*